C0-AYG-848

Interpersonal Messages
of Emotion

ALLEN T. DITTMANN

Springer
PUBLISHING COMPANY, INC., NEW YORK

020839

SPRINGER PUBLISHING COMPANY, INC.
200 Park Avenue South, New York, N.Y. 10003

International Standard Book Number: 0-8261-1340-0
Library of Congress Catalog Card Number: 72-81248

Current printing (last digit)
10 9 8 7 6 5 4 3 2 1

Printed in the United States of America

ALL RIGHTS RESERVED

Preface ————————————————————————————

The work which culminated in this book was begun in Milan, Italy, in 1964. I spent a year of special study there at the Agostino Gemelli Institute for the Experimental Study of the Social Problems of Visual Information, learning about research techniques in the psychological effects of the film situation and in the design and use of films for different purposes. While I was there I had the privilege of using the library of the Catholic University of the Sacred Heart, through the courtesy of Leonardo Ancona, who was then Professor of Psychology and Director of the Institute of Psychology there. The library contains one of the very finest collections in psychology on the continent, and Professor Ancona gave me every encouragement and assistance in using it as much as I wanted.

My search was for a body of literature on social communication which might serve as a way to make sense of the communication of emotion. I had been working for many years on process research in psychotherapy, or the details of the interchange between patient and therapist in the clinical interview. The moment-to-moment rise and fall of feelings is of prime importance to this sort of research, since it can serve as a dependent variable in many designs: from the patient's side, it can tell us how he has responded to therapist interventions of various kinds; from the therapist's side, it can give us a look at his response to different kinds of resistive maneuvers, and the like. How patient and therapist communicate feelings to each other, then, and under what circumstances their exchange is furthered and under what others it is blocked — these are the substantive aspects of the process. How all these interchanges can be communicated to the research observer so that he can study the entire process is the methodological aspect. It was perfectly reasonable in the beginning, therefore, to look to the literature on communication in social psychology and sociology as the one most applicable to my search.

As time went on I found that more was needed. To be sure, much has been written in this area of social psychology, but it was not immediately applicable to the problem I had set out to examine. Social psychologists have been interested more in how people influence each other than in how they learn about each other; and where they address themselves to the latter, they are interested in longer-term personality organizations and traits rather than in passing feelings and emotions. So I extended my search to other fields. The most natural of these was language. I had had more than a passing acquaintance with certain linguistic methods earlier when Lyman Wynne of the Adult Psychiatry Branch of NIMH and I had studied suprasegmental and paralinguistic analysis of speech with George Trager. I returned to linguistics again, spurred on by the growing interest of my colleague, Donald S. Boomer, in linguistics and phonetics. I also read widely in the philosophy of language, from the works of Ogden and Richards, Morris, and others. And since I had done some empirical research on body movement and facial expression as means of emotional interchange, I became acquainted with a number of other workers in this same area. I have found it invaluable to be able to exchange manuscripts with these investigators, to correspond with them about differences, and to discuss many points at conferences and symposia.

In the course of this developing acquaintance with human communication, I found that many writers were using a number of terms from engineering — some derived from the everyday language of radio broadcasting and telephony, some from the theoretical work of Claude Shannon. I approached Shannon's basic papers, "The Mathematical Theory of Communication," with some trepidation, partly because I lacked what seemed to be the necessary mathematical background to understand them, and partly because I had serious doubts that a theory designed for signals in telecommunication could be applied to the stuff of human communication without straining both theory and facts. On the basis of better acquaintance with the engineering literature, I was relieved to find that I was not always lost in the mathematics, and that the theory could indeed provide the framework I was looking for to tie many of the facts of emotional communication together.

In spite of the enormous usefulness of Shannon's theory, however, it did not provide a complete conceptual framework for theorizing about emotional communication — social science would have been in for a rude awakening if it had. For some of the necessary additional leads, several other theories presented themselves, some of which had been derived at least in part from Shannon's. Many of these are not usually thought of in connection with emotional communication, as is the social psychology of communication I started out with; on closer examination, however, they turn out to be highly applicable to the topic. Broadbent's theory of selective attention in perception is perhaps the best example of these. I therefore needed to search through a wide range of literature in psychology and in related fields.

The work of pulling these theoretical statements together, of relating theory to the available facts in this area of human communication, I have called theoretical research, and this book may be considered a report of the results of that research. It has been a complicated procedure. I would sometimes take a theoretical point and see if there were any facts that could be considered germane to it. At other times I would start with a set of research results and try to find some part of the theory where they might fit in. When I was setting forth on these small internal hunts, I would often have no idea of the outcome, whether theory or facts would be found wanting. It never seemed reasonable to believe that any one theory could really encompass all of emotional communication, and I almost welcomed those occasions where some other theory needed to be introduced. But the occasions arose with disquieting frequency when the facts, while not wrong, were inadequate for all the theories, or were missing altogether. These occasions, too, were welcomed. After all, in any effort to apply theories designed for other fields, we hope to be able to look afresh at what we are doing in our own field, to see gaps in how we have been doing it, and to find ways of filling those gaps. I believe that such results have been obtained from this theoretical research. In most cases I was clearly not the first investigator to see the possibilities, while in some I probably was. As I look at all of them, however, it is apparent that even those which had been seen before were made visible only because their authors were intuitively using one or another of the theories outlined here as their guide, chiefly Shannon's communication theory.

Thus the principal structure on which this work rests is the mathematical theory of communication. It is well known outside of its original area of telecommunication, for it has been used a number of times in psychology and in other social and biological sciences, with varying degrees of success, and will undoubtedly find use in still others. I must point out that I have applied it to only a limited aspect of human communication in my work, to a small corner of the myriad ways in which people interact with each other. I should not like to leave the impression that what seems to have been a successful application of communication theory to emotional communication is a precursor of sure success in all other areas of human communication as well. But even as I make this disclaimer, I realize that I believe the theory's applicability to be much wider than my efforts have shown it to be. How much wider is, in a sense, an empirical matter: one would need to try it out in more areas of human communication and see if it turns out to be useful — just as investigators have actually been doing right along.

This book consists of an introductory chapter and two main parts. The introduction sets the stage by looking at the broad field of human communication generally and seeing where emotional communication fits into it. Part I is the main expository section of the book. It starts with a brief overview of the mathematical theory of communication, plus some comments on how closely that theory fits the facts of emotional communication. Subsequent chapters take up the several topics of communication theory, with an additional chapter on the psychology of the communicating persons. Part II discusses problems of research on emotional communication, some of which derive from the theory itself (as explained in Part I), while others grow out of the strategies which the research investigator must use to do studies in this particular area.

Throughout this work I have been fortunate in having wise counsel from a number of people. I have worked most closely on problems of human communication, and for the longest time, with Boomer. We have discussed and argued, had simultaneous "insights," and followed up on each other's findings, with the result that more of our empirical studies have been joint ventures than the authorships tell. I asked his advice freely while doing this work and writing, and he always gave it just as freely. I have valued John Campbell's comments on the manuscript from a different standpoint. Because his work as a social psychologist leads him to other paths than those represented in this book, the questions he needed to ask in order to understand some points showed that I often assumed too much of the reader. He was not, however, too distant to ask some embarrassing substantive questions in addition, which showed that I assumed too much of the theory, and forced me to clarify my thinking. Paul Ekman has been another source of considerable help in this work. His research approaches in the general area of nonverbal communication, and his specific comments on the manuscript at various stages of writing, have led me to greater consistency in my thinking at a number of crucial points. Several others have offered helpful suggestions and unsettling alternative explanations during the writing of this book. I have prized especially the careful readings and frank critical reactions given me by Harold L. Raush and David Shakow.

Finally I wish to express my appreciation for — and pride in — the NIMH Intramural Research Program as a setting in which this sort of work is not only possible, but also fostered. David Shakow, who was Chief of the Laboratory of Psychology when the work began, understood the need for theorizing early in our work on the process of psychotherapy, and actively encouraged me to explore as much as I needed. David Rosenthal, his successor, has continued in the same spirit. And Morris Parloff, Chief of the Section on Personality, has been more than patient as I became increasingly embroiled in this work, to the detriment of other research he and I had planned to do together.

June, 1972

ALLEN T. DITTMANN

Contents

020839

Introduction: Emotional Messages in the Context of Human Communication ——————————————

In the course of living day by day, we exchange messages with each other all the time. The messages come in an almost unbelievable variety of forms: we talk and listen to others talk, we read letters and write notes, look at newspaper stories and magazine articles, and watch television shows. We go to lectures and wade through textbooks, and we listen to political speeches and to rebuttals of those speeches. We tell and hear jokes, give advice to troubled friends, and receive other advice in return. We glance at ads, keep track of traffic signals, notice facial expressions, observe differences in style of dress — messages are around us from morning to night. While they are so different from each other in so many ways that it is difficult to conceive of them all under the same heading of messages, they are still messages, still packages of human communication.

This book is about one particular kind of message and one particular kind of communication situation. It concerns the messages by which one person comes to know what another person is feeling in ordinary face-to-face dealings between people in pairs or small groups. By delimiting the subject matter thus sharply I have reduced our conceptual problem enormously: I shall not have to face the entire diversity of human communication all at once. The problem is not one that can be altogether avoided, however. The fact that communication is diverse is itself a fact of life, and bears looking at for a while to determine where the exchange of emotional messages fits into other kinds of exchange. That is the task of this first chapter. It will include a brief overview of human communication, and a review of the functions which communication is said to serve. As the discussion gets closer to our topic of

1

emotional communication, a good many of the references will come from works on language, since man has been thinking about that form of communication for millennia and has been writing about it almost as long as he has been writing about anything. These writings do not apply exclusively to language, however, but to any form of human communication, and I shall draw upon them freely in order to examine what has been said in this whole area of human activity.

THE FIELD OF HUMAN COMMUNICATION

Communication has been a central concern of a number of established disciplines for a very long time. Among the social sciences this has been especially true of both sociology and psychology, in which the founding fathers began writing extensively about communication in one or another of its forms in the late nineteenth century. In a number of other fields, such as speech, journalism, and radio broadcasting, communication is even more obviously the focus of the activities of these fields. In still others, such as education and business management, the communicative aspects of their various tasks have come to be recognized more and more widely as the fields have developed. In the past two decades or so communication has crystallized as a discipline in its own right, and workers from many professional and scientific backgrounds have contributed to it. Since it is so new, it has been struggling with many of the same issues of identity which other fields grappled with when they were at the same stage of development.

A particularly conspicuous manifestation of the identity struggle has been a deeply felt need to delineate exactly what this new discipline consists of. In fact, few aspects of human endeavor have been as blessed by attempts at definition as communication. The reason is obvious: Communication encompasses so wide a range of activities that trying to gather all of them into one's thinking seems like equating communication with life itself. Many writers have consequently tried to be logical about the subject by defining the area of their work, hoping that they will then be less likely to stray too far, and hoping, too, that they will be better understood by their readers. This certainly is a useful approach to writing a book on the topic or introducing a conference about it. G. A. Miller gave a definition in the former context, for example (1951,

p. 6), and Stevens offered one in the latter (1950, p. 689). Yet the need to define communication goes beyond these uses. Whole articles have been written with definition as their main purpose. The pair by G. R. Miller (1966) and Gerbner (1966) are good illustrations. And apart from articles devoted entirely to defining the field, there are many comments on the problem in other papers. For example, Thayer (1963), in the opening paragraphs of a discussion of some issues of theorizing in this discipline, notes that in reviewing six years of literature on communication he found "more than 25 *conceptually different* referents for this term" (p. 219).

There have even been two formal studies of the many existing definitions of communication. Minter (1968) surveyed a number of experienced workers on their opinions about the relative merits of a dozen definitions of the term. Dance (1970) examined 95 such definitions by content analysis of their main themes in order to find some bases for clarification of the concept. In could almost be said that definition is a subfield of communication.

The problem of organizing the many diverse aspects of communication has manifested itself in other ways than struggling with definition. There have also been many efforts to fit the available facts together into some theoretical structure. But building a theory of communication is an even tougher job than defining it, and the authors of a number of attempts at theoretical formulation have hinted at their awe of the task in their titles: "Toward a theory of . . . ," "An approach to . . . ," and the like. Krippendorff (1969) believes that a theory of the entire field is impossible at the present time, arguing that several theories about specialized aspects of communication will coexist for some time within a broad discipline. Thayer, in the article just cited, lists several obstacles to productive theory, such as some unwritten assumptions and some forms of conceptual sloppiness, which seem to him to characterize much of the thinking about communication. Driessel's discussion (1967) is more general. He writes about levels of theory, the functions of models in theory building, and the like. His comments could quite as well apply to any area of science. And finally, another survey: Andersen (1964) polled experts in the field on their choice of the ten most significant books on communication in the past decade, and on their opinions about the important trends represented in those books. Clearly

many people in communication want to know what their discipline is
all about and where it is going.

Of course the fact that diversity in a field gives conceptual problems
to its workers is not new, especially in the social sciences. There have
been many articles, too, on what psychology consists of, and sociology,
and so on. It is a problem that bothers the first workers in every discipline and returns periodically to plague subsequent generations. But it
does not impose too much inhibition on daily research activities:
everyone knows that when an investigator studies part of a large field,
he should not expect his results to be immediately applicable to all other
parts. By the same token, theorizing about one particular subtopic does
not neccessarily impose the responsibility for writing a theory of the
entire area of endeavor. That may be impossible for most social sciences,
and at the present time it almost certainly is for communication.

The danger of diversity, on the other hand, is that one can work
in what is usually called splendid isolation, and miss out on work in
seemingly distant areas that surprisingly would add a great deal to
one's own progress — if one only knew about it. There will be some
examples in later chapters where I call upon research results from quite
distant areas of communication. True, I shall be doing it almost out of
desperation, since those results will comprise just about the only available
evidence for the point I am trying to make. We often remain blissfully
unaware that such seemingly distant evidence is applicable, that there
is unity as well as diversity in a large field.

Stating the topic of this book as face-to-face communication of
emotion between people in pairs or small groups serves to locate it
within the general field of human communication in two ways: (1) it
narrows down the settings or occasions in which the communicative activity takes place, that is, delineates the who and the where of the message exchange; and (2) it specifies the subject matter thus communicated.
As to the first point, the definition limits us to studying individual people as the senders and receivers of the messages of interest. This means
that our work lies closest to those areas of communication research in
which people are involved as individuals, or in which the results may
be extended to people by analogue. Just how close the area must be
for the analogue to be applicable depends partly upon the ingenuity
of the investigator, of course; but there are some topics in communica-

tion which seem on the surface rather farfetched: machine-to-machine communication, for example, where the focus is computer interfaces, or such transportation networks as canals and railroad systems. The face-to-face feature of the definition further locates our topic as close to those which include the possibility of spontaneous behavior on the part of the participants: small group interaction is clearly one of these.

The second main part of the definition — specifying the subject matter as emotion — is a different way of slicing the pie. The factors we have just been considering are structural ones: they concern the communication chain itself, the sender and receiver, and the setting in which it operates. The introduction of emotion as an aspect of the definition adds content: what sort of message is exchanged by means of this chain, whatever the occasion might be. There are, to be sure, some "natural" combinations of structure and content in communication. Messages consisting entirely of numbers in the form of *bits*, for example, are far more likely in machine-to-machine communication than in the mass media. But many sorts of content can be communicated many ways, and emotion is just one of the possibilities in face-to-face situations with small numbers of participants.

Functions of Communication

To say that emotion is just another type of subject matter for communication brings us to a controversy that has been going on in the philosophy of language for some time. We may extend the various aspects of the dispute from language *per se* to communication generally with little loss in the substance of the argument, and we will need to keep this more general approach in mind because this is the section where most of the citations we shall be using are about language specifically.

Briefly, the argument is that language is one of the highest forms of human accomplishment, along with reason itself, and therefore the purpose of language should be to communicate logical, reasoned information. As Newman (1939) put it, "The official function of language is rational communication" (p. 177). The trouble is, however, that man is not always rational, and neither is the language he uses. The official function, instead, is an ideal, and over the years many writers have noted the many ways in which the ideal is interfered with in day-to-day dealings between people. Newman continues:

> The notion that language has its nonrational and personal aspects is by no means new and unfamiliar. It has often been pointed out that words carry emotive overtones that merge with their referential content. Affective implications have been recognized in many of the phenomena of speech, such as intonation, accent, timbre, speed, etc. Freud has shown that slips of the tongue are significant indicators of personal motivations. Yet the dogma persists that the function of language is intellectual and collective. Although other functions can be demonstrated, they are regarded as of distinctly minor importance, or, even worse, they are felt to be illegitimate intrusions upon the essentially rational and impersonal business of language (p. 178).

We thus have what seems to be a simple division of language use into the rational and the emotive. Many pairs of words have been used to refer to the two sides of this dichotomy: referential, scientific, cognitive, and so on, for the first; and affective, expressive, noncognitive, and the like, for the second. This dichotomy is closely allied to our oldest ideas about man himself. He is partly divine, and partly a beast; capable of reason and serious deliberation, yet prey to unthinking appetites and passions. These ideas, of course, are at the heart of the psychophysical dualism of Plato, perhaps best exemplified in passages from *The Phaedo*, where the soul and the body are compared. Through the soul we can "be pure and hold converse with the pure, and know of ourselves the clear light everywhere which is no other than the light of truth," but the body "fills us full of loves, and lusts, and fears, and fancies of all kinds. . . ." (Jowett translation, pp. 66, 67). It is no wonder that with the mind-body dualism of Plato so firmly established on the philosophical scene, the dichotomy of the rational and the emotional in language should be called linguistic dualism by philosophers of language (Frankena, 1958a, p. 122) and treated as such by many workers in the field.

Any dualism poses many problems, and thinkers about language have been far from satisfied with this one, just as philosophers have been unhappy with the neat Platonic division of mind and body. It is a curious fact, however, that resolution of this problem has never been sought by positing a monism in place of the dualism, by saying that the two sides of the dichotomy are only descriptively separable aspects of a single underlying process, as Spinoza had done in the case of the mind-body dualism. Instead, efforts to deal with the linguistic dualism have gone in the reverse direction. Most writers argue that there are really not simply two functions of language, the rational and the emotive, but more than two — three or five, or whatever — thus tending to dilute the strong polarity of the dichotomy. Elaborations have accordingly been offered by a succession of writers, so that lists of "kinds of language" or "functions of language" have by now proliferated beyond any usefulness. Despite the many elaborations, however, there remains a kind of primitive sense to the original dichotomy. I believe in fact that all the lists really retain the dualism, even while their authors are trying to do away with it. Let us examine some of the history of this thinking.

Ogden and Richards (1923) were the first of the modern philosophers of language to see the need to distinguish what they called the symbolic and emotive functions of language. To differentiate the two in any given instance, one poses a question: " 'Is this true or false in the ordinary strict scientific sense?' If this question is relevant then the use is symbolic, if it is clearly irrelevant then we have an emotive utterance" (p. 140). Their view of the dichotomy is not as simple as that, however, for they separate each function into two sides — that of the speaker and that of the listener. Thus the speaker may be expressing something from within himself, or he may be trying to evoke a response in the listener. Ogden and Richards later (pp. 223-228) divide the emotive function into four separate ones: the expression of attitudes toward the listener; the expression of attitudes toward the subject matter being talked about; evoking response in the listener; and, finally, what they call support of reference, in which the speaker indicates to the listener the clarity or relative ease of connecting symbol and referent. Still later (pp. 232-235) they recognize that while individual words may serve to indicate these various functions, there are longer-term effects, as well, such as choice of words and appropriateness to the situation at hand, which may also get the idea across.

Morris (1946), following upon the work of Ogden and Richards, also distinguished between smaller and larger units of language in referring to signs and sign complexes (ascriptors), on the one hand, and to other behaviors on the other. In his opinion, signs may have four modes of signifying (some of them sound emotive in the sense we have been using that term, but are not necessarily so, as Morris views things): identifying (signifying location in time or space); designative (specifying the characteristic of the referents to the sign); appraising (evaluating the referents according to some criterion); and prescriptive (signifying some action to be taken). Sign complexes are groupings of signs, in which some referent is introduced and something further said about it, thus forming a somewhat larger unit. Emotion appears to have come into the picture in the third and fourth functions of signs, the appraising and the prescriptive. But Morris holds that his analysis involves only the signs and the properties inherent in them. Words which refer to emotions may or may not be emotional. Emotion is not inherent in a sign; it is introduced by the hearer. It may mean something to him that the speaker is producing this particular set of signs and not others, and he may use this information itself as a sign about the inner state of the speaker. Morris argues that this is on a different level of analysis, and has nothing to do with the modes of signifying that are inherent in the signs themselves. These interpretations of emotion by the listener are very reminiscent of Ogden and Richards' longer-term effects, mentioned above. Perception of emotionality rests upon inferences which the listener makes from the speaker's behavior.

Ogden and Richards' book contains an essay by Malinowski (1923), who was struck by the importance of their analysis of language for anthropologists who were trying to understand vastly different tongues. On the basis of his field work, Malinowski felt that a quite separate language function should be posited to add to the main two which Ogden and Richards had written about. This consists of small talk whose content is so stereotyped as to lose meaning, such as many greetings and chats about the weather, and talk that accompanies ongoing work but is quite unrelated to the task at hand. The purpose of this sort of talk is not to convey information in any scientific sense, nor is it necessarily emotional. The real function, according to Malinowski, is to cement bonds between speaker and hearer, "a communion of words . . . to establish links of fellowship [akin to] breaking of bread and communion of food" (p. 314). Malinowski calls this function phatic communion, "a type of speech in which the ties of union are created by a mere exchange of words" (p. 315). This social function of language was spelled out more completely a few years later by de Laguna (1927), who argued that it was the main function, eclipsing that of communicating ideas. "Speech is the great medium through which human cooperation is brought about," she wrote. "It is the means by which the diverse activities of men are coordinated and correlated with each other for the attainment of common and reciprocal ends" (p. 19).

De Laguna's separation of the functions of communication of ideas and social regulation has been echoed more recently by Birdwhistell (1962). He writes that the passage of new information from one person to another is only "one aspect of the communicative process [but] no more important than what we call the *integrational* aspect of communicative process" (p. 196). The integrational includes keeping the systems operating, regulating interaction, placing the communication in context, and keeping contexts straight. The importance of these functions is stressed even more strongly by Scheflen (1963), a colleague of Birdwhistell, who sees " 'new' information exchange as a relatively unusual function, much less frequent than other functions, such as the maintenance of established relationships" (p. 128).

Another influential writer, Bühler (1934), started not from the rational-emotional dichotomy, but rather from a three-part schema of language function: the expressive, expressing the inner state of the speaker; the release or signaling function, designed to elicit a reaction from the hearer; and the descriptive, in which language symbols are used to refer to other things. Bühler listed these functions in hierarchical order from the simplest to most complex; and the order had another feature, too: the higher functions included the simpler ones, but the lower ones did not necessarily include those which were more advanced. In addition, "simple" in this scheme means more primitive. Animal communication is made up entirely of the lower-order expressive and release functions, according to Bühler, while the most complex function, the descriptive, is exclusively human. The old dichotomy thus remains in the shadows of this scheme since only the descriptive function can be considered "rational," or the result of human thought.

Several writers have built upon Bühler's classification. McGranahan (1936) subdivided both the expressive and release functions into the rational and the emotional, and then added what he called the material, consisting of those features of speech which do not represent anything symbolically in the sense that linguistic forms do, but which still tell about the state of mind of the speaker. These features may also have a direct effect on the hearer, as in the case of an angry tone of voice, for example. Thus McGranahan also maintained, along with Ogden and Richards and with Morris, that information about emotion can be communicated in two ways: by linguistic forms that are completely descriptive in Bühler's terms, and by other behaviors from which the hearer may infer emotion.

Bühler and McGranahan both claimed a "primitiveness" for emotional expression, and they were not alone among writers on language. Ogden and Richards agreed that "the emotive use of words . . . is probably more primitive" [1923, p. 145]. Sapir (1923) went even further than this, saying that the emotional was first in the development of language in man. To make this point he developed a theory of the origins of symbolism both in gestures and in speech sounds. In both cases some act first occurs which is an emotional response to some stimulus. Then some part of the act is used as a recognizable substitute for the whole act, and this substitute becomes accepted as such by the society at large. Only after such universal acceptance can the substitute act be thought of as a symbol, for then it can be used to refer to the original events, even though the emotional content — and indeed the event itself — is no longer present. Once the act has become a symbol and not just a pictorial reminder, it may be simplified by its users so that it loses all resemblance to its historical roots and appears to be a completely arbitrary sign for the situation.

In the light of recent research it is no longer possible to assert simply and categorically that language is exclusive to man. Techniques used by the Gardners (1969) and Premack (1970, 1971) have opened the way to learning more about this fascinating possibility than we could ever have known before. The Gardners have reported preliminary findings on teaching a chimpanzee American Sign Language, a means of communicating apparently ideally suited to the manually oriented chimp. The learning of this young animal is predictably much slower than that of a human child learning to talk, but her learning curve of signs is a positively accelerating one, like that of children's vocabularies, and had not leveled off at the time of the report. She has shown evidence of using signs to refer to people as well as to objects which are not present and which she is not simply asking for, as she does for food when she is hungry. While this use of language is not very complicated, the young chimp was still learning at a faster and faster pace at the time of the report, so we cannot tell how far she may go. To answer the repeated question about whether this animal "has language," the Gardners feel the need for some new formulations of what "language" is.

Premack's approach was to teach an adult chimpanzee a form of written language, in which pieces of metal-backed plastic represented words and were placed upon a magnetic slate to form sentences. Through this means he has explored the animal's ability to handle 8 different concepts which we ordinarily think of as being linguistic in nature, such as words, sentences (including order relationships), and the logical connective if-then. While Premack (1971, p. 809) disclaimed any logical sequence to these concepts, they are plainly ordered in complexity, as evidenced by the animal's performance in learning them. It took her almost no time to learn that pieces of plastic could 'stand for' objects and activities in the real world, while teaching her the logical connective required a good deal of painstaking training which built on all she had learned before. At some point along this continuum we should be able to call her behavior, and the understanding which her behavior evidenced, language in the true sense, and indeed Premack referred to the "prelanguage phase" of her training while discussing her difficulty in mastering the if-then relation (1971, p. 820).

The accomplishments of these two animals and their trainers clearly raise the question of what language really is in relationship to other sorts of behavior, and in turn of what anyone could mean by 'primitive language' in the context of the discussion in this chapter. Perhaps later results of these and other experiments will force new conceptualizations in this muddy area.

To return to elaborations of language functions, we have seen that McGranahan built onto Bühler's three-part scheme by specifying in greater detail the nonrational end of the hierarchy. Popper (1963) extended the system at the other end. He found that not enough of the strictly human function of language could be accounted for in the descriptive category, and added another, the "argumentative" or "explanatory," on top of the original hierarchy. This function consists of "the presentation and comparison of arguments in connection with certain questions and problems" (p. 135). Jakobson (1960) lengthened Bühler's list of three functions in a different way. At first accepting Malinowski's (1923) phatic communion as a fourth function, he then added two more of his own: the poetic, in which the form or beauty of the message is the main interest, and the metalingual, which is about the language itself, as the name implies — checking to see that speaker and listener are using the same code so that they can be sure to understand each other.

Thus far we have looked at several lists of language function, all having the same linguistic dualism built in somewhere of what is strictly human in the sense of the most rational and lofty capabilities of *Homo sapiens* compared with what is shared between humans and other animals. Beyond this the proliferation of other language functions is based upon a number of factors, but we are left without much basis for choosing one list over another. Miller and McNeill (1969) put it this way:

> It is obviously true that we use language differently when we give and obey orders, describe an object, report an event, speculate about an event, form and test a hypothesis, make up a story, play-act, sing, guess riddles, tell jokes, translate, ask, thank, curse, greet, or pray. But why should we believe that these diverse functions . . . are finite in number, or that any short and generally useful list can be constructed? (p. 752).

The answer is that lists may be built on many bases, but they do not really erase the basic dualism. Frankena (1958a, 1958b) came to this conclusion in two carefully reasoned essays. In the first he proposed a list of nine functions of language, or "aspects" as he called them; in the second he set out to determine which of these were cognitive or rational and which were noncognitive or emotive. He found that these two terms may apply to any of the nine aspects, and furthermore that a given utterance might be cognitive in some aspects and noncognitive in others. The three "aspects" most obviously related to emotional communication are: the emotions and attitudes which are expressed by the speaker in the words he uses, his tone of voice, or whatever; the emotions which the speaker's utterance may stir up in the hearer; and the feelings, beliefs, or attitudes which the speaker may reveal to the hearer, with or without intending to. This last aspect is quite similar to the instances dealt with by other authors, from Ogden and Richards on, in which the listener must make some inference on the basis of what the speaker has said. The most cognitive aspects listed by Frankena have to do with conceptual content and assertional attitude, or how much the speaker claims truth for his utterance. Again, Frankena, like McGranahan, notes that words referring to emotions, or utterances referring to emotional situations, can be completely cognitive.

Looking back now at the extensive thinking about language function which we have reviewed, how might we use it to pin down what emotional messages are? Two main points may be made: one about the various attempts at classification, and the other about what it takes to tell that an emotion has been expressed.

First, about classification. There are clearly many uses or functions of language and — to generalize now beyond that medium — of communication. They are not easy to list with any conviction, and few of the writers cited here has claimed that his particular list was exhaustive. One thing stands out in all the lists: despite attempts to get rid of the old rational-emotional dichotomy, the thread of it still remains — a more than usually slippery thread, since there are many exceptions when one tries to apply it in classifying given instances of communication function. Still its persistence, and the arguments it has engendered, are instructive. Perhaps the greatest use of the arguments is to remind us that communication is more complicated than simply classifying things into either of two categories. The hope is that some of the elaborations which have grown out of the old dichotomy will enable us to think more clearly about specific instances of communication that come to our attention, and to avoid a number of not-too-obvious slips into naiveté in our work.

Now to the second point: how we know that an emotion has been expressed. While many emotional aspects of utterances may be contained in words, the intrinsic "meanings" of words are sometime things, and cannot always be relied upon for knowing what goes on inside the speaker. Furthermore, the same words may be used to further any of a number of functions in any communicative act. Almost all the writers I have referred to are at one on this point. How, then, can we know about the emotion? Surely the listener is not always in the dark, making wild guesses about what is going on in the speaker. Instead, the listener makes repeated inductive leaps about many aspects of the communication, including emotion in the speaker. He does this by paying attention to all the cues he can get hold of — the very words that have been spoken; the fact that certain words and not others have been uttered; the voice quality used in their utterance; visible evidence of bodily tension; and so on. The process is as follows: most utterances have several communicative functions, and the listener cannot identify all of them all the time, since trying to do so would be too distracting while he attempts to keep up with the conversation. He will likely be interested in only one of these functions at any given time, and he can only make an off-hand judgment of whether that one is being served by the utterance at hand. Some of the various possible functions may involve emotion; some may involve it very little, or not at all. The point is that when emotion as part of the communication comes to the fore, the listener will come to a conclusion that something new has been added, and he will do this on the basis of some aspect of the speaker's behavior. Whatever aspect it was will have attracted the listener's attention as a cue, and from it he will infer that the speaker is now expressing himself emotionally in addition to, or instead of, some other way.

Thus we have arrived at a behavioral referent for emotional expression and at a locus for its conceptualization. By behavioral referent I mean that the cues the listener uses to make his inductive leap about the presence of emotion are behaviors, visible or audible, on the part of the speaker. By locus I mean that the listener or observer is the one who makes the inductive leap. This combination of referent and locus, one worth looking at closely, has a major implication for this book. It focuses our effort on the interaction between speaker and listener, on the relationship between the behaviors of the one and the interpretations of the other. As a corollary it effectively shuts the door on some kinds of analysis of emotional expression, except insofar as the results of these other analyses might corroborate our main evidence. The phenomenological is one approach that is excluded, particularly the analysis of the speaker's experience of his own emotions as they ebb and flow within his own awareness. I do not believe that the study of emotional communication could proceed otherwise, at least in the terms we shall

be using to study it—the channels used for expressing emotional information, for example, and the relative amounts of information conveyed by different sorts of messages; these must rest upon observables
for their primary data.

What we have gained from this survey, then, is a delineation of
the area of human communication on which we wish to concentrate from
now on— emotional messages. I do not expect to be able to remain
very pure in subsequent discussion about those other messages which
may be going on at the same time. Sometimes they will be uncomplicated
information exchange, sometimes orders or exhortations, sometimes status-
seeking ploys, and so on. I shall be inclined to call all of them "cognitive messages" and let it go at that, but I hope that this will not
constitute a license for forgetting that there are other kinds of communication besides the emotional, and that they, too, are complicated
and deserve study in their own right.

PART I

THE TRANSMISSION OF EMOTIONAL MESSAGES

The first main section of this book is about communication. As indicated earlier, I have chosen the most general theory in the field, Shannon's mathematical theory of communication, as the main framework into which to link both thinking and facts. Chapter 2, an exposition of that theory, will explain how the facts about emotional messages can and cannot be fitted into its outline. It would be surprising if they all could, since the messages the theory was designed for are so different from those that occur in human social interaction. It turns out that Shannon's theory cannot cover everything we would like it to cover, even though at a certain level of abstraction it can meet our requirements. But the fact that other theories will have to be called in from time to time in this work should not detract from our admiration of the one set forth by Shannon. Its generality is really astonishing. It is not news, of course, that a psychologist should find the theory promising, since it has been used for almost two decades in psychological research; but the way the theory is applied here is quite different from the usual psychological application. The outline of the theory in Chapter 2 will consequently need to be somewhat more detailed in some aspects than might be thought necessary after all these years of familiarity.

The next five chapters are about emotional communication. Chapters 3, 4, and 5 are arranged in roughly the same order in which the various topics are usually taken up in texts on communication theory: the measurement of information, channels, and noise. When I say "roughly the same order" I mean that there are two exceptions. First, there is no single chapter on coding, or how things are translated into alphabets for easier handling. Different aspects of that topic are dealt with in chapters 3 and 4. The other exception is that, since we are talking about humans as communicators, most of one chapter — again the fourth — is about their psychology, their fears, intentions, and capabilities, and how these factors affect the communication process. At that point we have to add to Shannon's theory by going to other sources to frame our thinking. Psychoanalytic theory is an important other source here, and signal detection theory receives more than casual mention.

Chapter 6 (the final one in the set of five about emotional communication proper) is a treatment of the way in which emotional messages are exchanged in social situations. Using all the concepts and thinking developed in the preceding parts of the book, it traces the details of the process in social interaction, with attention to the inevitable interferences which block communication from time to time, and to theoretical and research efforts that have tried to account for these blocks. Again we need other theories in the course of this chapter, and Broadbent's formulation of attention serves us very well.

Chapter Two

The Theory of Communication ⸻⸻⸻

Thus far we have made a general statement of what emotional messages are, and we have had a brief look at some of their characteristics. They consist of behaviors on the part of one person which serve as cues for another in inferring something about the first person's emotional state. Thus two people are involved, and the focus of the communication is on the interaction between them. The purpose of this chapter is to describe the theory by which this interaction can be studied in greater detail. The one I have chosen is Claude Shannon's mathematical theory of communication. This theory was developed in the quite distant field of telecommunication, but it is sufficiently general that since its original publication it has been found to serve very well in a number of other areas, psychology included. It cannot be a complete theory of human communication, as will become clear here and in later chapters, but it does provide a broad framework within which to discuss what emotional messages are and how they are evaluated, and a number of factors that affect their transmission and reception.

Shannon's _The Mathematical Theory of Communication_ was published in 1948, and reprinted in Shannon and Weaver (1949). The theory has been outlined several times in books and journals in psychology, but I shall do so again here for two reasons. The first, and less important, is convenience for the reader. The second and main reason is that psychologists and others outside of communication engineering have tended to use only part of the theory. With few exceptions, all the articles and books in psychology and in neighboring disciplines using communication theory have dealt only with the information measure which is part of the theory. While I shall go into the reason for this in more detail later, let me say briefly that most writers have analogized from the communication net involving transmitter and receiver to a closed system consisting of an organism with inputs and outputs. Indeed, part of the useful generality of the theory lies in the fact that it lends itself to such analogies. As a result, what Shannon called "communication theory" is widely known as "information theory" — in the Library of Congress catalogue, even to some extent in the field of communication engineering, especially in England. The first books on the subject in psychology use the phrase "information theory" in their titles (see Quastler, 1955, and Attneave, 1959).

The history of communication theory, as we will be using it, is the history of telecommunication, and includes the well-known names of Morse and Edison. Pierce gives a fine presentation of this development (1961, Chap. 2); but lest the reader conclude that the scene has been dominated by American workers, he might also consult Cherry's review (1952). The early attempts to conceptualize information as the commodity of communication came during the 1920's as a result of the burgeoning of radio broadcasting and the need to explain limiting factors in speed of telegraphy and telephony. Impetus for newer developments came during World War II, when more complicated problems had to be solved. In the course of finding solutions to quite different problems, two men came to the conclusion that signals and the noise that corrupts them can best be described in terms of statistical probabilities. These were Norbert Wiener, who was working on problems of prediction and control in directing guns onto their targets by means of automatic machines, and Claude Shannon, whose field was secrecy codes and telecommunication. They developed the same definition of information quite independently, although each acknowledged a debt to the other in the development of their respective ideas. There has been almost no overlap in their subsequent work.

In psychology, information measurement was first proposed by Miller and Frick (1949), and given in greater computational detail by Garner and Hake (1951). It was Garner and Hake who proposed using the communication model in the way most psychologists have followed, as I shall explain after we have had a first look at the communication network which the theory follows. A general article on the statistics which could be derived from information measures was soon given by McGill

(1954); a subsequent one by Garner and McGill (1956) related these statistics to analysis of variance. A recent article by Binder and Wolin (1964) clarifies a number of related statistical problems derived from the theory as it has been applied to psychological research. In the meantime a good deal of experimental work had been in progress principally in the field of perception, using the Garner-Hake application of the model as the basis for the experimental design and analysis of results. Garner used many of these experiments as examples in his *Uncertainty and Structure as Psychological Concepts* (1962) as he developed ideas about structure, meaning, and concept formation.

The model used in the mathematical theory of communication is essentially that of a telecommunication network. Figure 1 shows the several elements of this model as presented by Fano (1961). The components are connected in the form of a flow chart, and messages pass from one to another of these components, being transformed and retransformed on their way from originator to recipient. At this level of generality the messages can consist of anything from speech to the output of measuring devices, and the originator and recipient can each be either man or machine. It is perhaps easiest to trace the whole process by referring to the original application of telecommunication, the telegraph. The message from the source is first transformed into dots, dashes, and the spaces between them. These in turn are made into pulses of electricity to be sent over a wire. At the other end of the line the pulses are transformed back into dots, dashes, and spaces, which are then translated into the letters of the message.

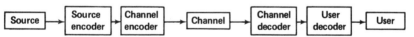

Fig. 1. A model of a communication system (after Fano, 1961).

In a telegram the message as handed to the user is a reproduction of that given by the sender to the telegraph operator. Reproduction, of course, is a relative term: some will serve the purpose better than others. As Fano (1961) says, "One could claim that the very word reproduction implies the existence of a criterion of acceptability. For instance, we do not expect Western Union to deliver a piece of paper looking like the one submitted by the sender. Furthermore, the ad-

dressee is inclined to regard a telegraphic message as satisfactory even
if some of the letters are incorrect, as long as he can understand its
meaning" (pp. 3-4). Indeed, in some situations of machine-to-man communication, reproduction of the original message would serve no purpose. When a computer has solved a problem, the original message inside the computer, the answer to the problem, consists of the status of
a series of flip-flops, which would be meaningless to most persons using
the machine.

Before we continue, let us see how this model in this form can
be applied to social communication in a face-to-face situation. Suppose
that the persons involved, instead of being in separate cities and having
to send and receive a telegram, were in the same room and could talk
to each other. In this case the sending person (source), having an idea
to get across, transforms his idea into linguistic forms (source encoding); and since he is going to talk instead of writing a telegram, he
shapes these linguistic forms by means of his vocal apparatus and
articulators into sounds (channel encoding) rather than into letters and
words on paper. The receiving person hears the sounds through the air
between them (channel) and groups them together into linguistic forms
(channel decoding), which he finally translates centrally (user decoding)
into the idea the sending person had wished to communicate, thus understanding what was said (user). The same functions of all the components in Figure 1 are all being performed, but an important difference is that in the telegraph situation the components are all independent
of each other, while in the conversation they are not. In direct, face-
to-face communication the first three functions all reside in one person, and the last three functions are all within the other person.

Ideas, linguistic forms, and speech performance are all intimately
related, so nonindependence of these functions means mutual influence.
It may be that on this account cognitive messages like the one depicted
above are not easy to fit into the model. Parenthetically I believe that
at some level of abstraction all messages are candidates for the model,
but we have a lot to learn about thought and language before we can
say how. Yet are we any less likely to confuse the different functions
in the case of emotional messages? As an example, one of the people
in the conversation might have a feeling, such as pleasure at hearing
something the other person has said. First he recognizes this feeling

as pleasure; then, instead of commenting on it in words, he simply smiles. The smile is formed by the complicated musculature of his face, and is seen across the space between the two persons in the room. The receiving person sees the expression, interprets it as a smile, then translates it into the idea of pleasure. He understands this idea perhaps as a feeling of pleasure within himself, or at least as evidence that the sending person has felt pleased.

If we look at this course of a relatively uncomplicated emotional message as it travels through the communication system, we see the same nonindependence of components that obtained for cognitive messages. The functions before the channel are all performed by one person; those after it are performed by another. The question is whether this nonindependence spells mutual influence as much in this case as it does with cognitive messages. The smile may actually illustrate the greatest confusion among emotional messages, and a relatively common one. Facial expression is particularly well suited to emotional messages, and among facial expressions especially the smile, just as language, is very well fitted to cognitive expression. But there are other combinations of expressive means and emotions, and among these the dangers of confusion may not be so great. In any case, confusion on this score does not necessarily preclude our using the communication model. It may mean that we have to use it at a higher level of abstraction, as I have noted that we might in the case of cognitive communication, or better yet that we must supplement the theory at certain points to achieve precision in our work. Indeed, in chapters to follow, we shall be taking this latter tack from time to time. In the meantime we must return to the outline of communication theory and to its application to human interaction.

When the two people are not in the same room, but are using the telegraph or telephone or television, the channel becomes extended, as depicted in Figure 2. All the events within the sending person become the source for the electromechanical network; those within the receiving person become the user. The nature of the extending device will impose limits on the sort of message the source person can send and the user person can detect, and will thus affect the channel encoding and decoding processes within both persons. Laughter, for example, is an appropriate expression on both telephone and television, but a smile can be trans-

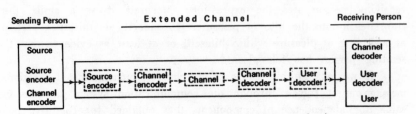

Fig. 2. A model of a person-to-person telecommunication system.

mitted only on the latter — despite the fact that people constantly smile while using the telephone. Neither a laugh nor a smile, however, can be sent or received in a telegram unless they are first translated into words.

Now that the general outline of the communication system has been presented, we have the terms with which to explain the use of the model in psychology as proposed by Garner and Hake (1951). These authors were working in the field of perception, where the experimenter presents stimuli to the subject and records his responses. They took the view that the subject himself could be regarded as the channel, with the experimental stimuli being the input in place of the source and the subject's responses being the output, where Shannon put the user. Thus instead of a system composed of two parallel sets of components, one in the transmitter and the other in the receiver, Garner and Hake put the entire system within the one person. Figure 3 shows this arrangement of the original components of the communication network derived from Figure 1. The advantage of this use of the theory is that it permits the experimenter to study the stimulus-response relationship in statistical terms that have been derived from the theory, such as contingent probabilities over stimuli and responses. It also allows him to compare the results from one study with those of the next in terms of how efficiently the subjects have discriminated the stimuli. I believe that there is an attendant disadvantage: one is likely to think of the information statistics as coterminous with all of communication theory, and consequently to believe that the theory only gives us "just another statistic," and that is all. Garner is not thus persuaded, and his book

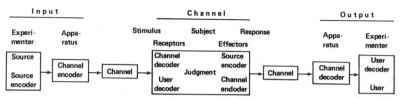

Fig. 3.   Representation of the Garner-Hake (1951) use of communication theory.

(1962) attests to his own understanding and use of the theory as a whole.

I have said that the Garner-Hake use of the terms from the communication theory model is analogical. It may also seem that the way I have used them in talking about social communication is an analogy, though perhaps of a different kind. I believe, however, that in principle, social communication events actually occur in this sequence, and that the model has sufficient generality to include the communication of emotions in social situations. It will be one of the major uses of the model to learn, as we fill in the details, what aspects of human communication can and cannot be covered by the theory, and for what reasons the model fails at those points where it proves insufficient. In some cases it may turn out that there are not enough data from studies of social interaction to know whether the model fits or not; and where it is possible to collect such data, the theory will have helped us to enlarge our knowledge. At other points it may be that the gaps lie in the model, not in the facts, when applied to our field, and here the theory will need to be enlarged or perhaps even abandoned in favor of a better one. One of these outcomes — and we should hope both of them — must result from any application of theory.

The mathematical theory of communication takes up four topics within the model already presented: (1) the nature and measurement of information; (2) the coding of messages in terms of the language being used in transmission (the topic of coding includes, of course, decoding at the other end); (3) the nature of channels, their capacity, and the constrictions they place upon transmitting messages; and (4) the effects of noise on the successful transmission of information. These various parts of the theory are interrelated, rather than a series of steps in which each step follows directly from the preceding one. The result is that the order in which they are discussed varies from one presentation to another. In addition a number of other topics are usually included, such as the various types of stochastic processes and their implications for coding efficiency. In some texts a good deal of probability theory is included, and one author, Brillouin (1962), devotes considerable thought to the relationship between the theoretical loss of information in communication nets and the limitations of measurement at the subatomic level in physics. In this presentation of the theory we shall take up the four main topics in the order listed above.

THE NATURE AND MEASUREMENT OF INFORMATION

In communication theory information consists of what the source in the model of Figure 1 submits to the source encoder: it may be letters, numbers, complex waveforms, pulses, or whatever. Here, however, we depart from the usual usage of the term "information." The theory is not about the information itself, but about its measurement and its transmission. Thus the source may not be particularly interested in it, and it may serve no purpose of the user. In Weaver's words, "*Information* must not be confused with meaning. In fact, two messages, one of which is heavily loaded with meaning and the other of which is pure nonsense, can be exactly equivalent, from the present viewpoint, as regards information" (Shannon and Weaver, 1949, p. 99). Brillouin (1962) puts it this way: "We completely ignore the human value of the information. A selection of 100 letters is given a certain information value, and we do not investigate whether it makes sense in English, and, if so, whether the meaning of the sentence is of any importance. According to our definition, a set of 100 letters selected at random, a sentence of 100 letters from a newspaper, a piece of Shakespeare or a theorem of Einstein are given exactly the same information value. In other words, we do not define 'information' as distinct from 'knowledge,' for which we have no numerical measure" (p. 9).

So fullness of meaning is not the measure of information, nor is the value it may have in the eyes of the user. What then can communication theory be talking about when it uses this word? What it means by information is, as I have said above, simply anything that the source submits to the coder for transmission to the user, and its measure lies in its scarcity, its surprise value, its oddity. Scarcity turns up in two ways: (1) the number of categories into which elements of a message may be cast, and (2) the relative frequency of use of these categories. To understand the first of these let us compare messages made of the binary digits *0* and *1* with those made up of the letters of the alphabet. In the case of binary digits there are only two categories, and if the two are used equally often the chances of selecting one of them are even, or .5. In the case of the alphabet, on the other hand, there are 26 categories, and the chances of finding one in 26 are .03846, again assuming that all are used equally. Each of the letters is thus much more rare than each of the binary digits, and for this reason can carry more information per message element although, as we shall see in a moment, not 13 times as much as the above proportions might imply. A letter from the alphabet, then, has much greater potential for carrying information than a binary digit. The letters *may* not mean anything, but they *could* mean a great deal. Each one, for example, might stand for a person's name, for a city, for an item in an inventory, for a location in a file drawer, for a book. Twenty-six categories are available when using the alphabet, whereas only two are available when using binary digits.

We usually think of using letters to form words, not simply to name categories, and this brings us to the second way that scarcity affects the amount of information. When letters make up words, the language imposes a number of restrictions on the use of the letters, so that the relative frequency of letters used becomes unbalanced, both singly and in combinations. Thus in English, *e* is the most frequently occurring letter, whereas *x* and *z* are very rare. To go one step further, the words formed by letters occur with vastly different frequencies, so that *the, is,* and *that* appear far more often than *factory, mountain,* and *antelope.* When we come to the word *that* in a message, we are less surprised than when we come to *mountain,* simply because we have seen *that* so many times before. At the point where *mountain* appears, something relatively unusual has happened, and we learn relatively more from that part of the message. In short, the infrequent words convey more information than the common ones. Similarly, in a message composed of binary digits, the same principle applies. If the entire message were composed of *1*'s, we would learn nothing from the next occurrence of a *1*. If only 90 per cent of the digits were *1*'s, we would learn something, but not much, from the next *1*, and so on. Were *1* to occur only

10 per cent of the time, it would be a high-information digit — like *mountain*, in the case of words.

Thus far we have been talking only about the information value of individual elements of messages. How about the message as a whole and its value? The answer is that the value is simply the sum of the values of each of the elements. This is where equal use of the categories makes a difference. Suppose that, in the case of the *0*'s and *1*'s in the above paragraph, *0* were to occur in only 10 per cent of the elements of the message and *1* in 90 per cent. The *0* would convey far more information than the *1* each time it appeared. But a message made up of such unequally used categories would total far less information than a message using the categories equally. If this is true of two-category situations, it is much more true of language, where the potential number of categories (at the word level) is enormous, but most of the total output is made up of a few words, which, appear over and over again.

To sum up this discussion of the amount of information based on scarcity, we may state the general principle as follows:

> The amount of information in a message element is a direct function of the number of categories into which the message may be cast, provided that the categories are used with equal frequency. When the categories are used unequally, the amount of information in each message element is an inverse function of the frequency of the category in which it occurs, and the amount of information in the whole message is the sum of that of the elements.

The unit of measurement of information has been based upon logarithmic functions in communication theory. Shannon (1949, pp. 3, 4) gives three reasons for this choice: (1) logarithms fit in with many basic engineering functions, such as time, bandwidth, and number of relays; (2) the logarithmic function is closer to our intuitive impression of what would be a proper measure of information; and (3) it is mathematically more suitable to deal with logarithms than with raw numbers of categories or raw probabilities. Because of the first reason, most measurements in communication engineering have taken the base 2 logarithms. Relays, flip-flops, *on* versus *off* — when one of any of these is added to a circuit the number of possible choices is doubled, and yet only one component has been added. Logarithms to the base 2 transform the number of choices into numbers that operate in just this way. Doubling a number increases its base 2 logarithm by 1: $\log_2 2 = 1$; $\log_2 4 = 2$; $\log_2 8 = 3$; and so on.

Applying the logarithmic measure of information to our original comparison between the number of categories represented in the alphabet and in binary digits, we can easily see why the alphabet does not convey 13 times as much information as the binary digits. Using the logarithm to the base 2, the binary digits can convey 1 unit of information, compared with the alphabet's 4.7. And we can also fill in with some numbers our discussion of the amount of information a set of unequally used categories can convey: where the *0* category was used 10 per cent of the time and the *1* 90 per cent, each *0* would convey almost 2 ½ times as much information as a *1*. When these amounts of information in each message element are added up, however, the low-information *1*'s appear far more often (90 per cent of the time) and reduce the average amount of information per unit. The total for the whole message would be less than half the information which a two-category system could convey if the categories were used equally. Psychologists will find this an entirely congenial way of looking at things, for the basic findings of psychophysics since the pronouncement of the Weber-Fechner law have been stated in logarithmic terms. And intuition — Shannon's second reason for using logarithms — also favors the point of view.

I shall not go into the mathematics of the information measure because it has been presented quite fully elsewhere. It is more necessary at this point to understand the general outline of communication theory and to see how it can help us to explore our subject more fully. Very clear presentations of the mathematical details can be found in Shannon and Weaver (1949) and Fano (1960) from the engineering standpoint, and in Attneave (1959), Garner (1962), and Binder and Wolin (1964) as applied to psychology.

CODING

To code a message, one represents its elements in the symbols of some alphabet. Thus, to take up again our familiar example of the telegram, the letters of the original message are represented by dots, dashes, and

020839

spaces as functions of time. The dots, dashes, and spaces, and the time relationships among them, are the alphabet of the code.

This seems very simple, and one might wonder why so much time is devoted to this topic in communication theory. The reason is that engineers in this field have sought to code in the most efficient way, and this has led to the study of the properties of messages so as to find the codes that can achieve the highest efficiency for each type of message. As a matter of fact, quite efficient coding systems were developed very early in telecommunication, mostly on an intuitive basis. The recent work in communication theory has only systematized the whole undertaking, making it possible to predict how any given process will work out and establishing rational criteria by which coding systems may be evaluated.

For our purposes the findings can be stated quite simply. In the case of messages of the lowest level of complexity, that is, where we can assume that each message element is independent of those which have gone before, the code must be capable of carrying at least as much information as the original message. It need not, however, be any more complicated than the message itself. And since the measure of amount of information in the message we just discussed is applicable to the code as well as to the message, the code can be designed to match the message. For example, where the categories have different probabilities (computed over large amounts of material), we can capitalize on this fact by assigning shorter symbols to the most frequently occurring ones and longer symbols to the rarer ones. Morse did this in setting up the original telegraph code. He determined frequency of use of the different letters of the alphabet by counting the number of letters in the type cases of a printer's shop, and then assigned one-unit codes to the most frequent (e and t), down to five-unit codes for the least frequent (x and z). Were Morse to invent a telegraph code today, more precise mathematical tools would be available for making the code more efficient. His intuitive understanding of the principles involved, however, led him to devise a code that modern methods could improve upon only very little.

Where the probabilities of some categories are higher than others, as we saw earlier, those more probable ones add less information to the message as a whole. They are, in this sense, redundant. Many messages, such as language, are highly redundant, and some means of making more efficient codes for them consist in reducing the redundant elements. Block encoding is one such means, carried out by assigning a single code to a group of message elements rather than coding each element separately. Giving numbers to entire words instead of coding each letter is an example of block encoding for short blocks. The "canned" greetings one can send by telegram exemplify longer blocks: each message may contain 10 to 15 words — they could, of course, contain many more — and yet all the messages in a long list covering many occasions for greeting and several choices for each occasion could be uniquely identified with only two or three decimal digits. In the case of very long messages, then, block encoding can save an enormous amount of time. We shall see later how this method makes possible error corrections for getting around problems of noise. For an excellent exposition of block encoding, see Pierce (1961, pp. 74-76).

Sources whose coding categories do not have an equal chance of occurring are more representative of human communication processes than those where the categories are equi-probable. There is yet another characteristic of these processes, which makes the probability relationships even more complicated: the way in which sequences of message elements are arranged. In language not only does *that* appear far more frequently than *mountain,* but the probability of its appearance is also determined by what words have gone before. The probability of *that* would be very low if the preceding word had been *the,* and considerably higher if the preceding word had been *is.* The probability of *mountain,* on the other hand, would be quite high if the preceding word were *the* in comparison with its probability if it were to follow *is.* These sequential probability relationships apply to many types of messages in human communication. Their properties over finite numbers of events have been extensively studied from a mathematical standpoint and are known as Markov processes. In the case of language the results are probably not capable of accounting for all the possibilities, even though Markov began the work by studying sequential probabilities in language in sequences of just two words (see Cherry, 1957, p. 39). Chomsky (1957, Chap. 3) has argued that language cannot in principle be accounted for by appeal to Markov processes, because an infinite set of sentences can be generated within the grammatical structure of any language, whereas Markov processes can encompass only finite numbers of events. While it is true that the rules of grammar are configurational and not based upon sequential probabilities, the subject we are dealing with here — emotional messages — may operate differently. I do not believe that anyone has looked at emotional messages by asking whether they are subject to any structure that could be likened to grammar. When we have learned more about many types of emotional messages, it may turn out that the mathematical model of the Markov processes, or something like it, may be applicable to this kind of communication.

We do not need to decide at this point whether emotional messages can be conceptualized as Markov processes; it will be more relevant in later chapters when we take up the properties of these messages and the research methods that are applicable to their study. To return to the process of coding, sequential probabilities impose an additional requirement upon the encoding (and decoding) systems: rather than using a code which can carry as much information as the source, the coding system must be able to account both for the categories of the code and also for the information needed to go from one category to the next. Since there may be different code words used at each step in the message, the coding device must be able to store the code words so that it can refer to them as the message unfolds. Hence this more complicated type of message demands a more complicated type of coding system. But it is still possible to design a coding device that is just as complex as necessary, and no more so, so that the goal of efficiency in coding can be reached quite precisely.

TRANSMISSION CHANNELS

Fano (1961) describes a channel "as consisting of a device capable of generating any one of a specified set of physical events and a device capable of observing the event that has been generated. Since energy is absorbed in the observation of any physical event, the existence of a physical channel implies the existence of a medium through which energy can propagate from the device generating the physical event to that observing it" (p. 8). Fano gives as examples a voltage source generating a set of time functions connected by a pair of wires to a recorder or meter; the same voltage source and recorder, but sent and received by radio across the space between them; a sailor on one ship waving semaphore flags and another on a nearby ship watching through binoculars; and an Indian moving a blanket over a fire while another observes the resulting smoke signals. These, of course, are vastly different types of channels. Furthermore, within each type, different messages could be sent simultaneously by varying the methods by which the medium is used. Radio broadcasting furnishes the best examples of this: amplitude modulation and frequency modulation are the two most common ways of using radio waves; and within each of these, in turn, many different channels are distinguished on the basis of the frequency of the carrier waves modulated by the signals.

In the telecommunication field, where communication theory was developed, it is a simple matter to identify a channel. If one is transmitting over wire, as in the case of the telephone, we need to know only which wire is assigned to the parties at either end of the line, and to keep track of the connections between them. If several signals are being sent over the same wire using different frequency bands, the situation is somewhat more complex. In the case of radio transmission, assignment of frequency bands and type of modulation are governed by national and international agreements, and broadcasters guard the accuracy of their frequency standards very jealously. Since so many of these channels are in use, very involved methods are used to identify which one belongs to whom and to select the correct one to transmit on or receive from. And the different channels are so close together that very complicated techniques are used to keep them separated, so that the user of the signal on one channel will not be bothered by interference from the next one. Still, the channel identification system is *conceptually* a simple one. If I refer to television channel 6 as it is used in the United States, broadcasters all over the world will know what frequency band I am talking about, what ranges of it are used for the video and audio components of the signal, and what is transmitted by frequency modulation and what by amplitude modulation. They will also know many other things about the system, such as the resolution possible on this type of TV, and the sorts of equipment used in transmitting and receiving it. Users of the signal may not know anything about how television works, but when I say channel 6 they will know what to do to the control knobs on their television sets to receive this channel with the best quality of picture and sound possible on their sets and in their geographical areas.

The situation is far different in the case of human communication.

I shall be talking in Chapter 6 about several channels over which emotional messages are sent: spoken language, facial expression, body movement, and so on. Some of them will be easy to define in the same sense that channels in telecommunication are; that is, the sender will be clear what the channel is, what its limitations and possibilities are, and the receiver will be able to "tune in" on messages sent on that channel. Other channels will be harder to define, or even to think about as communication media. Further, we shall see that it is often difficult to separate messages from these different channels. There are no wave traps and sharply tuneable filters to accept only short-term spoken language and reject vocalization when two people are talking to each other. Sometimes an outside observer will be in a better position to separate channels than the participants, especially if he is a researcher who has complicated recording apparatus at his disposal. Most of his results, however, will have to come from later study of the material, and therefore cannot be available to influence the current social situation. How all these facts affect the classification of channels in human communication, and indeed the definition of "channel" in this context, will be taken up in the sixth chapter.

Channel Classifications

In communication theory channels are classified on two main bases. The first classification is the discrete channel as compared with the contin-uous, referring to the type of information the channel is capable of trans-mitting. Most of communication theory is devoted to the treatment of discrete channels, since they lend themselves to the output of modern digital devices. Furthermore, continuous data can be transformed into discrete form with little loss of information. Some examples will make the distinction more clear. Morse code is clearly discrete information. The dots and dashes are *on* states and the spaces are *off* states. The code is made up of time relationships among these *on*'s and *off*'s: the dot is one time unit *on*, and the dash in three units, while the space between dots and dashes within a letter is one time unit *off*, and the space between let-ters is three. The channel transmitting such a code must be capable of a discrete difference between *on* and *off*, like current of a definite, known amount flowing for *on* and no current of any amount for *off*. The infor-mation from a GSR record, by contrast, is continuous; that is, the value of the GSR may be anything between the extremes for the person whose responses are being measured, say, 50,000 — 150,000 ohms. When we say that this continuous range can be transformed into discrete steps without much loss of information, we mean that for most practical purposes a change in GSR from 56,378 ohms to 56,379 ohms has no significance, and it may suffice to note only 10-ohm or 100-ohm changes. Thus, instead of an infinite number of values between 50,000 and 150,000 ohms, the values would be 10,000 or 1,000 steps of resistance, respectively. Exactly how many steps we end up with depends upon how exact the user wishes his measurements to be. The channel on which this information is sent must be capable of registering all of the steps required by the information to be sent on it — 10,000 or 1,000 in this example, rather than the two required for Morse code. But this is clearly a finite number of discrete steps rather than the infinite number in the original GSR output.

The other main classification of channels has to do with the probability dependencies of the events transmitted on it. If all events are independent as they are transmitted, the channel is called constant. If the probability for any event depends upon the preceding ones, as in Markov sources, then the channel is said to possess memory. In most cases this memory would be a function taken account of by the channel encoder as it transforms the incoming information into the actual signal to be transmitted, and by the channel decoder as it operates on the message it receives.

Channels of human communication are certainly more difficult to describe in the terms of these classifications than the continuous waves and the pulses of telecommunication, just as the information itself is more difficult to describe. At first blush it would seem likely that the channels for transmitting emotional messages would have to be continuous, since the information involved seems continuous. Smiles, for example, vary all the way from the almost sober expression to the very broad grin. For all we know, however, the person to whom the message is being sent distinguishes only discrete information — the sober expression, the smile, and the grin, in discrete steps, with nothing meaningful in between. And certainly one person either looks at another directly eye-to-eye or he does not, and even an outside observer watching from some angles can tell with uncanny accuracy whether or not there is direct eye contact (see Exline, Gray, & Schuette, 1965). Looking at it from the standpoint of the researcher studying the process from the outside, moreover, it may be that the most fruitful way of studying many expressions would be to set up observations as if the channels were discrete, to quantize the information, in other words, in the same way that the GSR signal was quantized into 10-ohm or 100-ohm steps in our example above. As to the other classification of channels, the constant and those which possess memory, human communication channels seem, again, obviously to possess memory, since the probability of any message element definitely depends on the past. The past, moreover, consists of the past message the person himself has sent, as well as of the context of past events in the social surroundings which have elicited this message. But the problem with accepting the obvious here, too, as in the case of the discrete-continuous classification, is that we have very little evidence on which to base any sweeping conclusions. As a matter of fact, as was pointed out earlier, many aspects of emotional messages may well be constant information sources, and I shall go into the first data relevant to this possibility in Chapter 8.

Channel Capacity

The most important characteristic of a channel is the most practical one: how much information can it transmit? In the case of the original message, the information can be measured in the terms we have already met with. When we talk about a channel, however, we must add something, for we are talking about something dynamic and ongoing: the use of the channel for transmitting messages over some period of time. Thus the measure of a channel, called its capacity, is in terms of *rate* of transmission, or units of information per unit of time. If the channel is of limited capacity, we must either send less information at a given speed or slow down the transmission in order to get the entire amount of information through the channel. Channel capacity stated in these terms is of obvious importance in telecommunication, where time is a commercially valuable commodity. It is no less important in communicating emotional messages, where the social situation sets the pace, and messages must often be transmitted with great speed or be out of context. Coding methods must be able to keep up with the channel capacity if the channel is to be used to its fullest, but they must not outrun the capacity because errors will be the inevitable result. Here is where efficient coding procedures pay off: when the code is used optimally for the messages to be transmitted, one can get the maximum amount of information through the channel in a given time, thus making the best use of the communication system as a whole.

NOISE

A limitation on the use of channels for transmitting information is that they always introduce noise. In the sort of channels which communication theory was designed to cover, this noise consists mainly of thermal agitation in the molecules which make up the wire between the transmitter and receiver, or atmospheric disturbances in the air between them. In addition, some of the same sorts of noise are introduced by the components in the circuits of the transmitter and receiver themselves. This kind of noise is random in character; that is, it does not occur at any one frequency, but at all frequencies, and it also occurs randomly for all time intervals. Since the frequencies and amplitudes involved are distributed according to the familiar Gaussian normal curve, random noise is often called Gaussian noise. The signals of the messages being transmitted, on the other hand, are systematic in character, as determined by the coding scheme. It would seem, then, that signals would be easy to distinguish from noise, and they are, as long as there is enough signal to be heard over the noise. But little bursts of noise can mask the signal at random points, leading to spurious reception of the signal and introducing errors. Common sense would therefore lead us to expect communication theory to treat noise as a reducer of channel capacity, as a restriction on the amount of information that can be transmitted and received in a given time interval, and as a potential cause of errors.

The most surprising result of communication theory is that these expectations are not borne out. True, the presence of noise requires us to work harder to make use of the channel than if it were noise-free, but noise is not an absolute restriction. Perhaps the most far-reaching finding of Shannon's theorizing is that, given a source producing messages of a certain information value, and given a noisy channel of a certain capacity, there exists in principle a code whose use allows the messages to be transmitted through the channel with vanishingly small probability of error, *provided* that the messages do not exceed the channel capacity; where the channel capacity is smaller than the source's information rate, some errors will inevitably result from any code. This not to say that the ideal coding system has been found for any channel, but it does place limits on what can possibly be done.

This finding does not mean that noise reduction comes free with the theory, as I have already said. The kinds of codes that have been developed since the publication of Shannon's theory all require effort on the part of the channel encoder and the channel decoder, and they take up channel capacity as well. The most successful methods have been built on block encoding, which we have already discussed briefly. Recall that this is a way of making coding more efficient by capitalizing on the redundancy of the source material and reducing this redundancy as the message is finally transmitted. Error-detecting codes can be added to each block so that the receiver will know *if* there is an error in any block of the material he receives, and error-correcting codes can be added so that the receiver will know *where* the error is and what to do about it. Both of these require extra digits added onto the block, digits that are in a sense redundant. But as blocks become longer, the error-correcting elements take a smaller proportion of the total block length, and make possible a considerable saving of channel capacity. The problem with many of the error-correcting codes already developed is that what they cost to add is more than what they save in channel capacity. The encoding and decoding equipment needed to put them into operation may be very complex and expensive, and there may be a delay between the source and channel (and between channel and user at the other end) which is more time-consuming for the total system than a slower transmission would have been. And the original redundancy of some messages like language may make it possible for users to correct errors while they are reading the output material. Nevertheless, error-correcting codes are necessary when numbers are transmitted, since numbers, unlike language, do not have a structure to help the user read them; and when the user is a machine, built-in error-correction is an absolute necessity. Again, Pierce gives a fine description of these matters (1961, pp. 159-165). For a review of recent accomplishments in engineering, see Gilbert (1966).

All this discussion, we must remember, concerns noise of a very special character, namely, random, white, Gaussian noise. This, as I have pointed out, is the main sort of noise that communication theory is concerned with. Noise of a systematic nature occasionally occurs, too, usually in the form of unwanted signals from other channels, like station interference on the radio, and is appropriately called "cross-talk." In radio broadcasting this sort of noise has become increasingly important as the airwaves have become more and more crowded with communication channels; fortunately, however, cross-talk is easy to reduce. The standards by which the frequencies of broadcast carrier waves are maintained have grown more stringent, and receivers have become more selective, so that only the desired frequency is amplified and its signal decoded while even very closely neighboring frequencies are effectively rejected. In addition, directional antennas for all practical purposes eliminate signals coming from any place other than the desired station. In the case of this type of noise, then, more complex equipment can reduce the noise itself, hopefully to the point where the only noise present is of the random sort which we saw communication theory deal with earlier. In addition there are nonrandom noises that are not introduced by competing channels. Shannon (1949) has given approximations for one sort of this nonrandom noise, that is, impulse noise, but cross-talk is apparently not a subject that has been tackled by communication theory. In the case of understanding speech, a good deal of work on cross-talk has been done and some theoretical conceptions have been developed to account for it (e.g., Broadbent, 1958), which I shall review in Chapter 6. Since the work and the ideas introduce a number of theoretical notions beyond Shannon's communication theory, I shall not go into them here.

Discussion

Now that an outline of the major points of communication theory has been presented, it is time to compare the situation in which the theory was developed with that of social communication. The similarities are many and obvious, yet writers have varied widely in their willingness to apply the theory to the relatively more complicated social situation. Shannon, the major pioneer of the theory, was quite relaxed in this respect; Cherry (1957), who wrote about it for a more general audience, was more wary: "These concepts are not easy to acquire, or simple to apply correctly. They are essentially mathematical and, what is most important, they are primarily of application to certain technical problems (mainly in telecommunication) under clearly defined conditions. It is only too easy and tempting to use these terms vaguely and descriptively, especially in relation to human communication — by analogy. The concepts and methods of communication theory demand strict discipline in their use" (p. 197).

With this *caveat* in mind we will have to be careful to spell out in each instance how closely our use of the ideas of communication theory adheres to the original use. In many cases the relationship will be close; in some, rather tenuous; and in some there will be no relationship at all, since the nature of the entire communication situation is so different. I shall concentrate here on the last category, just to make doubly sure that we know where we stand. There are three areas, as I see it, where we run into trouble trying to apply communication theory to emotional communication: (1) the nature of "information"; (2) the lack of independence of the source from the encoding and decoding; and (3) the form of the noise. I shall only outline them here, since their full delineation will take up much of the later chapters of this book.

1. The nature of the information exchanged in emotional communication is hard to specify, and even harder to measure in such neat terms as log transformations of category probabilities. Communication theory, we saw earlier, takes as its basic input whatever the source submits. It does not care — indeed, it cannot care — whether the material is of any use or human value. If it comes in discrete packages, it can be dealt with in one way; if it consists of continuous waveforms, it can be handled in some other way. One can sample the source and describe the statistical parameters of the messages it will produce, thus opening the way for measuring the amount of information in the messages to be processed. Not so in emotional messages. Feelings are often so fleeting that it is hard to tell whether there is a message "on the air" or not. If the receiving person finally concludes that there is one, his first reaction is to try to figure out whether it is important or not — both to the sending person and to himself. His next reaction may be determined by many things. One receiving person may wonder if the sender is pleased or pained by this feeling, and if it is the latter, what could be done to help. Another receiver may only hope that whatever the feeling is, he will not be blamed for it. Can the same measure of information be used for both

of these two receivers? Is the message continuous for the first receiver and discrete for the second?

2. One of the characteristics of the telecommunication situation, as I pointed out at the beginning of this chapter, is that the components depicted in Figure 1 are completely independent. The manner in which the source encoder does its job is not influenced by the source, nor does it influence how the channel encoder gets the message out. In human communication, on the other hand, all three of these components, or processes, reside in one person. The same person has the feeling or idea; he chooses the words, selects the channel, and monitors the whole enterprise from start to finish. All of the sending person's intentions, both good and bad, and all of his current hopes and fears are involved at every step. Conflict at one point will affect choice of channel, length of message, or whatever, and make it harder for anyone to understand what is going on. Then, at the other end of the chain, the last three components of the diagram are all embodied in the receiving person and a complementary set of complications arises. Finally, to make matters worse, the two people are each both sender and receiver, not only serially in time as they exchange roles in the conversation, but also simultaneously, since a person can be a receiver on one channel while he is sending messages at the same time on another. The result is that what the receiving person thinks of as a message may be a direct image of what is going on "inside" the sender; it may be more a reflection of the last message he, the receiver, has sent; or it may be some combination of these; a pale image or a gross distortion of what was actually sent. The message may be read as two different ones by two different receivers, and not recognized as a message at all by a third — and an uninvolved observer of the whole situation may see something quite different occurring. It is no wonder, then, that clear findings are rare in this field, let alone clearly interrelated findings which could be called a body of knowledge. When this issue came up earlier in this chapter, I said that the confusions were greater for some message-channel combinations than for others. The issue cannot be blinked, however, and will force us to look to other theories to supplement communication theory when we get down to the details of using it.

3. Noise in communication theory is random noise, and although lip service has been paid to other sorts, those nonrandom noise sources

have been dealt with chiefly by getting rid of the noise itself, as I have indicated above, not by developing methods of reading the desired signal through it. Random noise analogous to the thermal agitation of molecules exists in human communication only in rare instances — the chirping of late summer crickets or the wind of a winter gale might sometimes make it difficult for two people to hear each other, but these are unusual circumstances for a conversation. The fact is that most noise in human communication is cross-talk, and the sources of the interfering signals are varied. Emotional messages from different channels may be very different. And even before this, the work of decoding rational messages is so great that the emotional messages also being sent are often overlooked. In addition there are interferences from the different components all along the communication chain because of the above-noted lack of independence of these components. How often these various interferences are in play and what means there are to combat them is an area in which there are very few findings, but as we shall see, there are some beginning indications to build on.

So there are vast differences between the telecommunication situation, where communication theory was developed, and human interaction. I do not believe, however, that the relationship between them is, as Cherry fears, purely that of an analogy. The differences will put us on guard to use the theory carefully as it stands, and to add to it consistently, so that our present knowledge can be expanded, not merely restated.

Chapter Three

Emotional Information

By now we have laid the groundwork for our theoretical analysis of emotional communication. In the introductory chapter, where the domain of our topic was mapped out, we traced some writings on it by philosophers and psychologists. That gave us the content for our work. Part II opened with an account of the theory that will form the framework for most of our future investigation of that content. We are now ready to begin the substantive work of the book: measurement of the information value of the messages of interest.

Information value of emotional messages is measured in essentially the same way it is for any other kind of message, that is, by its scarcity or unusualness. The data to which the measure is applied come from the behaviors of people, as was discussed in Chapter 1. Let us recall that most of the philosophers of language have agreed that linguistic forms about emotion are not necessarily emotional in themselves. One can talk *about* emotion in a coldly rational way. These writers have agreed, on the other hand, that many behaviors of a speaker, including his use of language, can serve as cues for recognizing emotion. The latter point interests us here since emotion, as recognized, is the crux of the problems of emotional communication. The linguistic forms chosen by the speaker to use at this particular moment, his tone of voice, hints from other aspects of his behavior about tension or relaxation — all may serve as material for inferences about emotion. We can now take up these matters in detail: behavior, and inference from that behavior about the emotional state of another person.

WHAT IS COMMUNICATED ABOUT EMOTION?

I shall take as my text for this discussion two complementary lines of reasoning — one by Hebb (1964), the other by Frijda (1953, 1958, 1969). Hebb began with the problem of how one recognizes emotion in chimpanzees, then went on from there to the process of recognizing emotions in man, and finally tackled that of the individual person's recognition of his own emotions. All of these, he held, are based upon observations of behavior and upon the inferences about the inner mental state that stem from these observations. In the case of chimpanzees the conclusions were an outgrowth of a two-year experiment of careful observations at the Yerkes Laboratories of Primate Biology, during which the staff carefully avoided using "mentalistic" and "anthropomorphic" terms in their records of the animals' behavior. The resulting protocols consisted of disparate descriptions of specific acts, with nothing to tie them together so that they could provide any sensible guide to behavior. The strictly behavioristic cautions left out something very important, but when the staff talked about and recorded the animals' behavior in frankly human terms, things fell into place. Staff could understand each other when they were discussing the animals, and even newcomers could learn quickly how to deal with the different individuals — and with such powerful animals, safety rests in large part upon this sort of understanding. Hebb concluded that "references to emotion, attitude, and so on, whatever they may seem to imply about conscious entities that may not exist, even in man, have value as summary descriptions and predictions of behavior" (p. 89). Based on this, Hebb reasoned that it would be useful to take the "intuitive" names of emotions and analyze what sorts of behavior they were based upon.

Hebb's working definition of emotion was a cautious one: *"Emotion* explicitly does not mean any conscious process, nor any pattern of motor or glandular activity, but designates certain neurophysiological states, inferred from behavior, about which little is known except that by definition they predispose toward certain specific kinds of actions" (p. 89). When one "recognizes" an emotion, he is making an inference that such a state is present. The inferences consist of classifying deviations in behavior from some base line; this may be done directly, as in what Hebb calls *naming primary emotional behavior*, or indirectly, as in *naming emotion from associated behavior.* In the case of the first, little inference is necessary, since the actions speak for themselves. Actions are not the only data the observer use, of course; he can also see the situation surrounding them, and he must have some background knowledge of the habitual behavior of the animal or person he is observing. But acquaintance with present stimuli and past experience is secondary in naming primary emotional behavior. The behavior itself is distinctive enough to be named as soon as it is clearly perceived.

In the case of naming emotions from associated behavior, more knowledge of past behavior is required and more inference is involved. "Associated" here means that a behavior has been known in the past to have been associated with a sequence of primary emotional behavior. Currently, in the light of the stimuli now impinging on the animal or person, the behavior has no meaning; nevertheless, because the observer has seen the behavior before in accompaniment to a primary emotional response, it serves as a sign that something similiar is going on now even though it may be hidden from view. The examples Hebb gives of this in a chimpanzee indicate that although the animal is in a heightened state of excitability, he is controlling or avoiding the response. A little more stimulation, and the full outburst follows — inappropriately if one looks only at the final stimulus and response, but quite predictably if one is really acquainted with the animal's habitual emotional response patterns. Absence of response, in the light of one's knowledge of the stimulus and of the individual, may thus yield valid data about an inner emotional state.

Recognizing emotion in man, as Hebb continues his reasoning, is no different from recognizing emotion in a chimpanzee, since both are based on inferences from behavioral deviations. The final step in his argument says that the same processes are involved in recognizing one's own emotions. This last point takes a bit of explaining, since common sense tells us that we need no behavioral observations to tell how we feel because we have direct experience of our feelings in consciousness. Not necessarily so, according to Hebb, and he bases his arguments on hunches about the development of emotion naming in the child. Hebb reasons that the child's behavior is first interpreted by his parents, who are continually naming his emotions as they see them. Furthermore, he observes emotional responses in others and learns to name them. As the child grows, he develops controls for emotional expression and his overt behavior becomes less extreme. As his behavior changes, so does his evidence for his own emotions. Remember that Hebb's working definition of emotion posits inner states as *predisposing* toward action, not as always producing action. Thus tendencies toward expression in the growing child, his intentions, his fantasies, and all the rest, become associated signs of emotional response. This means that the person himself will have more evidence for what emotional state he is in than the outside observer; but it does not mean that on this account the person himself will always be more correct in his interpretation of them. He can make errors of infererence just as well as the outsider, and often does. Hebb cites as an example the situation where a person feels annoyed, indignant, and disapproving of someone's actions. Other people watching the scene disagree with him about what his feelings are. They all agree from what they know of him, and of the relationship between him and the object of his emotion, that he feels jealous (1946, p. 101). In this case there is a definite social desirability angle, of course: jealousy is "babyish" and "weak," and few people will admit to the feeling, even to themselves.

Hebb has given a very clear statement of the conceptual basis for considering behavioral deviations as the data of emotional communication. It is not behavior itself, isolated from its context of other behaviors and stimulus patterns, but deviations of behavior, implying that the observer must know what the base line is and what the provocations are. Hebb believed that taking an expression out of its proper context in experiments on emotion, such as those using still photographs of facial expressions, leads to erroneous conclusions. The fact that interjudge agreement under these conditions is often low does not mean that emotion does not exist or is named solely on the observer's knowledge of the stimulus situation, as early investigators had claimed (1946, pp. 98-99). But under the circumstances Hebb was writing about, making judgments about chimpanzee's emotional states, the observers did know the stimulus. We must therefore ask what aspects of his recognition of the subject's emotion can be attributed to the stimulus and what to the expression itself.

This question has been investigated by Frijda in a series of studies that tackled the problem in quite different ways. In the first (1953), motion picture records were made of the faces of two young women in response to a number of stimulus situations, 31 in one case and 37 in the other. Oddly enough, Frijda does not list all the stimuli, but some are mentioned in the course of the paper: hearing an explosion, smelling hydrogen sulfide, being offered a box of candy, remembering a personally disagreeable event, trying to understand the experimenter while he is whispering, pulling hard on a cord that is tied to the floor, receiving a slight electric shock, talking thoughtfully, listening to a poem. The films of the subjects' responses varied from 2 to 15 seconds, and a masking noise was always present in the room so that the subjects could not tell when the camera started and stopped. The stimulus situation was not included in the films. After each stimulus presentation the subject was asked for introspection of what she had felt. These introspective reports, plus the experimenter's knowledge of the stimulus situations, served as dual criteria for correctness of later judgment of the emotional expressions. From each scene one or more frames of film was enlarged onto lantern slides to be shown as still pictures for comparison with the motion pictures.

The judges were 20 male and 20 female observers from a wide variety of occupations and backgrounds. Judging was done individually, with instructions that the judge was "to relate what 'went on' in the subject's mind; that he could do it in his own words, and if he liked, by describing the situation; that the poses for the most part were spontaneous, and that not all were taken during ordinary conversation" (p. 300). The responses totaled almost 6,000 in all, and were scored on a five-point scale of correctness, using the criteria mentioned above. As expected, the motion picture presentations yielded substantially (and significantly) more correct judgments than the still pictures. For the purposes of the present discussion, however, the most important results come from the qualitative analysis of the responses.

Frijda found that most subjects took the instructions as a suggestion, and imagined what the stimulus situation might have been. Only a very few were satisfied with simply naming an emotional response. But instructions were not the only determinant of this method of responding:

The fact that descriptions of this kind are so much more

frequent than simple naming of the emotions, is not only a
consequence of the instruction to formulate the expressions. It
is certainly easier to express them in this way than to search
for emotion-names and to give each of these . . . [its] proper
weight. But often the answer came so quickly, that it looks as
if the impression is at once transformed into a view of the
subject-in-a-situation. The instructions did not ask for con-
cretization, and the introspections of the observers do not give
any indication that they consciously tried to do this. Rather
the contrary is true. Some O's worked directly from a concrete
attitude. "Sometimes I saw at once what it was, on the basis
of the first impression. But sometimes I had to try hard. The
answer came when I tried to imagine myself in a situation which
checked with the face." Another O: ". . . With the films, I
placed myself in a situation, 'what would happen?' (p. 313)."

Thus, by making up a situation to account for the expression, the
observers in Frijda's experiment added a concreteness to the general expression they saw. Then it became possible for them to name an emotion compatible with the expression they saw in the film. A general
expression of withdrawal and tenseness may result from a number of
situations, such as a slight electric shock, smelling hydrogen sulfide, or
hearing a disapproved remark. Seeing the expression *and* knowing the
situation, one could be specific in naming the "emotion": pain, disgust,
or indignation, respectively. The expression itself is general; the situation makes it concrete. Frijda tells us what this "general expression"
expresses in this way:

It then appears, that *the configuration of facial expression is
the expression of the person's specific position towards a nonspecific content,* that is, of the specifically structured relation
he has with an object, person or his entire world (p. 326).

The way that knowing the situation influences the observer's interpretation of the general expression is taken up experimentally in
Frijda's next report (1958). In this study four still photographs were
presented, with a brief description of the situation in which they were

supposed to have been taken. There were two different sets of situation descriptions, however, one for each of two groups of 32 subjects. Instructions were to describe the person's feelings or emotional states in the subject's own words, with as much detail as he liked. Again most subjects gave fairly extensive descriptions. Frijda developed categories for the responses to get at both those elements that were situation-related and those that were more general. Comparing the responses of the two groups, it was found that there was disagreement on the more situation-related responses and agreement on the more general ones; more disagreement on those categories which included emotion names, and more agreement on those which described the general orientation of the person in the photographs. Thus "facial expression represents only a general pattern: a general behavioral attitude, containing the state of attention and withdrawal of the person, the degree to which he is involved in his own reaction; or the mere presence of 'inner' events" (p. 153). Frijda relates these general attitudes to the dimensions of emotion posited by Schlosberg (these will be mentioned in more detail later in this chapter).*

By 1969 Frijda and two students had followed up on this experiment to try to explicate further the interlocking roles of expression and situation in recognizing emotions. Again they used small numbers of stimuli, and again they paired some with situation descriptions that were compatible, and with others that were incompatible, with the expressions. The results showed that both the expression depicted in the

---

* Rump (1960) criticized Frijda's 1958 experiment on the grounds that similar agreements and disagreements would be found if the subjects were not shown any photograph, but only told to imagine one. Using one of the pairs of situation descriptions Frijda had used, Rump categorized the responses by the titles of the brief summaries Frijda used to illustrate the categories in his article, and found that the same patterns obtained. Some differences did occur between the two sets of results, and Rump attributed these to chance variation or to differences in language usage between his English subjects and Frijda's Dutch subjects. Frijda (1961) was then led to perform this control operation on all of his situation descriptions, using the complete set of scoring categories, so that he could compare these results with those of his original experiments. There were strong differences between the results using real and imagined pictures, and in a direction that clearly upheld Frijda's original conclusions.

photographs and the situations in which the photographs were supposed to have been taken were important in the subjects' responses. In all cases, expression was the dominant cue, especially when the expressions and situation descriptions were incompatible, but the situations were never without influence, and usually that influence was strong.

This discussion of Hebb and Frijda began with the question of what is communicated about emotion. We can now look at the answers their work provides. First, all an observer has to go on in recognizing an emotion in a person is what the observer can see or hear. From then on, all his conclusions are based on inference. In some cases the inference seems to be minimal, as the expression speaks for itself. In other cases the inference looks like a long and complicated maneuver, as the observer makes use of all the cues he can get from the situation and the entire history of his acquaintance with the person in drawing his conclusions. Whether he can draw a conclusion or not, and whether his conclusion is "accurate" or not, depends upon the clarity and compatibility of the information he can bring to bear on the estimation process. There are two sources of information, as Hebb outlines the process. Recall his position that the basic datum the observer uses is a behavioral deviation. This, he goes on to say, is composed of two parts: the behavior itself or (in some cases), the absence of it, and the observer's knowledge of the animal's or the person's habitual mode of response. To be a deviation, the behavior must deviate from some base line. But present behavior and base-line behavior are not separate sources of information. They are interrelated: the base line tells the observer how deviant the present act or expression is. Here, then, is the first information source: the current behavior as evaluated in terms of the base-line behavior. The second source is the stimulus in the current situation which seems to have led to the present response. The basis for evaluating its information lies in the present situation, which serves as its background. It may be the structure of the social situation, the modal behavior of the people who are part of it, or whatever.

THE INFORMATION IN EMOTIONAL MESSAGES

Now, what does information mean, and how is it measured? Remember that in communication theory the information in any message element is measured by the scarcity, the surprise value, the oddity of elements of that category as compared with the other categories whose elements make up the message. Where there is known to be a finite number of possibilities for the next element — 0 or 1, for example, or letters of the alphabet — the information value of the next element can be specified with great accuracy. In the usual social situation, on the other hand, the number of "next" events that could possibly happen is not so neatly limited, as we all know. Still there are equally well-known limits on next-possible behaviors: the culture in which a person lives sets the outside range on behavior, and regional, family, and idiosyncratic patterns superimposed upon the cultural norms restrict the range even further. And these behavioral limitations are especially relevant to behaviors in which emotions are expressed, as Hebb and Thompson have pointed out so imaginatively (1954, pp. 555 ff.). Moreover, since so much of human behavior is codified, or covered by sort of unwritten rules that are agreed upon by the group, the members of the group know a good deal about this range, at least subliminally, and recognize deviations from it quite easily. Thus when we say that we are surprised at seeing a given behavior, we are making a phenomenological statement about the information value of that behavior: if it is surprising, it must be unusual and therefore have high information value. Again, "unusual" means that this kind of behavior occurs relatively infrequently in comparison with behaviors of other kinds.

In telecommunication the frequency distribution of the various possible categories is often known in advance to both coder and decoder: there will be about as many 0's as 1's in a long message, for example. In other cases it is known approximately, but not exactly: Morse based his telegraph code on frequencies of letters in a printer's type case rather than on the more precise frequency counts of letters in English which were available at that time. In still other cases nothing about the frequency distribution is known in advance, and one must collect a sample of this type of message and describe its statistical characteristics in some way if he wants to measure the information value of the next element. In emotional communication we have a combination of these last two cases. The other person's behaviors are not completely unknown because he has grown up in our culture. Even where he has not, there are probably some universals of human conduct — Hebb (1946,

p. 95) writes of species differences which are, of course, even more basic than the cutural differences we might meet in observing a foreigner. So a roughed-out frequency distribution of next-possible behaviors is already available to the social participant against which to compare any given current expression, even if he does not know the other person. Herein lies the meaning of Hebb's concept of naming "primary emotional behavior": a warm smile or a cry of fright does not take much inference to interpret. Long-term acquaintance with another person enables the observer to refine the frequency distribution even further and to estimate more exactly the information value of the next act. Hebb's naming emotions from associated behavior makes use of these more complete background data.

The other information source, the stimulus that sets a behavior in motion, is cut of the same cloth, for we know that the stimuli for most human behaviors are other human behaviors. Both stimulus and response occur within social settings whose structure dictates some of the possibilities. Thus the very processes we have just discussed apply here, too: the social situation provides the background against which to evaluate the information value of the antecedent act which serves as a stimulus for the present expression.

We do not know yet precisely what aspects of the social situation control the probability levels in this process, but Ekman and Friesen (1969b) have suggested some excellent directions for us to pursue. First, the sorts of events that stir up emotion are vastly different from one culture to another, and the sorts of emotion that are stirred up may be quite different for the "same" situation. An example of the former is the reaction to being spoken to by a cousin of opposite sex: in many places this would produce no emotional response, while in others there would be shocked fear for the lives of both parties. To illustrate the latter, we need only think of the range of response to funerals. For most people it is a sad occasion, but for many it is a happy one, filled with joy for the departed person's new role in the scheme of things.

Another aspect of emotional expression, which Ekman and Friesen find very much subject to cultural control, is what they call display rules. These are the rules by which one regulates the expression of emotion. One might play down some emotions, and exaggerate others, try to look completely neutral when still others are stimulated, or cover up by displaying some opposite emotion. These rules vary not only from one culture to another, but across status and age groups within any one culture. They are undoubtedly very powerful influencers of behavior, and certainly affect very strongly how people feel about themselves. Failure to live within those rules may lead to quite devastating loss of self-esteem, as in the young man in our culture who finds himself weeping over what he considers a relatively minor loss. And others from the same culture or background, seeing his behavior, can assess more accurately the depth of his feeling because they know the rules themselves. Display rules, of course, apply to both participants in an emotional episode: the one who produces the antecedent act and the one who responds to it.

I have been emphasizing the rules and regulations of human responses here to make the point that all is not chaos, that the information value of acts is not infinite, but is rather subject to estimation. It is true that our behavioral repertoire is limited because we cannot do whatever we like. Man has been decrying his sufferings on this score for centuries; but despite these protestations, the possible behaviors a person may emit are many, and the information value for any one of these behaviors is high, in the same sense that the information value in any of the 26 letters of the alphabet is high when compared with the 0 or the 1 of the binary code. We know also that behaviors occur with markedly different frequencies, as letters do when they spell words and as words do when they make up a language. These differential rates of occurrence make up the real meaning of cultural restrictions — not that certain behaviors never happen and others always do, but that some happen very seldom and some happen often in comparison with all the others. Also, as in language, sequential probabilities form still other limitations. Following the first act in a sequence, the probability of certain other acts goes down, while that of still others goes up. And to make things worse, there are times when absence of behavior may be considered an act in the same sense, and assigned a probability level.

So the information values of different behaviors are different *in general,* to begin with, and they constantly keep changing in the ongoing specific situation. In free social interaction the computation of all of these probabilities appears to be impossibly complex, yet people perform the computations all the time, or at least they try to. Accuracy may not always be high for any given behavior. but there are many behaviors in a social situation. Fortunately for our self-esteem, we do not have time to respond to every one of them and thus expose the extent of our inaccuracies. Still, the complexities are also unfathomable, and terms like "attitude," "intuition," and "clinical judgment" are applied to our understanding of other people's behavior instead of "calculation of sequential probabilities."

Some Beginning Research Evidence

Using the concepts of information measurement to talk about attitude and intuition appears to be stretching a point beyond recognition. It is a far cry from the clean and exact figures of dots, dashes, and spaces in telegraph transmission to the vague and unstructured field of social response. I believe, however, as I have said earlier, that both social interaction and telegraphy are communication situations and that the same principles must govern both of them. But this belief is cast in very abstract terms. At the present state of our knowledge about these two sorts of communication, do I have any evidence that the same — or even analogous — measures can be applied to both of them? My answer is that the same measures are already applied, and I point to two sources for evidence: reactions in the social situation itself, and methods used by the research investigator who does observational studies of social interaction.

The first of these is as yet largely anecdotal. Consider the remark, "I never saw him go that far; he must really have been angry." Here there has been a surprising episode of behavior, surprising, because the speaker had base-line information about the actor; he had some notion of the relative probabilities of various actions given this sort of stimulus, and the one which did occur was relatively improbable. This high-information act, then, leads to an inference about the inner state of the actor, an inference the speaker is quite certain of.

At the present time our knowledge of the individual participant in social interactions is likely to remain at the level used in this illustration, but a number of existing experiments can be viewed from this standpoint. An example is one reported by Kelman and Eagly (1965), in which the message did not happen to be a directly emotional one, but had definite emotional overtones for the particular subjects in the experiment. A standard message was embedded in a variable context of background information about the person who was communicating the message to the subjects. Three different contexts were used, and the resulting total messages given to each of three experimental groups. Subjects' understanding of the message, along with changes in their attitudes related to it, were the dependent variables. The "central message" was assumed by the experimenters to be the same for the three groups and the authors speak of "misperception" of it by subjects in one experimental group (p. 67). Yet a second look at the stimulus indicates that the messages were not the same. The context material was part of the message in that subjects used it to build probability distributions for the communicators' responses. When the communicator got to the "central message" in each case, the meaning of the words and certainly the intent of the communicators were interpretable only in terms of what the subjects had been told about the communicators. The authors recognize this in part as they discuss source orientation and content orientation (pp. 74ff.). In the case of what they call source orientation, where the perceptual distortions occurred in this experiment, the authors reason that the context information touched off self-definition problems in the hearers and led them actually to hear different messages from the communicator. My point is that there was an actual difference between the central messages under the three experimental conditions because of the structure of the relationship between the "message" and its context. This is only one example of many recent social-psychological experiments where we can see something of the information processing that goes on in social situations.

The other line of evidence about these events comes from watching a research investigator whose methods may be compared directly with those of a social participant. A most happy example is given by Raush (1965), who has written about social interaction among children, both from the inside of the experiment by reporting results and from a slight distance by discussing as he goes along how the methods are being applied. To make the similarity even more complete, Raush uses information transmission as his general model. When I say that we may watch an experimenter as he acts like a social participant, I mean that in studies like Raush's the experimenter himself takes all of the steps taken by the participant in a social situation, and the methods he uses let us in on what these steps are, much as a slow-motion movie does. Raush makes it clear that "the findings tell us what we have always known" (p. 497), but with considerably greater precision.

Recall that the two information sources are the present act and the stimulus to that act. Raush evaluates the information in the present act by comparing it with other acts expected of this kind of person. He uses the group of which the person is a member as his data for what is expected. Then, to evaluate the stimulus act, he compares it with the specific context surrounding the stimulus, using the social situation to obtain the necessary data. There were four groups, all preadolescent and early adolescent boys, who differed in diagnosis (hyperaggressive patients vs. normal controls, the patients being observed at two different times in treatment, and the normals being groups from two different countries). There were six social situations in which all the boys were observed, sampling different times of day and different activities. The behavior observed was scored on an affectional dimension in a dichotomous pair of categories: friendly and unfriendly acts. Thus the probability of friendly as compared with unfriendly responses could be computed as they were preceded by friendly or unfriendly stimulus acts, with knowledge of who the children were and what the current social situation was. Raush notes (p. 493) that it would be possible to add more exactness to the computations by taking individual differences into account as well, the characteristic ways in which each child responded to the group, the situation, and the antecedent act. To do this, however, he would have had to collect unwieldy quantities of data in order to end up with stable numbers in all the myriad subcells of the analysis.

The information unit Raush used in these analyses was the binary unit, since all acts, whether of one group or another, or one situation or another, were scored as either friendly or unfriendly. The maximum amount of information in a two-category situation is one such unit, and one determines the outcome of predictions on the basis of what proportion of this unit has been accounted for. This assumes, as we learned in Chapter 2, that the events in the two categories are equally likely, or, in this case, that over the long haul, friendly acts are emitted as often as unfriendly ones. In the case of the patient group under study, this was indeed the case, but the normal control groups were decidedly different.

Far more of their responses were classified as friendly than as un-friendly. Thus the total possible information available from describing behavior in these terms may depend upon the subjects one sets out to observe. In a similar way the current social situation altered the response probabilities: American normal controls responded in an unfriendly fashion to friendly acts 30 per cent of the time in game situations where there was built-in competition, but only 4 per cent of the time at meal-times, where there was none.

Another kind of look at the same data is reported in Raush's article, rounding out the analogy of the research investigator and the participant in a social situation. This is the study of the sequential probabilities of acts, again as seen in the dichotomous variable, friendly versus unfriendly. The first step in the sequence has been covered in the analysis we have already examined: given one act, what is the probability that the next one will be the same kind? In the analysis now under discussion, this process is carried further: from this first pair of acts one can extrapolate to what the next one will be, and the next. One can then ask whether the next acts as they actually occur conform to the pre-dicted course of the series.

Briefly in the case of the patients, when they first arrived their actual behavior deteriorated toward greater hostility than would be ex-pected from the first acts in the sequence. Later on in their treatment their sequential behaviors changed so that they would continue from a first act behaving about the same way they had started out. Normal children, on the other hand, counteracted any initial unfriendliness, so that sequences ended in a more friendly atmosphere than they started. In these analyses of sequences, Raush was able to present only one of the variables taken up in the first part of the study, namely, differences among groups. Here, too, individual cell frequencies became impossibly low when entire episodes of behavior were used as the basic unit and further subdivisions were also used. These practical limitations should nevertheless not obscure the similarity of the research investigator's operations and those of the social participant. They should, if anything, only make us wonder all the more at the complexity of the calculations accomplished by the social participant at split-second speed in the course of interacting with other people.

There are a number of differences between the research investigator's methods and the way a person perceives emotionality in the social situation. Most of these have to do with the ways every investigator must simplify his material in order to get a research handle on it. The acts in Raush's observations were neatly marked off from each other, so that in following sequences of them one can talk about antecedent and subsequent acts. And the acts were either friendly or unfriendly, with nothing in between. Similarly the social situations in the study were treated as distinct and non-overlapping. Finally, comparison of "adjusted" controls and "hyperaggressive" patients implies that the pathology in the patients affected all their social behavior all the time, and that the controls were always normal. Investigators know about these simplifications, and worry lest they be oversimplifications, thus rendering their results unrepresentative of the aspects of life they wish to generalize to.

Making things simple in order to handle them in the most economical way is, of course, no stranger to users of communication theory. Complex waveforms are cast into relatively few categories for transmission, and while an absolute reproduction of the original signal is impossible by this means, the recipient can still make use of the output. And in human communication, the participant in social situations sends and receives codified messages which cannot possibly contain all the nuances of his thought and feeling, but they still serve to communicate to other people. There is good evidence to indicate, too, that different communication channels can carry different amounts of information about emotion, information perhaps even about different dimensions of emotion. We will learn more about that in Chapter 5.

THE ALPHABET OF EMOTIONAL COMMUNICATION

In Raush's work the dependent variable, the emotional tone of the interactions, was a simple dichotomy, friendly versus unfriendly. Clearly there are many other emotions in addition to this pair — if indeed this is a pair on any rational grounds other than presence or obsence of the prefix "un-." What emotions are there, and how can they be conceptualized in the terms we are using here?

Psychologists and others have been producing lists of emotions for many years. No one believes that the number is infinite, although Allport and Odbert (1936) produced a list of some 2,500 terms, most of which refer to feeling states that should probably be called emotion. Darwin (1872) lists some 30 feeling states that are organized into eight general categories. The differences among the states within the categories are based sometimes on intensity of emotion, sometimes on whether there is some distinctive aspect of facial expression for expressing these nuances. Tomkins (1962) and Ekman and Friesen (1969b) have been particularly influenced by Darwin's conceptualization and have performed experiments following directly from it. Tomkins argues that affects are the primary human motivations, and that they consist of facial behaviors, each of which is genetically patterned. Even though these facial expression patterns are motivations, they are at the same time responses, and the individual becomes aware of them through proprioceptive feedback from the facial musculature. This feedback, in fact, *is* the experience of the affect, especially in the young child. In later years of development the individual can generate the experience of emotions from the memory of various facial expressions. Tomkins lists eight "primary" affects in an order that implies an underlying dimension of positive and negative, although these terms are mainly used descriptively. To some extent, too, they can be the basis for some commonsense predictions of confusions among affects. The primary affects are the positive ones of interest and enjoyment, and the negative ones of distress, fear, shame, contempt, and anger. Surprise is called a "resetting" affect, located between the two main groups.

Tomkins and McCarter (1964) used this set of eight primary affects in an experiment on recognizing facial expressions from posed photographs, and found impressive evidence that the categories are distinctive. A variety of people, not only actors, posed for the photographs, and the 24 judges who responded to them were everyday people, not specially trained at reading facial expressions. The responses were recorded in terms of the same eight categories of affect, each exemplified by four or five words. One extra category was included which is not often used in this type of research: a neutral one. I shall comment on its implications in a moment. General results for the total pool of 69 photographs are presented, and complete data for a subset of three of the most typical photos from each category selected in advance to represent the designated affect (or neutrality). In this subset an average of 72 per cent of the responses were "correct," that is, the subject's judgments of the photos coincided with the affects for which the actors were instructed to pose. This percentage varied considerably from affect to affect, of course: *enjoyment* was seen as enjoyment 92 per cent of the time, while *fear* was seen as such only 60 per cent. Among the overlaps of judgment, the photographs of *interest* were seen as *neutrality* almost half as often as they were seen as *interest*.

A number of other studies using Tomkins' approach are under way, though not all necessarily follow his theoretical ideas completely.* Ekman, Sorenson, and Friesen (1969) have explored the universality of the basic emotions and their recognition by showing a series of carefully selected photographs to people of different cultural backgrounds. Subjects of as great a diversity as Europeans and Orientals may not give us a satisfactory answer, the authors reason, since looking at photographs is common to all literate peoples, and the mass media may have taught everyone certain cues to the emotions generally portrayed, with the result that subjects may not be so different as experimenters might hope. Ekman, Sorenson and Friesen therefore sought nonliterate as well as literate subjects for their study, two subsamples of the fairly Westernized Fore in New Guinea and one of the Sadong in Borneo for the former, and samples from the United States, Brazil, and Japan for the latter. The photographs, all of Caucasians, were chosen to represent pure instances of six of Tomkins' eight primary affects (interest and shame were not included), and subjects were asked to say which of the six affects was depicted in each photograph.

The outstanding result is that the *happy* photographs were almost unanimously identified as such by both literate and nonliterate subjects. Beyond this there is a definite split between these two large subject-groups. The literate subjects identified the affects correctly in the pre-

---

* Since this book was edited in its final form, two books on facial expression of emotion have been published: Carroll E. Izard's *The Face of Emotion* (Appleton-Century-Crofts, 1971) and Paul Ekman, Wallace V. Friesen, and Phoebe Ellsworth's *Emotion in the Human Face* (Pergamon Press, 1972). Both acknowledge a strong debt to Tomkins and his thinking and report complementary lines of cross-cultural research. Izard's emphasis is on the concept of emotion itself, and he uses the results of facial expression studies as evidence for many points in his theory of emotion. Ekman, et al., focus more on the observer's process of decoding facial expressions and on methodological issues in research on facial expression of emotion.

ponderance of cases other than the *happy*, especially in the *disgust-contempt* and *surprise* categories, and no rate of correct response was less than 63 per cent for any affect-group combination. Among the almost nonliterate groups, on the other hand, 64 per cent was the highest figure other than for *happy*, and this was for *anger*. *Sadness* also yielded fairly high agreement. The language barrier was enormous for the preliterate groups, of course, and a different method was devised for a later study of an even more isolated group. Instead of naming emotions with single words, short pre-tested stories were used. For each trial three pictures were shown, including two which earlier studies had shown to be frequently confused with the correct emotion. A large number of subjects were selected again from among the Fore, excluding any who had seen motion pictures, who spoke English or the local Pidgin, had lived in a Western settlement or town, or had worked for a Caucasian. The rate of correct responses for these people with this method matched that of Western subjects in the earlier study. One confusion of responses was puzzling: when the *fear* story was told and the pictures given the subjects included *surprise*, correct responses were way down. In fact, given *fear*, *surprise*, and *sadness* pictures, they chose surprise 67 per cent of the time. From these results we can conclude that most affects show themselves in facial expression very much the same everywhere, and that the *happy* expression, probably mediated mostly by the smile, is in a class by itself on the score of universality.*

We thus have partial support for Tomkins' theory of built-in programs of facial expression for different emotional states. As for the smile, we may as well say it is part of the genetic heritage of man, as Darwin posited. Beyond this, how much is cultural will take some time to unravel. Ekman and Friesen (1969b) have done much to start on the process by distinguishing (a) the antecedents to an emotional episode

---

* Ekman and Friesen (1969b) have also reported the beginnings of work in the opposite direction, presenting stories or films designed to elicit affect, then photographing the resulting expressions. Ekman gave preliminary findings of this work at a Conference on Nonverbal Dimensions of Social Interaction, sponsored by the Association for the Aid of Crippled Children, in June 1969, analysis of which will add a great deal to our knowledge of this area.

together with the controls exercised on certain affects, both of which are culturally determined, from (b) the actual facial expression, which may not be. We shall be referring back to Ekman and Friesen's analysis when we discuss the degree to which different emotional expressions resemble language as true codes in the communication theory sense of that term.

Earlier I mentioned that Tomkins and McCarter had included a neutral category as a control in their list of affects. Photographs posed for neutrality were quite frequently interpreted as interest (and vice versa), and significantly often also, there were confusions between neutrality and shame. Nevertheless, the neutral expression was correctly recognized more often than were several of the named affects. This finding raises an interesting question: Is absence of emotion a distinct event in the same way that the presence of one or another emotional quality is? It certainly is noticed at some times when a person does not react as expected, and we even have a technical term for it as a part of the symptomatology of one diagnostic entity: flattened affect in schizophrenia.

Tomkins and those who have been influenced by his thinking, then, have conceptualized emotion in terms of discrete categories, and have posited a number of these in the order of eight as the basic alphabet of emotional communication. The only other writer who has adhered to the categorical notion of emotions is Titchener (1900), who stated flatly that there are only two qualities of emotion, the pleasant and the unpleasant. Within each of these classes is a large number of "special emotive forms" (p. 232), but he finds it impossible to classify these on any rational basis.

Most other writers have thought in quite different terms, those of a few dimensions of emotion. The earliest set was proposed by Wundt (1907):

> Three such chief dimensions may be distinguished. We call them the series of *pleasurable* and *unpleasurable* feelings, that of *arousing* and *subduing* feelings, and finally that of feelings of *strain* and *relaxation*. The fundamental feeling qualities can be represented in the form of a three-dimensional figure the central point of which is the indifference point. . . . A given feeling may lie in one or more of these dimensions (pp. 91-92).

Wundt's proposal was not universally accepted, to say the least; Titchener was the most critical, as he adhered to his position that feelings could be only pleasant or unpleasant. The evidence from other investigators was about evenly divided between one side of the argument and the other. Beebe-Center (1932, Chap. 3) gives a very good review of the several studies that bore on the question.

It was several decades before psychologists returned to the question of the dimensionality of emotions. Even though factor analysis, the method of choice in recent work, was developed in the early 1930's, research applying this method to emotions did not begin for another twenty years. At that time another method, the semantic differential (Osgood, 1952; Osgood & Suci, 1955) appeared and was found useful in studying the relationships among emotions as concepts. The importance of this work for our discussion lies in the relative lengths of the dimensions that have resulted from the analysis of semantic differential data, that is, from the relative amounts of common factor variance which the dimensions account for. The semantic differential was first applied to a wide variety of concepts in an effort to find some concrete basis for thinking about the meaning of words. In that analysis, and in many others reported since then, the longest dimension is the one labeled evaluation. The other dimensions, usually called potency and activity, are only about a fourth as long as the first one. It appears that the psychological space of judgments of meaning is a three-dimensional one, long and round in cross section, with the most evident dimension being concerned with good-bad, pleasant-unpleasant, or the like.

Applying the semantic differential to words that name emotions, Block (1957) came up with results very similar to the general ones described above. The shape of the space is shorter and flatter in Block's analysis, a difference easily attributable to the difference in technique (Osgood and Suci intercorrelated the descriptive scales, while Block intercorrelated the words described) and in the number of variables in the matrix submitted to analysis (Osgood and Suci studied 50 scales; Block, 15 emotions). The first dimension is still clearly an evaluative one, with *contentment, love, elation, sympathy,* and *anticipation* at one end, and *guilt, worry, humiliation, grief, envy, fear,* and *boredom* at the other. Block's second dimension corresponds to the activity one of Osgood and Suci's results. It is defined by the extremes of *anger, pride, anticipation, fear*, *elation*, and *envy* at one end, with *nostalgia* and *boredom* at the other. The third dimension does not have any counterpart in the earlier study. It accounts for only 5.4 per cent of the common factor variance, and is unipolar, having *sympathy*, *nostalgia* and *grief* as the only prominent loadings. Block calls it interpersonal relatedness, and it certainly does not seem at all similar to the potency factor in Osgood and Suci's results.

Two other works should be mentioned here, although their methods of data collection led to results that are really not comparable with the others being discussed. One is the series of studies done over the years by Burt (summarized in 1950), where subjects were rated in many settings — from tests to real-life situations. It is not easy to tell if the studies were about specific emotional responses or about traits, since Burt uses both terms in his descriptions. Clearly those subjects who responded emotionally in the different situations were expressive people, and it is not surprising that general emotionality as a first factor accounts for about half of the total variance of the correlation matrices, and that the second factor is demonstrative-inhibitive. The pleasant-unpleasant dimension comes in third in Burt's analyses. The other somewhat different type of study is G. Ekman's (1955). He presented subjects with emotion names in pair comparisons, and asked them to rate the quantitative similarity of the emotional states represented by the words — from not at all similar to identical. The similarity matrix was then treated as if it were an intercorrelation table and was submitted to a factor analysis. Pairs of emotions which are ordinarily considered polar opposites and those which are independent would both be rated low (that is, not at all similar) on Ekman's scale, thus accounting for the otherwise unusual result that *happy* and *glad* defined one factor, while *sad* and *depressed* defined another, and *restless, impatient*, and *agitated* yet another — all independent factors. It is difficult to recast the loadings on Ekman's 11 factors into a form comparable with those of the other studies in the literature.

The dimensional studies covered so far are about emotions in the abstract, or emotional traits, but not about communication of emotional responses. Research related to the latter may be found in the more usual recent literature on facial expressions of emotion — all, that is, except that by Tomkins and his collaborators, already mentioned. One line of research started with Woodworth's (1938, pp. 250-251) development of a scale of emotions from published data about identifying the emotions portrayed by actors in a series of still photographs. This scale was further examined by Schlosberg (1941), who found that the ends of Woodworth's scale were closely enough related that a recurrent continuum, or circular form, could best describe the results. In a subsequent test of this idea (Schlosberg, 1952), subjects were asked to rate pictures (the Ruckmick & Frois-Wittmann series) in terms of the two dimensions of the circle, pleasant-unpleasant and attention-rejection. They were able to do so with remarkable agreement, and the two-dimensional organization seemed secure. In 1954, Schlosberg posited a third dimension, that of sleep-tension or level of activation, and Engen, Levy, and Schlosberg (1958) tested this by having a new set of pictures, the Lightfoot series (see Engen, Levy, & Schlosberg, 1957) rated on this dimension in addition to the older ones. Again the subjects were able to do so. Triandis and Lambert (1958) followed up Schlosberg's three-dimensional conception by testing subjects in Greece for comparison. The dimensions seemed to serve their judgments of pictures quite as well as they did those of Schlosberg's subjects, although the shape of the conceptual space was somewhat different for the two groups.

Considerable doubt has been cast on Schlosberg's original notion of a circular continuum by Thompson and Meltzer (1964). Using live expressors who were selected from the usual subject pool instead of photographs of trained actors, they failed to find the overlap of the ends of Woodworth's scale which led Schlosberg to think in two-dimensional terms. They believe that the difference in methods of presentation may account for the difference in results. Two other studies found that Schlosberg's second and third dimensions may not be separable. Both used scaling methods based upon judgments of similarities and factor analyzed the results, and both used stimulus materials from the Lightfoot series of pictures. Abelson and Sermat (1962) presented their 13 stimuli in pair comparisons for similarity judgment, and found that the results accorded very well with Schlosberg's in the pleasant-unpleasant dimension, but that his attention-rejection and sleep-tension were almost completely redundant. Thus a two-dimensional space seemed sufficient to account for the data. Gladstones (1962) presented his ten stimuli in triads, and found three dimensions: one like Schlosberg's pleasant-unpleasant and one like his sleep-tension (this one also correlated highly with Schlosberg's attention-rejection), and a third which was difficult to identify. It is interesting to note that Schlosberg's third dimension, sleep-tension, comes out as the second in both of these studies.

Osgood (1955) used live performances instead of photographs as stimulus material to be judged. He gave 40 emotion names to students who portrayed them for their classmates; the latter, in turn, identified them using the same 40 words. The results were submitted to profile simi-larity analysis and yielded three dimensions: pleasant-unpleasant, quiet-intense or quiet-active, and what Osgood calls control, which seems to mean whether the emoter is in control of what he is emoting about or not. A later article (Osgood, 1966) reports a factor analysis of the same data by the centroid method, from which four interpretable factors emerged: pleasant-unpleasant; the control dimension formed earlier; activation (the second and third dimensions were simply reversed in the two analyses); and, finally, a dimension of something like interest — it may be related to Schlosberg's attention-rejection one, but accounts for too little variance to lend itself to precise naming.

Nummenmaa and Kauranne (1958) used G. Ekman's similarities method and found four orthogonal unipolar factors that resolved into Schlosberg's pleasant-unpleasant and attention-rejection. Later Kauran-ne (1964) had subjects respond by Osgood's semantic differential method to pictures, and factor analyzed the similarity matrix, with three factors resulting. One, a contempt factor, was interpreted as being a counterpart of Schlosberg's rejection; a pleasure factor was directly comparable to that end of Schlosberg's first continuum; finally, a hate factor was seen as corresponding to unpleasantness. Kauranne interpreted these results as supporting Schlosberg's two-dimensional conception of emotional space.

Frijda and Philipszoon (1963) used a set of 30 pictures selected from 150 in which an actress tried to portray a wide variety of emotions, including some everyday ones, more subtle and less extreme than those in the classical pictures. The investigators devised a series of 27 response scales from the free descriptions of the same pictures given by pretest subjects. Factor analysis of the resulting ratings yielded four dimensions: the first was the frequently found pleasantness-unpleasantness, and the third and fourth were expressiveness-control and active attention-disin-terest, respectively. The second dimension has no parallel in any other study: it is defined by *mildness, naturalness,* and *submissiveness* at one end of the continuum and by *derisiveness, artificiality,* and *authoritarianism* at the other. The authors find this dimension puzzling and difficult to reconcile with other published data. A laater analysis with a more complete factor analytic method (Frijda, 1969) yielded essentially the same first four factors, plus two others. These accounted for only 5 to 6 per cent of the variance, and were defined by too few loadings for easy assignment of names.

Royal and Hays (1959) used the multidimensional unfolding technique rather than factor analysis to analyze response to classical posed pictures. Three dimensions were needed to account for the judgments, and they were essentially the same as Schlosberg's three. In a subsequent study (Royal, 1959) using schematic faces as well for stimulus material and similar data analysis techniques, three dimensions continued to be found; but beyond the pleasant-unpleasant first one, they did not turn out to be the same. A temporal factor was the second, like the enduring-momentary, while the third was aroused-relaxed.

The last factor analytic study of emotional expression I wish to mention was one done in our laboratory, reported here for the first time. The stimuli were different from those in most of the other studies on two counts. First, they were not still photographs which the judges could look at for any length of time they chose, but were, instead, three-second segments from motion picture film. The second difference was that the persons photographed were not actors, but people participating in interviews, both diagnostic interviews and sessions held to test the motion picture recording facilities we were then developing. There were 25 such film segments representing six people, and we tried to select segments that covered a wide range of expression, although we had no "rational" method for determining this range other than the results of studies such as those I have just cited. The method of recording responses consisted of an Affect Checklist of 17 categories (each described by three adjectives) developed from a thorough search of the literature both on perception of emotion and on feeling and emotion generally. The form of the checklist turned out to be very similar to that of Dusenbury and Knower (1938, 1939), whose work had not yet been seen when we developed our scheme.

Sixteen judges were shown the film individually. After each segment the judge was asked to place a check next to all categories he felt were applicable to that segment. Any number of checks could be used, from

TABLE 1. SUMMARY OF DIMENSIONS FOUND IN STUDIES OF EMOTION

| STUDY AND YEAR | SOURCE OF DATA | | RANK OF DIMENSIONS | | | | | |
	Number and Type of Stimuli	Mode of Response	Pleasant-Unpleasant	Level of Activation	Attention-Rejection	Demonstrative-Inhibitive	Control	Other
Wundt (1907)	Introspective Data		1	2				3: strained-relaxed
Osgood (1952)	Variety of words and concepts	Semantic differential	1	3				2: strong-weak
Block (1957)	15 emotion names	Semantic differential	1	2				3: relatedness
Burt (1950)	Variety of situations	Ratings by observers	3			2		1: general emotionality
Engen, Levy, & Schlosberg (1958)	56 Lightfoot photos	Ratings on 3 Schlosberg scales	1	3	2			
Triandis & Lambert (1958)	6 Ruckmick photos	Ratings on 3 Schlosberg scales	2	1	3			
Abelson & Sermat (1962)	13 Lightfoot photos	Similarities of all pairs	1	2				
Gladstones (1962)	10 Lightfoot photos	Similarities in triads	1	2				3: unclear

TABLE 1. SUMMARY OF DIMENSIONS FOUND IN STUDIES OF EMOTION

Osgood (1955)	40 "acted" emotions	Pick best from list of 40	1	2		3	
Osgood (1966)	40 "acted" emotions	Pick best from list of 40	1	3	2		4: unclear
Nummenmaa & Kauranne (1958)	27 Ristola photos	G. Ekman similarity method	1		2		
Kauranne (1964)	30 Frois-Wittmann photos	Semantic differential	2	1			
Frijda & Philipson (1963)	30 posed photos	Semantic differential	1		4	3	2: naturalness
Frijda (1969)	30 posed photos	Semantic differential	1		4		2: naturalness 3: intensity of expression
Royal & Hays (1959)	8 Frois-Wittmann photos	Similarities in triads	1	3	2		5 and 6: unclear
Royal (1959)	8 schematic faces	Similarities in triads	1	3			2: enduring-momentary
Dittmann (data presented here)	25 movie segments	17-item Affect Check List	1	2			3: trustful-mistrustful 4: unclear

none to 17. The next segment was shown when the judge finished checking the last one. The score for each segment for each category was the number of judges who checked it. Intercorrelations were computed of the categories across segments, and the resulting matrix was submitted to a principal components factor analysis. Four factors emerged: the familiar pleasant-unpleasant dimension was the longest one here, too, and level of activation was the second; the third dimension appeared to be a trustful-untrustful one, while the fourth gave such an unclear picture as to defy naming.

The results of all these studies are summarized in Table 1. Everyone from Wundt to recent investigators, using introspection to factor analysis and a great variety of stimulus materials, has found pleasantness-unpleasantness as a dimension, and as the first dimension in 14 out of 17 studies. The next most frequent dimension is level of activation, appearing in 13 of 17 studies, and it is the first or second dimension in 8 of these. The elements constituting this activation dimension are not always as clearcut as those that define pleasantness and unpleasantness, but not much inference is required to name it and to see that it has counterparts from one study to others. From here on the path is not so clear. One other dimension is approximately duplicated in six studies, or in seven if we include the hard-to-name fourth one in Osgood (1966). All investigators find attention or interest at one end; but at the other some find disinterest, some find rejection, and Osgood's results are unclear. The methods of arriving at these dimensions are so different, however, that this may not constitute excessive disagreement. As for other dimensions that have been found in one study or another, the differences must be attributed to the diversity of inputs to the analyses. Perhaps the most basic finding common to all the factor-analytic studies is that at least three factors are necessary to describe all of the matrices, and three studies admit of four factors. We can be certain about the nature of the first factor, and reasonably certain about the second, but we must wait for more data before we can know much beyond that.

Categories and Dimensions Compared

We have been surveying two approaches to conceptualizing emotions — both emotions in general, as studied by Wundt, by Osgood and Suci, and by Block, and emotions as recognized from facial expressions, as in all the other investigations we have cited. The first approach views emotions as a number of categories, discretely different from each other; the second searches for the dimensionality of the psychological space of emotionality. Several points need to be made about the difference between these approaches. First, the number of descriptive terms they yield is quite similar: eight categories according to Tomkins, and three to four dimensions that are *bipolar* in the results of the studies of dimensions. The content of the descriptive terms, however, is very different. The categories are specific and the words cannot be applied to anything but emotions, while the dimensions are general and the terms have been used before to characterize psychological states of all kinds, emotions included. The dimensions can provide a means of describing emotions, but they are not themselves emotions. How then are the two approaches related in the research we have been discussing?

Categories of emotion, such as those proposed by Darwin and followed quite closely by Tomkins, are conceptualizations based upon eons of human experience. Each person gets sight of them from time to time in their pure form, but generally they are shadowy essences of which daily events are only approximations — beyond early childhood, at least. We measure our experiences against these essences, for they are always available as memories of things that have actually happened to us or that we have heard vividly described. The measurement process is probably automatic or unconscious, with the result that we do not think actively of the essences themselves in the course of many of our days. Dimensions, by contrast, are not essences; rather, they are approaches, or ways of organizing many kinds of experience, including essences.

The experiments we have been surveying here, and the methods of analyzing the data they produce, have predestined the results to support either the categorical or dimensional points of view. Tomkins and McCarter, as well as Ekman, Sorenson, and Friesen, chose photographs carefully to represent the categories of emotion in their purest form. These investigators all recognize that pure affects are very rare in daily life, but for purposes of experimentation they eliminated blends of more than one emotion as completely as possible from their stimulus material. They also asked their judges to respond in terms of these same pure categories. In the dimensional studies, on the other hand, the set-ups were very different. Osgood did not, indeed could not, demand purity in the way he asked his "actors" to portray the emotions, and he used a list for them to act and for the judges to respond to which was five times as long as Tomkins's, and many emotions undoubtedly included what the students of categories would regard as blends. In the study reported here for the first time, stimuli were not preselected in terms of specific emotions at all, and the list of possible responses was twice as long as Tomkins's. Other investigators used various numbers of photos, but how they represented any universe of emotions is seldom clear from the reports. What is clear is that the way the subjects were asked to respond could hardly have produced results in the form of categories. In two studies, subjects were asked to rate the photos on preconceived dimensions. In five they were asked to respond in terms of similarities among pairs or triads of pictures, and in three they rated on semantic differential dimensions. Factor analytic methods were used to analyze the data in most of the studies, and the very purpose of factor analysis is to find dimensions. So the stimuli and the response methods, plus the data analysis techniques, dictated the form of the results.

Just how all this research represents what the social participant does in assigning information value to emotional messages is hard to say. There are a number of issues on which most or all studies are unrepresentative of daily interaction: (1) for the most part, subjects are allowed to look at a single instant— namely, a still picture— for a long time, something no one ever has a chance to do in social interaction (the exceptions are Osgood's study where the "actors" posed live, and my own which used short segments of movie film); (2) after they have looked, the subjects are allowed to ponder what they have seen long enough to make up their minds about the emotion depicted; (3) the subjects are asked to respond to every stimulus; (4) as has been noted, they are given a standard method for responding, i.e., the one concocted by the experimenter; finally, (5) although neutral stimuli are generally included in some of the studies, emotion is the topic of every experiment, so that the subject is on the lookout for emotional expressions in every stimulus.

Things are certainly different in real life. Social participants can receive input continuously, or as much as they wish to and can pay attention to. In comparison to the number of messages available, they respond very seldom — as I said a few pages back, they would not be able to respond to every expression even if they wanted to and still keep up with the conversation. And although we have no ecological map of these matters, identifiable emotions are probably not expressed very often, even if there is a general affective undertone to most social situations. When an emotion does come up it is a fleeting event, most often a blend of a number of emotions, and its place in the conversation has to be sorted out of all the other communicative events which are going on at the same time. In short, we get sequences of little glimpses at how other people are feeling.

On being confronted with an emotional event, the social participant does not always have to deal with it immediately. Usually he can wait for more information before he evaluates its importance or its kind, and decides how to respond or whether to respond at all. He gets a chance to correct his first impression because time is continuous and events keep happening. While none of the studies of emotional expression tell us anything about these sequential aspects of the social situation, they do tell us something about some of the details of the process. Those from the category viewpoint tell us how high one's accuracy *can* be under ideal circumstances, and may thus be classified as studies about competence. The dimension studies tell us more about how the person approaches an expression, and what sorts of things he pays attention to first — such as whether it is pleasant or unpleasant, and so on down the line — and may thus be classified as performance studies.

In measuring the information value of a given message, I hold that the social participant uses both dimensions and categories as his basis depending on how much information is available to him. The fleeting reactions of short duration, and many body movements, do not inherently contain enough information to apply categories, and are thus more amenable to dimensional thinking. Ekman and Friesen (1967) refer to these cues as those of gross affective states. The more definite expressions, such as the specific affect displays of the face, and many verbal expressions fall more neatly into categories. The relationship between these two degrees of emotional information and the two sources of inference proposed by Hebb as bases for naming emotions, namely, from primary emotional behavior and from associated behavior, needs to be explored further. Primary emotional behavior appears to be arranged in categories, according to the research of Tomkins and his colleagues. It is more clear-cut, pure perhaps in the sense of including fewer blends of a number of emotions. Just how associated behavior and dimensions fit together is not clear enough at this point for a neat package to be made of all these concepts.

SUMMARY: THE MEASUREMENT OF EMOTIONAL INFORMATION

In this chapter we have covered all the facts necessary to apply the communication-theory measure of information to emotional messages. It is time now to state this succinctly, so that we can take a hard look at it and ask ourselves how far we have come toward making use of it as we study emotional communication.

1. The information value of emotion, like that of anything else lies in its scarcity, and is measured in any behavior (including, in some cases, absence of behavior) as some inverse function of the relative frequency of occurrence of that type of behavior as compared with others in the behavioral repertory.

2. Knowledge about the behavioral repertory of the person under observation comes from: (a) general knowledge about the cultural background of the person, and, where available, (b) specific acquaintance with the person's idiosyncratic patterns as they are added to or modify the cultural norms.

3. Knowledge about the behavioral repertory of the stimulus situation comes from: (a) general knowledge of the cultural background of the persons who make up the situation, and, where available, (b) knowledge of the social structure of the situation as it further limits the cultural norm, and (c) acquaintance with the individual person or persons who make up the situation within which the observation takes place.

4. The contingent probability of the response and stimulus, evaluated as in (2) and (3) above, yields the information value of the current act.

5. The categories into which emotional behaviors are classified are the qualities in terms of the dimensions or other classifications that can be discriminated for those types of behavior. The relative frequencies of

behaviors so classified gives the unit of measurement for the information assessed as in Step 4.

Within this formulation Hebb's concept of the behavioral deviation is seen to refer to information value of the response, computed on the basis of cultural and personal frequency distributions of possible responses. If no information is available from the stimulus, response information is all there is to go on. In this case, Frijda's finding is pertinent: general response tendencies are seen unless knowledge of the stimulus is added to provide greater specificity to the judgment of the response. In short, the fewer the data the observer has at his disposal, the less precise his judgment can be. It seems entirely reasonable that specificity, precision, or exactness of inference should be an outcome of amount of information in the message. But this implies that there are different levels of specificity in the qualitative categories mentioned in Step 5, different qualities of qualities. It looks as though qualitative differences were hidden among the quantitative differences, and this is indeed a problem for the theory. We shall have a closer look at this problem in Chapter 5, where we discuss various channels of emotional expression.

The question of qualities being confused with quantities in information measurement comes up in another way in this application of communication theory. Throughout this chapter I have said that every emotional message is a behavioral deviation. But have I not also said that every behavioral deviation is an emotional message? After all, this latter is really the direction in which the observer's inferences go. What he begins with is the behavioral deviation, and he works his way from there on to guess what feeling might be behind it. But surely he cannot believe that an emotion is involved every time he sees something unusual. He must certainly have some way of telling the difference, for example, between the speech-falterings of embarrassment or fear and those of trying to put words to a very difficult conceptual point. Actually much of this differentiation is included in Step 2(a): acquaintance with the person would include knowing something of his manner of speech under different emotional and cognitive circumstances. Yet the qualitative difference remains; there is no getting around that fact.

We may be disappointed in the mathematical theory of communication, since it apparently leaves us stuck with the quantity versus quality problem in information measurement. Yet we really should not feel that way, for the theory was not designed to help us on this score. It was designed to measure the amount of information of messages at various steps along the course—from source to user— and to measure the loss and confusion resulting from interference at various places along the line. But the specifics of the devices through which the messages travel, or of what sort of information they contained in the first place, the theory does not indicate, and we should not expect it to if we wish to retain the theory's generality. It does not tell the engineer in telecommunication how to design a receiver to detect frequency modulation of a signal and to reject amplitude modulation, nor does it tell him how to account for one which does not do these things as well as he had planned. The engineer must do that. The theory can only tell him how to measure the amount of information of each type of modulation as the receiver actually works.

By the same token, communication theory does not explain the many confoundings and confusions which human beings are heir to as they try to make sense of emotional messages. As a theory it cannot distinguish between emotional messages and the many other kinds of message common in social interchange. The psychologist must do that. The theory can only tell us how to measure the information in the various types of messages that are actually present.

Chapter Four

Message and Person ———————————————

The main theme in the preceding chapter was the development of ways in which one might measure the amount of information conveyed by emotional messages. This was really our first application to emotional messages of communication theory, and more specifically of the information measurement concepts of the theory. True, emotional information turned out to be more complicated than the source information which telecommunication ordinarily deals with, but we could still fit facts and theory together without distorting either one. This is partly because the facts we were talking about were indeed facts, observables which lend themselves to measurement, either directly or by their effects. There are some other aspects of emotional communication, however, that do not fit so neatly into communication theory. In part the fault lies in the subject matter: the messages cannot be described completely in the terms we talked about in Chapter 2 because they are more numerous in form and vary in a host of ways from one occasion to the next. In part the fault also lies in the structure of the relationship between the sending person and the message and receiving person. In telecommunication, we must keep reminding ourselves, the components of source encoder and channel encoder are separate from each other and separate from the source — they could all be in different cities and still work — as are the corresponding three parts at the receiving end. In emotional communication the functions are still there, all being performed within people, but there are no separate components, and the functions are not by any stretch of the imagination performed independently of each other.

This chapter will deal with some consequences of this nonindependence, namely, the way in which people influence messages in communica-

tion situations. The discussion is cast under two headings — level of awareness and intentional control — both of which are clearly psychological in
nature. First, there is another topic which interacts with these influences,
but is really more closely related to coding in communication theory. That
topic is communicative specificity. For want of a better name, I call all
three of these topics structural variables. They are structural in that they
are relatively independent and must all be taken into account at the
same time that we talk about any emotional message, how it gets transmitted, or how we measure its information value. The term is to some extent
a misnomer, though, since the three are not variables in the usual sense
but are, rather, three quite complicated sets of factors. In connection
with level of awareness and intentional control, we shall be calling for
the first time on theories other than Shannon's communication theory.

COMMUNICATIVE SPECIFICITY

By "communication" here I mean much the same thing Morris
(1946) meant by "language", only somewhat more general and not limited
to speech. Language, to paraphrase Morris's definition, is a system of
signs, universally applicable, whose use is agreed upon by the members
of a group (pp. 35-36). This is one of those definitions in which every
word counts, and Morris goes into each element at some length: *system*
implies an organization, a grammar or syntax; a *sign* is a preparatory
stimulus which points the person toward some specific form of action;
universality indicates that the system of signs is not tied to any one
situation or time, but can be used in many; and *agreement* by the group
refers to the codification of this universal sign system by the language
community. The several parts of Morris's definition can be regarded as
a set of criteria, all of which must be met if a behavior complex may
truly be called a language.

"Communicative specificity," as used here, is a continuum which
has language — or "communication" as the more general term — at one
end and expression at the other. A message is more toward the communication end of the continuum, as it meets more of the criteria in Morris's
definition system. Spoken language clearly meets all the criteria, and can
carry many types of messages, emotional and others as well. The system of
sign language used by deaf people also seems to meet all the criteria of

communication. The recent analysis of signing from a linguistic point of view (Stokoe, Casterline, & Croneberg, 1965) shows that it has developed into a complete language, albeit different in structure from the spoken language used by people with normal hearing. Languages made up of gestures, such as the Plains Indian sign language, probably do not fully qualify, since they have no codified organization like a syntax to tie them together. They may still serve many uses, although their lack of organization would limit them to brief messages of the most practical sort, and make tedious, if not impossible, any extended discourse where abstract ideas are to be exchanged.

Along the rest of the continuum things have not been very well studied, but some indications can be given of the directions they may take. Facial expressions of emotion are very specific, and many of them are universally recognized, as the work by Tomkins and McCarter (1964) and Ekman, Sorenson, and Friesen (1969) has amply demonstrated. In this sense these expressions lie toward the communicative end of the scale. Even so, we do not yet have evidence that these expressions are made up by a system of rules from a set of components which are like Morris's signs, or that they serve as signs which are organized into some larger entity. Ekman, Friesen, and Tomkins (1971) have studied the components of facial expressions of emotion extensively, and have found that certain combinations of behaviors of the three parts of the face (brow and forehead, eyes and lids, and lower face) combine to give configurations that are expressive of certain emotions. They found, however, that there is a good deal of leeway in each of the six emotion categories as to how many combinations are possible. For all but one of the categories only one brow and forehead display was allowable, but in the case of that one (sadness), any of eight could be present. All the emotions could be made up of more than one display of the other facial areas, up to eleven in the case of lower face in disgust. One might predict that those emotion categories which permit the greatest variability of combinations of specific facial behaviors would be the most difficult to judge, that is, yield the lowest percentage of correct predictions. But that is not the case. Thus even though facial expressions of emotion are legible with an accuracy reminiscent of the words of speech, they are not constructed like speech as a linguistic system. In our terms they are quite close to the communicative end of the continuum, but not as close as language. Ekman and Friesen (1969b) appear to share this conclusion as they try to fit these expressions into their classification of different kinds of coding (see especially p. 78). Many other movements we see in the face, looks of tension, fatigue, relaxation, and the like, are not coded in the same sense that emotional expressions are. The very words like "tension," and so on, usually used to refer to them, are states-of-being kinds of words and do not bring to mind any facial expressions as specific as the emotion displays. Even so, the fact that one can use states-of-being words to describe these expressions indicates that they vary systematically with something about their wearer, some psychological states or passing physical conditions. The same may be said of movements of other parts of the body. To the extent that they do vary systematically and may be observed by some means, they are expressions of those states of being. In the terms developed in the last chapter, they are behavioral data from which inferences may be drawn. In the terms developed by Frankena (1958a), the expression end of the continuum corresponds to the aspect of language called emotions and attitudes revealed. "What is expressed and revealed is always some statement about the speaker, and this is only signalled by his utterance; it is not symbolized or asserted" (p. 133). Thus a person who fidgets a lot and looks "strained" is signaling that he is ill at ease, but he is not asserting this in any communicative system as defined above, as he would be if he said, "I am upset."

For the sake of completeness we should note that the communicative specificity continuum does not really end with "expressive" acts, but continues on beyond to what may be called random activity. I realize that calling an act random does not mean that there is no reason at all behind it. It may only mean that we do not know what the reason is. In the present context it may also mean that the act is random with respect to transmitting emotional messages, but may convey some other sort of information. If, for example, such acts do not appear in any regular way as accompaniments to other short-term changes in the person, or to the things that may be thought to stimulate him, they might provide some longer-term information about him, such as his more enduring mood states or personality traits, his activity level as compared with that of other people, or his age or cultural heritage.

At this point it may be advisable to point out a couple of things that the communicative specificity continuum is *not*, in order to help clarify some confusions before they become set. The first thing that the continuum is not is the familiar one of verbal, as compared with non-verbal, communication. To be sure, most messages toward the comunicative end of the scale are verbal, or at least these are the easiest ones to think about and give as examples. But there are many facial expressions that say it "in so many words," just as there are shifts of posture and changes in gaze direction. Leaning toward a person or leaning away from him, and looking toward or away, are eloquent communications of one's feeling toward him, just as a smile or an expression of disgust is. Thus many nonverbal messages can be communications in this sense. By the same token, there can be expressive messages sent by means of words. The listener may note quite late in a conversation, for example, that the speaker has brought up many topics having to do with danger, quite unrelated and interspersed with other subjects. He may conclude that this is a very fearful person, indeed, even if the person has never said "in so many words" that he is afraid in any of the situations he has mentioned. We will hear more of this sort of verbal-expressive message in the next section of this chapter, and again in Chapter 5.

Another thing that communication-expression is not is conscious-unconscious. That, too, we will discuss more fully later in this chapter, but some examples may clarify the issue for now. There are many times when the expresser is perfectly aware that he is putting out expressive messages. These may consist of nervous wiggling or stumbling over words in a tense situation, or of a soft warmth of voice when he is feeling affectionate. Thus, expressive messages certainly need not be unconscious ones. Examples of messages toward the communicative end of the scale (of which the person is not aware) are more difficult to think of, but certainly many tongue-slips say it "in so many words," as do passing facial expressions.

Now that we have looked at two variables which communicative specificity is not, it is time to consider what it *is*. As I mentioned earlier in this chapter, communicative specificity is closely related to, but somewhat more inclusive than, coding in communication theory. Acts at the communication end of the continuum are like coded information, that is, produced and responded to as if they were discrete forms cast into the terms of an agreed-upon code alphabet. I say "as if" here because in human communication, as compared with telecommunication, the process is not at all cut and dried. The details of it are only now being discovered, and are of considerable theoretical interest to the fields of phonetics and linguistics today, since recent research results have begun to shed light on how language forms are encoded into speech acts and how these are then decoded by the listener. Some explication of these results will help us to understand why I have said that communicative specificity is a continuum, not a dichotomy.

Speech sounds, like any productions of living beings, vary continuously; yet we all act as though they fell neatly into a group of well-separated categories. There are several types of categories of different sizes in speech — the word, the morpheme, the syllable, the phoneme — and these may or may not be arranged in hierarchical order. Most linguists believe that they are, but at least one dissenter, Garvin (1968), reasons that a couple of equally important but usually neglected dimensions complicate the picture. At any rate we know most about the phoneme, especially from recent research, and I shall take the results of that work as the model for discussing coding in emotional communication. We can then use that model to look at some other behaviors that are implicated in emotional communication.

The sounds produced by speakers of any language may be sorted into a set of abstract classes for the convenience of linguists and phoneticians in studying spoken language; these classes have been called phonemes. Within the range of sounds which fall into one phoneme class, no difference is recognized by the speakers of the language — for example, in English, the "t"-sounds in *team* and *steam*. Between categories on the other hand, the difference in sounds is considered significant, one that will change the meaning of words, as between the initial sounds in *team* and *deem*. In some other language the first difference may be considered significant, while the second may not — and an observer with acoustic instruments may find the two pairs of differences very similar in magnitude. The particular language, then, defines the categories, and both speakers and listeners of that language operate within the set of definitions as if it were a set of rules to live by, all but ignoring the "acoustic reality" of the situation. So strong is this tendency to categorize speech that the nativistic view of speech as an inborn characteristic of man has become increasingly attractive to thinkers about language.

A brilliant review of the evidence about the details of this process, and by now it is considerable evidence, has been provided by Liberman, Cooper, Shankweiler, and Studdert-Kennedy (1967), concentrating on their own work at the Haskins Laboratories but including that of many other research centers as well. Especially useful to the present discussion is the emphasis of the review on what the authors call the speech code. By code they mean restructuring and simplifying the phonemes in the stream of speech as the speaker produces it, and the complementary restructuring back into phonemes as the listener organizes what he hears.

The speaker believes he is producing the necessary, distinct sounds which, when put together, make up syllables and words. As the sounds are strung out in sequences, however, they flow into one another so that they are not really distinct sounds at all in the sense that letters are distinct as elements in written language. And in the overlaps between the sounds "representing" one phoneme and the next, there are mutual influences so that neither phoneme is represented as pure, but rather as transitory, in-between states, depending on what has gone before and what is about to follow. Phonemes do not exist, then, as acoustic phenomena, but only as the speaker conceptualizes language. The listener, in turn, organizes the tremendously complex acoustic output of the speaker along the same lines, simplifying it into words made up of a few, discrete "sounds." Recent results reported by Eiman, Siqueland, Jusczyk, and Vigorito (1971) show that this conceptualization is not all learned, since infants one month of age tend to respond to differences in sounds across phoneme boundaries but not to those within the phonemes, and at four months they definitely respond as if they "understand" phoneme categories. It is this simplification and regularization that Liberman et al. call encoding and decoding.

Different aspects of speech lend themselves quite differently to the restructuring process. Consonants change markedly with the context in which they appear, while vowels are relatively invariant, especially in slow articulation. This led Liberman, et al., to write of a "continuum on degree of restructuring" (fn. 15, p. 442), and to refer to "encoded phonemes" such as most consonants at the more highly restructured end, and to "unencoded phonemes" such as most vowels and a few fricatives (like the "ss" and "sh" sounds) at the other end. We are taught by communication theory that proper encoding can increase the density of information in messages so as to utilize any given transmission medium most effectively, and speech appears to provide a good example: it does seem to be the case that consonants convey more information than vowels. One can synthesize speech, using only a single midvowel for all vocalic positions, and produce quite understandable results. And in the Soskin method of eliminating intelligibility from speech while leaving emotonal information relatively untouched (Soskin & Kaufmann, 1961), a low-pass filter is used, cutting off sharply at 450 Hz, a frequency that quite effectively masks information about consonants, but not about vowels. Thus even within speech itself there are marked differences in the extent to which coding is instituted.

The continuum which Liberman et al., posited has been seen as a dichotomy by a number of writers, and is indeed easier to think about that way. Beginning in 1954 Ruesch published a number of works in which he dichotomized the variable. He called one category digital, equating it with language, and the other analogic, equating it with nonverbal behavior. In one article (1955) he referred to both the digital and the analogic as modes of codification. Ekman and Friesen (1969b) discuss coding under a similar, but more complicated, classification. They list two types of what they call extrinsic coding, in both of which the act or sound represents something else. In the iconic the act is a pictorial representative, so to speak, of what it signifies; in the arbitrary there is no obvious relationship. Their other main classification of coding is the intrinsic, in which there is no representation at all; rather, the thing signified is simply presented outright. The act of hitting someone, for example, does not represent anger; it *is* the anger being presented directly.

In both these conceptualizations the differences among the various types of coding are discrete, and all types are called codes. But only the digital of Ruesch and the arbitrary of Ekman and Friesen can be considered codes in the Liberman et al., use of the term, since only these have been restructured and cast into simpler form. And this process, say Liberman et al., is not one of dichtomous choice at all; it is a continuum. Even language possesses varying degrees of this restructuring, at least at the phonemic level, according to their results, and in the next section of this chapter we shall see another way in which words, discrete though they seem on the surface, can convey a somewhat more continuous sort of information. Actually, Ekman and Friesen's tripartite division can be viewed as three steps along this continuum. Arbitrary coding is indeed coding, as I have said, and there are acts as well as words that have resulted from boiling down a more complicated set of expressions into what is by now a quite arbitrary representation. In intrinsic expression no coding is involved at all, since act and thing signified are rolled into one. In iconic expression there is some boiling down, even though the form of the act serves to point out its own relationship to what it signifies. Thus iconic representation is coding to some extent, and falls somewhere between the arbitrary and the intrinsic along the continuum.

This discussion may be summarized by noting that coding in the sense of communication theory is a viable concept in human communication as well as in telecommunication, although it must be considered a more complicated process when people perform it by manipulating parts of their bodies than when activating external mechanical apparatus. There is a less clear-cut difference between coded information and noncoded activity, for example, in human communication than in telecommunication, but humans as they interact believe that they are coding quite unambiguously. Our illustration of these processes has been confined to speech, and to very small segments of speech, at that. Larger segments — syllables, words, phrases, and so on — may also be thought of in the same terms, with the additional complications of the rules that govern the relationships among them. But looking into coding at those levels would carry us far afield.

Emotional expressions use many means, language included, to get their messages across. Differences in extent of coding, or in communicative specificity (to use the somewhat broader term), are probably greater among these many means than they are within language itself. Emotional messages of the linguistic type are usually high on the continuum toward communication, while those of other varieties are always somewhat lower. Still there are strong differences among them on this score as well: many gestures are far more specific than most changes in tone of voice, for example. We shall be discussing these various means of expression under the term "channels" in the next chapter, and we shall be considering a number of differences among them, including communicative specificity.

How can we know whether a given act is communicative or expressive? The answer is that there is no way given by the act itself. In many cases, of course, one can be very sure that the act is communicative, as when the person emits a series of sounds which form the words "I am upset". In other cases one can be sure that the act is more toward the expressive end of the continuum, as in the case of the many psychophysiological responses that can be perceived only vaguely by either the sender or the receiver. But there are many acts whose status along the continuum would be a puzzle to the observer who did not know the social group to which the sending person belonged. In the preceding chapter we saw how the observer's cultural background gave him facts against which to evaluate current behavior. He needs the same acquaintance to know whether an act is a codified piece of behavior for the sending person's group. The act may be a formally coded expression for one people and thus make up communicative messages, while it may be a vague signal of arousal for another people and thus be responded to quite differently. (See LaBarre, 1947, for a number of examples.) Subcultural groups may also codify acts in their own ways, so that an act may have a specific meaning for one regional, social class, or age group, and either no specific meaning or a different one for another. Families, too, often have a few signs all their own. An imitation of a voice quality or movement may convey as succinctly as a word or phrase a reminder of an emotional situation that no one outside the family could possibly know about. The same thing happens among friends, patient-therapist pairs, and other small groups. Finally there are the idiosyncratic sign values which individuals attach to acts described by Krout (1954b). These are usually related to specific events in the history of the individual; and since others do not know their referents, the acts could not be used for communication purposes. The observer may learn of their meanings by intensive study of the individual, as Krout demonstrated that one could do; but barring this, he will respond to this sort of act as if it were more expressive in nature, if he responds at all.

In a way communicative specificity has to do with how closely various messages can be put into words, since we use words to describe messages, and words facilitate thinking about the whole process. On these grounds, language is certainly the easiest sort of message to conceptualize. Since notational systems of writing have been developed for many languages, their messages can be recorded, recalled, and thought about very conveniently. There are words, too, to describe other messages, but these must always be one step removed from the message itself. In thinking about messages in facial expressions, for example, we must use words to describe the expres·sion, and these can then tell of a feeling. This process is a roundabout ap·proach as compared with language, in which the words in the message may tell of the feeling directly. Of course, in social interaction we do not neces·sarily think about these expressions conveyed by means other than language. Instead, we simply respond to them in whatever way seems called for. We respond to a smile with a smile, not with a verbal discourse. It is important that we note the difficulty of thinking about expressions outside the realm of language, however, because of the problems it leads to in research. Since they are not so easy to conceptualize, they are not so easy to design studies around, and this may explain why our knowledge about them has not advanced as rapidly as it has about language.

LEVEL OF AWARENESS

This is a far more complicated topic than communicative specificity, since it involves not only coding and decoding methods but a great deal of the perceptual and personality processes of the participants in the com·munication situation. In addition, one continuum does not suffice to describe its ramifications; and to cap it all off, there are two aspects of messages that are at issue when it comes to level of awareness: the content of the mes·sage, and the fact that a message is being sent in the first place.

First, what are the continua, and how many dimensions are involved? I believe we can identify two dimensions, each having "aware" as one of its end-points. One dimension goes in one direction from "aware" to "re·pressed" at its other end, while the other goes in a different direction with "subliminal" at its other end. The first of these dimensions is the familiar conscious-unconscious one. Most of the attention of psychologists, so far as explanation is concerned, has been paid to the unconscious end of the continuum, and anything that is not unconscious is then said to be conscious or at least available to consciousness. In connection with mes·sages of emotion, the repressive forces are said to prevent the sending person from being aware of the messages he is transmitting, while at the same time the drive forces working against the repression still strive for expression and keep on producing the messages, even if these appear in an attenuated form. The receiving person is also affected by the same process: repressive forces in him keep him from being aware that he is receiving certain messages, while the drive forces lead him to be alert and on the lookout for them and attuned to their reception. If there are no repressive forces at work with respect to the particular sort of message to be transmitted, both the sending and the receiving persons may be fully aware of the message, or at least can be made aware if their attention is called to it. This brief description will be easily recognized as a condensed presentation of psychoanalytic principles that are so well known that we do not need any more detailed exposition here.

The other dimension, with end-points of "aware" and "subliminal," should be equally well known, but actually we are just beginning to learn about it as it applies to the field of emotional communication. By this I mean that, while there are a number of ways in which a stimulus can be below threshold, not all of these have been studied in the communication situation, with the result that there are a number of gaps in our knowledge of the nature of this dimension.

The most obvious reason for a stimulus to be below threshold is that the physical intensity of the stimulus itself is too low in comparison with the background against which it is to be perceived. In the case of emotional messages, this means that to be above threshold the message must stand out beyond all the other activities in the face-to-face situation. Some of these activities are relevant to emotional messages; some are not. Those which are may be relevant to both cognitive and emotional messages at the same time, and the emotional parts will have to be intense enough to be perceived through the welter of the combined input. And here is where the definition of threshold becomes complicated: the emotional messages must be strong enough to be perceived, and they must also be discriminable from the other messages exchanged in social interaction.

So we started out with absolute thresholds and ended up with a combination of thresholds and qualitative discrimination. One could argue, of course, that all threshold determinations actually involve precisely such a combination, but few would maintain that the processes involved here are as simple as those of the sensory threshold as it was dealt with in classical psychophysics. In talking about emotional communication we should probably start out by assuming that all messages are complex combinations of a number of things, the cognitive and the emotional among them. If the participants in an ordinary social exchange stopped to think about it, they could probably see emotional components in the most "purely cognitive" discussion: the eagerness of each to display his competence, the fun of the gossipy aspects of the conversation, and so on. How the participants can tell that these aspects are emotional, as compared with the specific steps in the logic itself, is another matter. They have probably learned it in the same way that they learned how to name emotions, as we saw in the last chapter. Still the fact remains that the emotional components of the communication can vary in intensity above and below threshold. In one discussion the eagerness to display competence may be an almost invisible background accompaniment to the work of developing the topic. In another it may be a power struggle where each point in the discussion is forced out between clenched teeth of rage. As to level of awareness, the emotional messages in the first of these discussions could be said to be subliminal, since we would have to get the participants to stop and think about them before the messages could be noticed, or we would need to apply special observational techniques to detect their presence. The emotional messages in the more heated discussion would be well within awareness in the sense of being so far above threshold that the logical or cognitive aspects of the argument would be difficult to discern (let us leave out for the moment the possibility that the participants might be repressing awareness of their emotional response).

Emotional messages may be subliminal, then, because their intensity is so low in comparison with other messages in the interaction situation that they cannot be noticed or are not noticed. The fact that two alternative phrases are necessary here — "cannot be noticed" and "are not noticed" — indicates another gap in our knowledge in this field. The first sounds like the real sensory threshold, while the second is mixed up with how closely the observer is paying attention to the message. How much the "subliminal" results from attention directed elsewhere is a moot point. In the classical psychophysical experiment on absolute limens we sidestep the problem by directing the subject's full attention to the stimulus, or to where it will appear when its intensity reaches threshold. In man-machine engineering, on the other hand, the problem cannot be ducked: the airline pilot must keep track of a large number of dials and controls. How far above threshold must a given signal be for his attention to be attracted to it? Modern psychophysics, based on statistical decision theory and the theory of signal detectability (see Swets, 1961, for a succinct overview), suggests that these two problems, that of the absolute limen experiment and of the airplane pilot, are related. In both cases the observer bases his responses on some criterion of certainty. The signal must be intense enough for him to be at least this certain before he says it is present. Part of setting the criterion involves how much difference it makes to the observer if he errs in one direction or another. The decision is the same as that involved in evaluating the dangers of Type I and Type II errors in testing hypotheses with statistical methods. Just as in communication theory, the noise above which the signal must stand out enough to be detected is random noise, and thus not immediately representative of the situations we are discussing here. We shall hear more of this in Chapter 6, when we talk about noise and its effects on the process of transmitting emotional messages.

Other reasons for a message to be subliminal have to do with the duration of the stimulus. In one case the exposure is too short to be perceived; in the other the events that make up the message occur over too long a period of time. The first of these is familiar in psychophysics: the stimulus is not available for enough time to be distinguished from the random transients which make up the background noise level. The problems are related to what we have just been talking about in connection with low-intensity stimuli. In emotional communication the background is not random — it has its own meaning — and thus the "threshold" is higher than in the simpler case. There is evidence for this in one study which has already been done on these very short messages or stimuli. Haggard and Isaacs (1966) examined the appearance of, and some of the correlates of, what they call Micromomentary Facial Expressions in filmed records of psychotherapeutic interviews. Running the film at very slow speeds (four frames per second rather than the usual 24), they found easily discernible expressions that were too fleeting at the normal speed to be seen as such. Expressions lasting three to five frames (about a fifth of a second) could be seen at the slow speed, but not at the normal speed. Expressions lasting about twice that long produced something midway between this and complete perception of the expressions: at normal film speeds two-fifths-of-a-second expressions made the judges aware that something had happened, but they couldn't say what. They knew there was some change, but were not able to identify its content. Preliminary examination of the events surrounding these expressions left little doubt about their nature: they were not random events, but contained messages of emotion. It seems reasonable to believe that similar phenomena occur elsewhere than just in facial expression, but we need a good deal of research before we can make firm statements about them.

The idea of stimuli being subliminal because of very short exposure time is a familiar one; but the other case, where too long a time is involved, is not usually thought of in terms of limens. Let us take spoken language to illustrate the principles involved, since it is the easiest sort of expression to conceptualize about. We may divide language into short-term and long-term carriers of messages — as I shall do in listing a number of channels of emotional expression in the next chapter. "Short-term" means that only a small amount of material is necessary to detect the message. These messages are the immediate ones, in the focus of attention, and can be perceived easily by both speaker and listener. The long-term messages, on the other hand, are made up of a number of short-term messages, with other material interspersed so that the connections are not immediately apparent. I have already cited an example of this where the speaker mentioned dangerous situations quite often during a conversation. Long-term messages of emotion consist precisely of such recurrent themes, of the patterning of short-term messages. The widely dispersed elements of the long-term message may be a little bit different each time they come up, or they may each time include a stereotyped phrase or other act which serves as a marker. In any case the repetitiousness itself is a message in its own right, and comes to be perceived as such. The listener says to himself, in effect, "Oh yes. I remember hearing something like this before; he seems to be preoccupied with that sort of thing." An interesting aspect of long-term messages is that the elements constituting them may not individually be emotional in content at all. They may be newspaper stories, things that have happened in the neighborhood, small talk about the weather, scientific topics, or whatever. It is the fact that these elements recur that leads to the conclusion that the person is preoccupied with the topic. The recurrence itself means that the topic is more emotionally loaded than it might seem on the surface.

Recurrence, of course, is only recurrence, and is thus just another sort of behavior from which inferences may be drawn, as we have previously discussed at length. It is a bit different from other sorts of behavior which we usually think of as expressive, however, in that it requires a certain kind of conceptualization to be perceived in the first place. The whole process should have a familiar ring to it for the reader, since the methods for detecting these messages in social situations are related to methods developed by social psychologists and by psychoanalysts: content analysis in the first case, and the psychoanalyst's method in the second. Frequency of recurrence of topics is the basis of the earliest form of content analysis, and the whole method may be both praised and blamed for its reliance on this basis. George (1959) saw two assumptions underlying content analysis of this sort: first, that "each individual item counted as falling under a designated content category is of equal significance for purposes of inference," and, second, that "the inferential significance of explicit propositions, themes, or statements is dependent upon the precise frequency of their occurrence" (p. 23). It is upon the rigid adherence to these assumptions in the early content-analysis studies that George built his criticism of the method, and he advocated a more qualitative approach in which communicative style, changes in the writer's strategy, and the occurrence of unusual words or phrases guide the investigator's development of hypotheses.

Needless to say, content analysts are usually not so naive as to suppose that frequency is the only criterion of importance. Other quantitative methods have been developed, notably contingency analysis, to give more body to the results. Osgood (1959) has written an excellent account of these methods. In contingency analysis, inferences are drawn not only from the total frequency of occurrence of the various content categories, but from the relative frequency of their occurrence in association with each other. Thus two categories that are mentioned together with far greater than chance frequency are thought of as being associated. The investigator can infer not only the fact of preoccupation with a topic, but also some of the qualities of this preoccupation from the other topics with which it is associated. In some analyses significantly nonassociated categories are also subjects of interest. Inferences about defensive avoidance and the like may be drawn from them. In a still more complicated procedure, evaluative assertion analysis, Osgood seeks greater objectivity by transforming all statements in the material to be analyzed into simple assertive sentences, with codings of the writer's or speaker's evaluation as judged by the investigator. These are subjected to frequency and contingency analyses in the same way the other materials are. This method is much more painstaking, but serves our discussion by being even more representative of the way the social participant detects long-term messages. While these methods have been used chiefly with such social-psychological documents as propaganda materials, they have also been applied to clinical documents, such as psychotherapeutic interviews and Thematic Apperception Test protocols, and by some workers to Rorschach responses.

The other area where recurrent themes are systematically used as the lexicon of messages is psychoanalytic therapy, where the analyst listens to his patient's "free associations." These are free in the sense that the usual amenities of social discourse are deliberately suspended, so that consistency, propriety, appropriateness, and the like, are less controlling of the outflow of ideas and feelings, leaving the true relationships among things to show themselves more clearly. It is the analyst's job to listen just as freely, without weighing the associations in terms of his own theories or prejudices. If he can really do this, he will become a remarkably effective information storage system for items whose interrelationships will become clear only much later. In Freud's (1913) words, "Those elements of the material which have a connection with one another will be at the conscious disposal of the physician; the rest, as yet unconnected, chaotic and indistinguishable, seems at first to disappear, but rises readily into recollection as soon as the patient brings something further to which it is related, and by which it can be developed . . ." (p. 325). As a consequence, when the patient compliments the analyst on his feats of memory, this is only a sign that the analyst has been performing his job correctly. Using these connections in the patient's associations as the basic data for interpretations is the primary technical task of the analyst. Fenichel (1935) put it this way: "As we may assume that the unconscious strives for expression again and again, the best way for the analyst to find out what is actually meant is to look for a common factor in the various utterances of the patient" (p. 34). Further, Fenichel (1941) said: "Usually we first endeavor to do away with general isolations by showing the patient *connections* between events, feelings, and intentional attitudes, connections which he had not previously noted, although they were obvious" (p. 35).

Thus we see that in principle the study of contingencies in content analysis and work with free associations in psychoanalysis draw upon the same sources of data and are based upon the same assumptions. The data derive from the repetitiousness of topics in manifest content, as they appear in association with each other. The basic assumption is that repe-titiousness is a sign of preoccupation, the association between topics indicating the qualities of that preoccupation. But how closely are these processes and assumptions related to active channels of communication in free social situations? I believe that in principle the phenomena are the same, but not so clearly visible in face-to-face contacts as in the special situations of content analysis and psychoanalysis. Two reasons may account for this: first, it is not the primary task of people conversing with each other to pay attention to long-term trends and to detect the messages contained therein. In fact, when a person does, others look upon him somewhat suspiciously as though he were trying to check up on them and to catch them in inconsistencies, or otherwise to expose them in some way. So even when we do notice long-term trends, we usually do not let people know how much we are drawing conclusions from them. Indeed we may not even let ourselves know that we are doing it at all.

Another reason that detection of long term messages is not so visible in social interaction has to do with the old, familiar perceptual problem of span of apprehension. The participant in a social situation, engaged as he is in the interaction — both listening to the other person and trying to get his own points across — is in a position antithetical to that of the psychoanalyst. He cannot hold in abeyance all judgment and logical at-tention to developing ideas in order to allow his companion's expressions to be registered in memory with no strings attached. Therefore he may not notice recurring themes unless they are unusual, unless they do not follow logically from what has gone before, or unless there are "markers," such as a characteristic word or phrase, each time the theme comes up, or a fixed accompaniment in some other sort of expression. In short, we can expect the social participant, simply because he is busy with other things, to be slower to "catch on" than the psychoanalyst as he listens freely or the content analyst as he examines a typescript of the interchange later on. We might expect a third party who is not actively involved in the conversation to have a wider span of apprehension, and to see con-nections which the other two could not. Many long-term messages, then, require many repetitions or special attention attracting markers to be perceived; many others, are never perceived at all.

Spoken language has served as an example for long-term messages in this discussion, as I said it would at the outset. This does not mean that the same processes do not take place in other channels of communication, but only that it is easier to write about spoken language than about other media of exchange. And since content analysis as a method was originally developed in connection with written language, the terms "word," "phrase," and "conversation" are naturals in making the point that there is information to be had from long-term sources. Once the point is made, it is easy to think of examples in connection with other sorts of expression: the slight hardness of voice in one person, which occurs only occasionally or only in certain situations; the repeated sigh in another, which happens only when he is alone with a certain person or with persons of certain statuses relative to his own. It may, however, be more difficult to separate short-term and long-term modes of communicating by these sorts of expression than it is with language, which has such a special relationship with cognitive processes, and whose messages may lend themselves so much more readily to memory.

Under the topic of level of awareness, we have taken up two dimensions, one with aware and repressed as its defining end-points, and the other with aware and subliminal. I have treated them separately in this exposition because conceptually they are separate: it is for quite different reasons that we are unaware of things under these two rubrics. When it comes to studying behavior, on the other hand, it will not always be easy to tell when a person is unaware of some message because he is repressing or because the message is subliminal for him. One reason for this is the tremendous opportunity there is for interaction between these two processes. This interaction, I think, can best be put in terms of signal detection theory, which was mentioned in the discussion of low-intensity stimuli. We saw there that the criterion by which a person says that a signal is present or not depends on some schedule of values. Among those values which motivate people strongly, there must certainly be counted the danger of anxiety if repressive forces are broken through, and the danger of frustration from unsatisfied needs. Efforts to maintain repression, then, will affect one's criterion of certainty, apparently altering his "threshold" for perceiving certain stimuli. Thus two persons exposed to a message from a third person may differ strikingly in what they are aware they have perceived. The message may be just above "threshold" for one person, and well below for the other, because of the relative repressive forces at work in the two people with respect to the message they were both in a position to receive. In Chapter 7 we shall consider how the investigator may separate these two continua of awareness.

At the beginning of the section on level of awareness I noted that there are two aspects of messages of which one might be aware or unaware: the fact that there is a message, and its content. These two have been lumped together in most discussions — indeed, they have been so far in this one. The reason is that in most cases they probably coincide. There are important times, however, when level of awareness is different for the two, and it is necessary to be able to conceptualize them separately in order to understand those occasions fully. If we simplify the level of awareness continuum by dichotomizing it, we have two variables in contingent relationship, with four resultant possibilities: aware of message and aware of content, aware of message but unaware of content, and so forth. The interactions between sender and receiver complicate the picture, of course, but they also help us to see what particular combination we are dealing with.

The simplest instance is the first, where the person is aware of both aspects of the message. The sender says in effect, "I feel excited," or whatever it is he feels, and the receiver gets the message. Each participant knows that there is a message and knows what it is about. There is no confusion here. Another simple instance is the opposite, where the person is unaware either of the fact of a message or of its nature. This is what we usually think about in connection with communications of which a person is not aware, and fits very well the classical (perhaps stereotyped) description of hysterical communication patterns. The person sends ardent messages of flirtation and desire, yet is completely unaware either of the desires or of the fact that they are being communicated. When the receiver of the message responds as though there were a romantic opportunity at hand, the hysterical person is baffled, and proclaims that he or she has been "misunderstood." Thus these two instances are easy to conceptualize: the person is wholly aware or is wholly unaware of the entire communication.

The other two combinations make the distinction necessary. The case where the person is fully aware of the nature of the emotion involved, but believes he is not sending any messages about it, will probably be familiar to most of us. The most commonplace examples of this pattern occur when the individual is deliberately holding back his expression because of the social consequences that might follow. Unbeknownst to the sending person, though, the feeling does leak out. He understands full well the reaction his behavior elicits, and he feels embarrassed and ashamed, unlike the hysteric mentioned above. Usually he sees, on looking back over his recent actions, that he has really sent the message he was trying to keep under cover. The final combination, being aware of the message but unaware of its nature, is difficult to find in pure form because of the possibilities of multiple messages, but it is frequent in social intercourse. The person says, in effect, "I feel excited and happy," but his message is more specifically one of affection for the receiver. Or he says, "I am very determined about this point," and his fellow participants understand him to be angry. In both of these cases the sending person realizes that he is sending a message, but misinterprets what it is about. In Hebb's (1946) terms, he has not named his own emotion correctly; we cited his example of the jealous person in the last chapter. In Ekman and Friesen's terms (1969a), he is engaged in self-deception. The multiple-message difficulty is that the individual could be said to be sending two messages, one which he is aware of, and the other which he is not, and it is hard for the observer to tell the difference between these two cases. It is easier to think of examples from the receiving person's side, where he knows he is being sent a message but identifies its content incorrectly — a polite smile being seen as a come-on and the like. Here the criterion of certainty has been distorted by the receiver's need to hear only certain messages and to be selectively on the lookout for them.

INTENTIONAL CONTROL

This structural variable refers to the control exercised over messages as transmitted or received, control over whether the message should be sent or not (or received or not) and how this should be done. It is not easy to define intentional control, since ordinary language is not clear about it. We are easily understood if we say that a person has intended to put a point across. On the other hand, when we say, "He didn't intend to say that," we can mean either of two things: he had no intentions one way or the other, he really wasn't trying to control the appearance of the message at all; or he had a very specific intention about the message, namely, not to say it, but it got expressed anyway. In this discussion the basic variable will refer to the first of these two meanings, and the continuum will be defined by end-points of intentional control and absence of intentional control. The control side will be further subdivided into positive and negative intentional control: positive control will refer to intentions to get the message across, while negative control will refer to intentions to prevent the message from being sent.

Most emotional messages are probably sent without controls, or with very little effort to control. This is, of course, especially true in small children, whose feelings are clearly written all over them as the feelings come and go. In older children and adults there is less of this emotional expressiveness to be seen, but only partly because controls are any greater. As the child gains more and more experience in living, things lose their all-or-none, life-or-death quality. Also, he is taken less by surprise all the time because succeeding events, as they occur in his life, are not so apt to be so new to him and so different. As things seem less crucial and less unexpected, emotional reactions are not so strong or so frequent, and so we naturally see them less often.

Of the emotional reactions that do occur, however, increasingly many are controlled as the child grows older. The question for us now is: why should emotions be controlled? When does one control his emotional messages rather than letting them be expressed freely? The most general answer is, I believe, that in each case of control some conflict is involved, conflict about the consequences of the expression. By "consequences" I do not mean anything so fine-grained as praise for one specific act or punishment for another. Most feeling happens too fast for such one-to-one response. The consequences that figure in most conflicts are rather much more pervasive, like making sure one can continue to be considered a "good person" in the terms he has been taught are important to his group. Ekman and Friesen (1969b) have spelled out this process as display rules for emotional expression. In addition to these more general consequences, there are naturally some specific conflicts over specific expressions, and these are dramatic enough that they are far more easily remembered. One may walk quite a long tightrope in a conversation, trying to avoid alienating his conversational partner by expressing one sort of thing, or keeping from embarrassing him by expressing another. Ekman and Friesen (1969a) have written very imaginatively of the situations in which one sets out to deceive in order to avoid certain consequences or to further others. We shall return to this in Chapter 7 when we consider some of the methods they have used and others they have proposed for studying these situations.

The concept of intention we are using here may be clarified by reference to a significant, but virtually forgotten, article by Fearing (1953), in which intent is used in a very similar way. Fearing is concerned more with cognitive communication than with messages of emotion, but he keeps the motivations of the sending person (the communicator) and the receiving person (the interpreter) constantly in the forefront. Emotional communication thus seems to be included in his thinking far more than it is in most works on human communication. Intent, for Fearing, is the communicator's focus on the interpreter, his directing his communication toward the interpreter's pattern of needs, expectancies, and demands. The communicator intends to produce an effect by communicating. Fearing writes:

> ... the interpreters are always in the psychological field of the communicator. The communicator's perceptions of the interpreters may determine the character of the content he produces. The degree of specificity with which these presumed effects are defined by the communicator may vary widely from one communication situation to another, but clearly or vaguely they are dynamically a part of the communication situation (p. 77).

How accurately the communicator will perceive the interpreters' reaction to his message will vary according to the situations and his own needs. In the face-to-face situation with which we are most concerned the communicator will have the opportunity for constant reevaluation, if he is willing or able to make use of it.

The more focus the communicator maintains on the effects of his communication on the interpreter, Fearing goes on to say, the more the power relationship between the two is involved in the communication. This is probably especially true with cognitive communication. He says, "all highly planned communications are power communications in the sense that specific behavioral effects are expected to follow specific contents" (p. 81), and he goes on to cite Lasswell's (1949) discussion of ruling elites struggling for control of channels of communication. In face-to-face interchange of emotional messages, on the other hand, we do not ordinarily think of power. When one is in conflict over how others might react, he might well be concerned with possible punitive action, implying that the interpreters are in a superior position, but he may also be looking for signs that the others have been persuaded or soothed. Work with certain clinical groups provides evidence for a number of power relationships mediated by emotional messages which Lasswell would not predict. The passive-dependent person, for example, who plays the martyr role, uses messages of suffering to control his interpreters with an iron hand. Saying always that he is the inferior and weak one in his relationship to them, he forces them nevertheless to do his will by playing on their guilt. Just how widespread any uses of emotional messages for power are, no one can say without a lot more study, but power is probably not a central characteristic of these messages as it is of propaganda, for example, or of educational efforts.

Fearing's conceptualization of intent is a useful addition to the structural variable of intentional control, for it gives us a lead in devising methods for getting at the variable in research studies, as we shall see in Chapter 7. We shall need to add one feature to Fearing's idea to make it serve our purposes here, an extension which I believe is quite compatible with his point of view — namely, that among the interpreters who receive messages and are affected by them is the communicator himself. We need to add this because many of the conflicts about the consequences of expression, in our terms, which lead to control of messages, are of how the person will think of himself if he expresses this or that feeling. True, if an outsider stopped him and asked him why he was controlling the expression, he might say that he was thinking of how his conversational partner might react to it; but since he cannot get as much information about the reactions of others as he can about his own, many of these explanations tell of projection upon others of the sending person's own values.

The relationship between intentional control and level of awareness is a complex one. Some of the conflicts of whether to express this or that feeling may be fully within awareness, so that one can stop to consider, just for a moment, the various aspects involved. Others may be the classical unconscious conflicts spoken of by psychoanalysts, in which repression is instituted at some point. The difference between these two sorts of conflicts, as they affect intentionality of emotional expression, can be

found in the results, in the effectiveness of control. To be truly effective
the conflicts must be conscious. The communicator can then evaluate his
interpreter's needs and possible responses more fully, in Fearing's terms,
so that the feeling gets into a message that gets across to the other
person or is prevented from turning into a message in the case of a
negating control. With unconscious conflicts, things cannot be so neat.
Recall that the aim of repression is not necessarily to discontinue an act,
but to keep out of awareness any knowledge of the act or any knowledge of the feelings that may be associated with it, or of the reactions
it elicits. By these means the anxiety that would result from such awareness can be avoided, or at least reduced (Dittmann & Raush, 1954, pp.
393-394). One way to satisfy this aim of repression is to reduce the
intensity of the act. A strong outburst of affect will more likely be obvious
to the person himself, while an attenuated expression of it may go unnoticed — but a message may still be formed which others can understand
and respond to.

 When we think of unconscious conflicts as a basis for controlling
the transmission of messages, we usually think of the motivation for the
control as unreasoned and unrealistic in the here and now, justifiable as
it may have been at some time in the past. The decision is made blindly
so to speak, whether to send the message or not. In the case of control
because of conscious conflict, on the other hand, real decision or choice
is involved. This is what we usually think of when we talk of intentions,
and it is certainly what Fearing wrote about. The whole sequence may be
carefully planned in advance, knowing what the other person's stand is
on the issue at hand: "He'll think better of me if he believes I feel calm
and relaxed in such-and-such a situation." Or, "His feelings would be
hurt if he knew this made me angry." Thoughts like this might be voiced
if there were time to stop and formulate them in the middle of the
ongoing social situation. Extended conscious deliberations however, are
probably unusual. Social situations proceed so rapidly, and responses are
so automatic, that it is impossible to consider, or even to know about,
the whys and wherefores of most acts, even when the person is quite fully
aware of the conflicts he has about expressing them.

 There is another kind of intention which appears to be less swayed
by conflicts over expression, and this is the intention *of how* to express
certain feelings. The inner question here is not "Should I express this

feeling or not?" but, rather, "Should I say it in words or should I smile?" or "Should I register my disgust vocally or will a brief frown do as well?" In making these decisions the sending person is strongly swayed by the structure or the tempo of the situation. Again, the various possible responses of the interpreter are at the focus of attention. A vocal expression of disgust may be considered rude in one circle of friends and not in another; saying something in words may kill the spontaneous flow of the interchange where a smile would keep up with it, or carry it further. Another factor affecting this sort of choice is the personal style of the sending person. One will have a characteristically unexpressive voice, but a very mobile face; another will be constantly stiff in posture, but have a colorful vocabulary. Each will still have a good deal of intentional control, however, over how he expresses his feelings as the social situation changes.

Since the conflicts which lead to controlling emotional expressions may be either conscious or unconscious, it follows that the decisions resulting from the conflicts, and the consequent intentions to transmit (or not to transmit) emotional messages, may also be either conscious or unconscious. The structural variables, level of awareness and intentional control, are probably not tied to one another directly — although it would be presuming too much of our present state of knowledge to maintain that they are really independent. One combination of the two presents a problem: the notion of unconscious intention seems contrary to common sense. We usually think of decisions and intentions as being thoroughly within awareness, as being part of man's more rational potential. Yet clinical experience provides us with illustrations of incompatible behaviors that must be born of repressed intentions. Coffey et al. (1950), for example, cite the case of a group therapy patient who "describes himself as nurturant-non-aggresive and says he sees the world as friendly. However, his social mechanisms in the group are consistently scored [by observers] as directive, defensive, and hostile" (p. 282). This man expresses one type of feeling in words, and a seemingly opposite one in actions. Since both of these expressions are so consistent as to be unmistakably present, we must conclude that he really intends to express both, despite the apparent contradiction between them. And we must conclude, too, that the two are at different levels of awareness, in intention as well as in content.

The relationship between intentional control and the other structural variable, communicative specificity, may more likely be thought of as an independent one, though common sense again dictates against this conception. Do not positively intended messages fall toward the communicative end of the dimension, and negatively intended ones toward the expressive end? This point of view is taken by Fearing in the article we have just been discussing, and by Haggard and Isaacs (1966) in the one we referred to earlier in this chapter. As an explanation of their findings, Haggard and Isaacs posit a temporal dimension in defense mechanisms. According to their argument (p. 165), ego controls regulate or inhibit impulse expression, but allow a certain amount to bypass the censorship for brief periods of time in Micromomentary Facial Expressions. Recall that these are subliminal in that neither the person expressing them nor the other participant in the situation can perceive them clearly. In this way responses from other people, such as retaliation, for example, are not risked. Haggard and Isaacs equate "intended" and "unintended" (or negatively intended as used here) in this connection with "communication" and "expression," respectively. But the facial expressions which these investigators found in the film at slow speeds could be named in such specific terms as "anger," "disdain," "pleasure," and the like. We may therefore conclude that they fell quite far toward the communication end of the dimension of communicative specificity, even though they were so brief as to be subliminal at normal projection speeds. At the same time it seems from the description that the person intended not to allow the expressions to come through — and indeed they did not in the actual social situation, even though observers watching the film at normal speeds could tell that something was happening.

In Fearing's (1953) paper, one of the dimensions of communication he discusses is what he calls specificity of intent — the degree to which the communicator plans to get his message across. It seems to me that this dimension is very closely related to intentional control. At the other end of his continuum, however, Fearing puts unplanned communications, which he reasons are really not communications at all, but expressions of the personality structure and emotional dynamics of the communicator (p. 80). I believe this formulation misses some important behavior, at least in the field of emotional communication, because it confounds communicative specificity and intentional control. Expressions, that is, non-coded, continuous activities which reflect what feelings are going on inside the communicator, can be highly planned means of getting emotional messages across. By the same token very discrete acts, communicative in our sense, can be used in messages over which the communicator sees no need to exercise control, and these, too, can tell of the communicator's inner emotional life at the moment. Fearing appears to allow for this possibility when he includes face-to-face conversations among his examples of unplanned communications, or what he calls expressions. Our reasoning so far has indicated that there is a good deal of planning in face-to-face interactions, but these are really not the focus of Fearing's ideas in this paper, even though the ideas are general enough to include them.

Summary: Structural Variables in Emotional Messages

In this chapter we have discussed some of the ways in which individual people who send and receive emotional messages complicate the nature of the messages themselves. It turns out that a message is not just a message, but depends upon who is sending it, what groups he belongs to, what the history is of his contact with this sort of emotional situation, and what his aims are in this face-to-face contact. The student who wishes to apply communication theory to the exchange of emotional messages must take all these factors into account because the processes of getting a message out are controlled by the same person who originated the message, unlike the situation in telecommunication where these various functions are performed quite independently. These, then, are the psychological influences on messages, and I have called them structural variables because they form the context within which any given message must be looked at if we are to measure the amount of emotional information it conveys. Three structural variables have been dealt with here:

1. Communicative specificity, referring to the degree to which the form of the message is codified by the groups that the social participants belong to: the cultural groups, regional, family, friendship groups, and the like. The model of coded communication is, of course, language, which makes use of symbolism and complex systems of syntax, can be applied to any situation, and makes up an important part of any cultural heritage. At the opposite end of the continuum are expressions, those visible or

audible reactions to situations by which another person can tell that there is a response, but not very specifically what the nature of the response is. Research on one of the smallest elements of language, the phoneme, was used to illustrate the nature of codes in human communication, and to show that there is a continuum of the extent to which acts are subjected to the coding process.

2. Level of awareness: two dimensions are posited here, one extending from aware to repressed, and the other from aware to subliminal. Messages whose nature or whose very presence is repressed are bound up with longtime psychodynamic problems in the individual. Subliminal messages may be so because the stimulus is too weak, too brief, or because the elements are interspersed in the interaction over too long a period of time for easy grasp.

3. Intentional control has to do with the degree to which emotional messages are allowed to go through freely, on the one hand, or are monitored and controlled, on the other. Controls are usually instituted where conflict over the message is involved, and the conflict has to do with the consequences, hoped for or feared, of sending or receiving the message. Thus in controlling his production of emotional messages, the sending person's orientation is toward the receiver, toward how the message will be taken and responded to. One of the receivers whose reactions matter is the sending person himself — he is also concerned with what this sort of message will do to his own self-esteem. In addition there is often some intentional control exercised over how the message is to be expressed, and this sort of control is probably less affected by conflict. The whole process of control may be fully within awareness or quite outside of it.

Chapter Five

Channels of Emotional Messages —————————

The last two chapters have dealt with how the information in emotional messages might be measured, and how these messages are affected by the psychology of the sending and receiving persons. There have been a number of allusions to different means by which these messages might be sent and received, these means being referred to as channels. In Chapter 1 various channels of human communication were explicitly mentioned — spoken language, facial expression, body movement; but we did not describe them in any detail or set forth any criteria by which to decide whether a communicative medium should be called a channel or not. This is quite in line with tradition, for the different media are referred to quite often in the literature on human communication, and the word "channel" has usually been used to cover them, but few writers have found it necessary to stop and define the term or otherwise to discuss it as a concept. As we shall see, the psychological literature is not unusual in this respect: many engineering works on communication theory, including Shannon's original exposition, have also neglected to define the term. I shall follow that tradition in the first part of this chapter, describing some commonly used channels without saying exactly what a channel consists of. Then I shall return to the problems of defining the term as it applies to emotional communication. This will prepare us for a discussion of how channels are classified and of the most important characteristic of a channel, namely, its capacity for transmitting information.

Choosing what channels to discuss is to some degree an individual matter, and a number of possibilities have been offered by various writers in the past. The test situations which Allport and Vernon (1933) used in their studies include many that lend themselves to the communication of emotional messages. The studies of gait by Wolff (1935) indicate clearly that here is another activity which plays a part in daily interchange of emotional messages. A different kind of channel is "object language" (Ruesch & Kees, 1961), the ways in which one displays one's possessions or arranges material objects, either intentionally or unintentionally. A final example is the recently presented channel of immediacy (Wiener & Mehrabian, 1968).

All these authors have had a different purpose in choosing the behaviors they studied than the one I am pursuing here. They have been searching for the ways in which personality or attitudes are expressed, ways an outside observer can use to know what sort of a person the expressor is in general or what he thinks about people in general. On the other hand, I wish to deal with carriers of emotional messages as they may be superimposed moment by moment upon the more enduring attitudes and qualities of personality. This is not to say that the acts described by these writers could not be used for sending emotional messages in the sense meant here, but only that one has to look at them from a different standpoint. Uprightness of posture and meticulousness of grooming, for example, are two behaviors that may go together to indicate a well-established trait of neatness in a person. For our present purposes, this trait becomes part of the background data from which to view deviations as messages conveying emotional information. Deviations can be seen more readily in those behaviors that are capable of change from moment to moment. The changeable ones, therefore, lend themselves more readily to transmitting emotional information. Thus, between posture and grooming, a person might change from an upright to a slumping posture quite rapidly, but he would not be able to dress any less neatly from one minute to the next.

Speed of change, then, is one basis for my choice of the channels to be listed here. Another is that the channels represent behaviors that can be observed in interview situations. This second basis for choice must be understood as an outgrowth of the research I have been engaged in, and of research reported by other investigators, rather than as a limitation on the generality of what we shall be discussing under the topic of channels. Much of the recent work on emotional communication has originated in psychotherapy research, and investigators have generally hoped that their findings could be applied to further analysis of therapeutic interviews. Of course, what happens in interviews is in no essential way different from what happens in other social interaction. The range of behaviors likely to be found in interviews is somewhat more restricted than that of other social situations, but the behaviors are not different in the sense that what we learn from studying the one cannot be applied to thinking about the other.

The channels I have chosen to list are classified as to how their messages may be perceived in the social situation: the audible channels and the visible channels. The audible ones are short-term spoken language, long-term spoken language, and vocalization. The visible channels are facial expression, body movement, and psychophysiological responses. This classification is not airtight — in a quiet room like a psychotherapist's office, for example, many body movements are clearly audible — but it does serve as a first approximation to how independent the information is from the different channels. The independence issue is a real problem for the research investigator in this field, and we shall hear a good deal more of it here and in later chapters. As I describe each channel, I shall mention some research in which it has been used to illustrate the kind of information transmitted on the different channels, and to specify to some extent just what aspects have been worked on so far.

A List of Channels

Audible Channels

Short-term Spoken Language. Messages on this channel consist of the content of speech at any given moment as it describes the emotional state of the speaker. Superficially it corresponds to McGranahan's (1936) subdivision of the Bühler "descriptive function" of language: those linguistic forms which represent emotions, feelings, or attitudes. It appears, again superficially, to be covered by Frankena's (1958a) expression of attitudes or feelings. An example of research using this channel is a study I reported in 1962: spoken language was the first criterion for selecting interview material to be used later for studying frequencies of body movements. When the patient said, "I am angry," or made some other direct reference to a current mood or feeling state, this passage of the interview was set aside for further work. A number of passages from each of several moods was thus selected for studying the frequencies and patterns of movements associated with those moods. In this case, only direct references to emotion, or manifest content, were used. By citing research using manifest content, however, I do not mean to imply that short-term spoken language is limited to conscious messages — that is why I included some qualifications in connection with the applicability of McGranahan's and Frankena's categories when I referred to them just above. The fact is that symbolic references, *double entendre,* and many other manifestations of "latent content" are also carried by means of short-term spoken language. Early research on these messages is epitomized by Freud's (1901) analysis of tongue-slips; more recent examples are George's (1959) method of content analysis, that of finding unusual words or phrases, or defensive maneuvers in the writer's strategy, and Wiener and Mehrabian's (1968) immediacy. In neither case is the short-term message necessarily within the speaker's awareness. Thus many messages come under Frankena's category of emotions and attitudes revealed about the speaker by the content of his discourse, his choice of words, and the like.

Long-term Spoken Language. These are the relatively hidden messages we discussed at some length in the section on level of awareness in Chapter 4, the ones that are often subliminal because the time between message elements covers too great a span. The reception of these messages does not depend on the hearer's adeptness at understanding the speaker's personal symbolism or upon his noticing anything unusual in phraseology. Instead, the messages come through in the way the discourse is organized, in the recurrence of short-term messages — and the short-term messages which form the long-term ones, as I mentioned before, need not themselves even be emotional ones. The long-term messages depend for their reception on the memory span of the listener. I have already referred to psychoanalysis and content analysis as being similar in their aim of recovering the long-term messages in social situations. A number of considerably more molecular approaches should also be included here, such as the work on word-frequency distributions and on the relationship among the occurrences of words of different grammatical classifications. A very useful review of these methods may be found in Mahl and Schulze (1964), specifically in the sections concerned with language style and with vocabulary selection and diversity.

The dividing line between short-term and long-term spoken language as two separate channels is, of course, obscure. We ordinarily think of the content analyst plodding painstakingly through large masses of data and of the psychoanalyst listening silently for many interviews, in order to discern any messages at all in the material they are working with. By contrast it takes almost no time to hear a person say he is happy or angry, and to understand the message. Thus, intuitively, the difference between short-term and long-term seems large, and we expect the participant in the social situation to need an extended acquaintance with the other person before he can begin to receive long-term messages. Yet a skilled diagnostic interviewer is usually able to make some decision on the basis of a single session; and while his basic data include all sorts of messages, he is particularly adept at picking up those themes (and their combinations) which recur over a relatively short period of time. Then, too, we need not think that all long-term messages are carefully buried in confusing context: a friend who one day is unusually witty in conversation and brings up many amusing topics is easily understood as feeling good.

Vocalization. Information from speech *other* than that derived from the words which are spoken comprises this channel of communication. It includes what is ordinarily called "tone of voice" and also nonfluencies of speech. Experiments on tone of voice have been conducted since the late 1930's, although the total number of them has not been large. Actors were used to produce emotional passages of standard content by Fairbanks and Pronovost (1939), a technique that was used in several studies collected by Davitz (1964). Meaningless material, such as letters of the alphabet (Dusenbury & Knower, 1939) and numbers (Thompson & Bradway, 1950), can also be used to assure that content does not influence judgment. Since the advent of electronic techniques, material from more natural settings has been used to control content. Soskin, in a symposium paper in 1953 talked about two communication channels in speech, the semantic and the affective, at a time when he and his associates were developing a way of eliminating the former so that the effects of the latter could be studied. Drawing upon results of research on speech intelligibility at the Bell Telephone Laboratories, they experimented with low-pass filters that severely attenuated the signal above 500 Hz. By this technique, intelligibility of a wide variety of test tapes was reduced to about 2 or 3 per cent, while the remaining sounds could still be used for judging the affective content of the speech. The method has been put to use in several studies (Soskin & Kauffman, 1961; Starkweather, 1956a, 1956b; Waskow, 1963; Kramer 1964), using tapes from interviews, recorded excerpts from Congressional hearings, and even recordings of actors reading the Fairbanks-Pronovost material.

Many more studies have been done on nonfluencies of speech than on tone of voice. These began with the independently developed but very similar methods of Dibner (1956) and Mahl (1956). Later work is represented by Kasl and Mahl (1965), Boomer (1965), and Siegman and Pope (1965); references to other recent work in their respective research centers may be found in the papers cited here. From the standpoint of linguistics the vocalization channel has been studied intensively by Trager (1958), and his developments in this field have been followed up by a number of investigators, beginning with a study by another linguist, McQuown (1957), and continued by people from mental health fields, such as Pittenger and Smith (1957), Eldred and Price (1958), Pittenger, Hockett and Danehy (1960), and Dittmann and Wynne (1961). The review by Mahl and Schulze (1964), referred to above, covers this area, too, perhaps in even greater detail, because of Mahl's long-standing participation in this research.

We have now covered the audible channels, those in the list which have to do with talk, its content and the manner of its production. Two of the channels are quite similar on first sight — short-term and long-term spoken language — since to receive them one has but to listen. But listening alone will not suffice in the case of language style and other things I have included under long-term spoken language. No one, for example, could do the tabulation necessary for the computation of verb/ adjective ratios during the course of a conversation. At best a listener might get a vague impression of a lively or a stilted quality in the sending person's speech which is thought to be associated with the ratio. The question then arises of whether such characteristics can make up a real vehicle for transmitting emotional messages. The same question will come up again in connection with psychophysiological responses. It has to do, of course, with both the nature of channels and the nature of communicative acts. These can be discussed more fully after the list of channels has been presented in full, and we get to the discussion of defining the concept of channel itself.

The first two channels, short-term and long-term spoken language, are alike in another way, one that is important to research in this area: information from these two channels can be typed out and studied without listening, while that from vocalization cannot. On the other hand, much of the information from the vocalization channel can be derived from filtered speech by Soskin's technique, thus eliminating the information from the two language channels. Within the audible channels, then, the research investigator can achieve some degree of independence of information sources and study the interaction among them without contaminating the data by his techniques. The two spoken language channels, short-term and long-term, are more difficult to separate in this way. Short-term messages can be isolated, of course, simply by restricting the amount of material available to the listener (or reader). Long-term messages, too, can be studied separately after they have been categorized, as in content analysis, or otherwise "predigested" before they get to the observer. But for many studies the separation cannot be accomplished as neatly as the typescript-filtered tape methods can do for the language-vocalization pairing.

Visible Channels

Facial Expression. Smiles, frowns, and the many other expressions of the face make up the content of messages transmitted over this channel. There have been a great many laboratory studies over several decades, using schematic drawings, still photographs, and motion pictures as methods of presentation; actors and amateurs posing, experimental subjects undergoing all kinds of stimulation, and news-magazine pictures of people in real-life situations as stimulus material; infants, children, and adults as subjects whose expressions were to be judged; children of different ages, college and graduate students, people of different occupational groups, and groups from different cultures as judges; with free response and precategorized response methods of data collection — all devoted to learning more about facial expression of emotions. Woodworth and Schlosberg review much of this literature (1954, pp. 111-121). A few recent studies have drawn upon material from interview situations (P. Ekman, 1964; Dittmann, Parloff & Boomer, 1965; Haggard & Isaacs, 1966), and one has used the natural stress situation of women in labor (Leventhal & Sharp, 1965). These many years of work are witness to the strongly held general impression that the face is a rich and reliable source of information about how the person behind the face is feeling. Indeed Tomkins (1962) has said that the face is the seat of the emotions and that expressions are biological givens. The work from our laboratory, just cited, shows that without special inclination or training to do otherwise, most people appear to look at nothing else but the face to find emotional information. We will return to this phenomenon later when differences in channel capacity are discussed.

Body Movement. We usually think of this channel as being made up of gestures, which are substitutes for words or phrases. The nod of the head for "Yes," and the jerk of the hitch-hiker's thumb for "May I ride with you", are obvious examples. But gestures of this sort are quite rare as compared with the nonspecific movements which have been studied by a number of investigators: "nervous habits" (Olson, 1929); "gestural movements" (Sainsbury, 1955); movements of different body areas (Dittmann, 1962); and "speech-accompanying gestures" (Renneker, 1963). These investigators have all focused on frequency of movements, often categorized by the body part in motion, but have not taken account of the form of the motion involved. The form of movements was studied most specifically by Efron (1941), who traced movements from motion picture records and found differences between ethnic groups among immigrants, but not among their descendants. Krout (1935, 1954a, 1954b) also studied formal aspects of movements; more recently Freedman and Hoffman (1967) and Ekman and Friesen (1968) have separated different forms of movement for comparison of their occurrence in different clinical groups and different stages in the course of illness. Finally, working from another standpoint, Scheflen (1964, 1965) has viewed movements and postural shifts of different forms as indicators of units of interactions in interviews.

Duncan (1969) and Mehrabian (1969) have reviewed this literature quite usefully. Interpretation of emotional meaning of movements and postures has been only one of the topics of this area over the years. A number of theories and conjectures have been offered, beginning with Darwin's classic *The Expression of the Emotions in Man and Animals* (1872), which includes explanations about facial expressions as well. Studies interpreting the meaning of movements and posture include James (1932); Carmichael, Roberts, and Wessell (1937); and the works of Krout, already referred to. Ekman and his colleagues (Ekman & Friesen, 1969b) report the beginning of a long-range project and, in greater detail, the necessary data analysis system (Ekman, Friesen & Taussig, 1969), which should yield very solid findings along these lines.

Psychophysiological Responses. The cases in which these responses can be seen and thus be considered to carry interpersonal messages of emotion in free social situations are probably rare for most individuals, although our present state of knowledge about their extent is woefully deficient. Some examples are blushing, very heavy or rapid breathing, profuse sweating that is visible or makes the person wipe his hands frequently, and a strong pulse that produces resultant movements such as a slightly swinging foot when the legs are crossed. Some manifestations of these procesess have been mentioned in clinical papers, but little systematic work has been done on any of them. The eyeblink has been related to momentary excitement and anger (Ponder & Kennedy, 1927), or to changes in incentive in a perceptual motor task (Meyer, Bahrick, and Fitts, 1953); but it could not be related to changes in interview topic which verbal-output measures did discriminate (Kanfer, 1960). A puzzling finding of increased eyeblink frequency among schizophrenics and a decrease among alcoholics in the Chapple stress interview (Wood & Saunders, 1962) further complicate the picture. An easily perceptible response, the belch, was related in a recent report (Tislow, 1964) to aversive thoughts, although the data were anecdotal, and it is probably produced only by certain individuals in any useful quantity for our purposes.

For the most part, investigators have bypassed the more visible and audible psychophysiological responses I have just listed, and have concentrated on those which require laboratory instrumentation to be detected, like galvanic skin response and heart rate. The results have shown that a great deal of information, with direct relevance to emotional states, can be derived in this way. Lacey's review (1959) is invaluable in this connection, partly because of its coverage of the relevant literature, partly because it points out the complications one gets into with the simple notion that autonomic response equals emotional state. In a summary of later work, Lacey and collaborators (1963) point out, with even more evidence, that autonomic changes result from many states, such as cognitive set, which may parallel or be independent of emotion. For this reason many interpretations of autonomic data are oversimplified and lead to confusion. To make full use of the available information, the investigator must take account of many factors in addition to the polygraph chart.

When we speak of these more subtle psychophysiological responses, detection of whose very presence requires special techniques, we raise the same question that came up earlier in connection with long-term spoken language: if the receiving person in the social situation cannot resolve the messages transmitted over the channel, should it be considered a channel at all? As I said before, we will be better able to deal with this question when we discuss the problem of defining the concept of channel.

We have now dealt with the three visible channels included in this list. They are not all visible in the same way, a situation parallel to the one we found among the audible channels: just as a listener would find it difficult if not impossible to collect all the information obtainable in long-term spoken language by simply listening, an observer would have the same trouble with many psychophysiological responses if he confined his observational techniques to looking. Nevertheless it is useful to separate these two general sets of channels, as we shall see in the next chapter, where different requirements for transmitting emotional messages in different social situations are compared.

In the case of the audible channels, we concluded that research investigators can separate incoming information into independent sources in certain combinations so that information from different channels can be compared. By the same token, the visible channels are also separable, but with somewhat greater difficulty. In some situations, using film or closed-circuit television, for example, one can study facial expression by masking the image of the body or by showing the head only in close-up view. Similarly, one can study body movement by showing only that part of the person on the screen. But discrete head movements, which have been shown in our laboratory to be an important source of body movement information, appear in the masked image that was designed to show only facial expression. So do those hand movements which take place near the face or the side of the head. And to complicate matters further, changes of posture, such as shifting position in the chair and uncrossing and recrossing the legs, usually produce passive head movements which can be seen in the "facial expression" image. In addition, some of the more visible psychophysiological responses, such as the eyeblink, can be seen in the face, while others, like heavy or very fast respiration, can be seen in the body. Masking techniques, then, will not necessarily eliminate information from one visible channel while one is concentrating on another. We should note, however, that some masking is possible: if one is studying body movements in such a way that the face cannot be seen, one cannot be influenced in this work by facial expressions, and those psychophysiological responses which can be observed only with the aid of laboratory apparatus cannot bias observations of either face or body. Thus we do have some control over sources of information in the visible channels, but it does seem easier to separate audible channels from one another than visible channels.

When we look at the question of separating information in the audible channels from that in the visible channels, it is plain that there are many more possibilities. In observing through a one-way screen, the investigator has only to shut off the sound system by which the subjects' voices are ordinarily brought to him in the observation booth. Unless he is particularly adept at lip-reading, the observer cannot then be influenced by audible channels. Using films or television, he can simply turn off the sound. The audible channels by themselves, in turn, can be studied by using the audio system only, or a tape recording of the session. We appear to have a hierarchy, then: it is most feasible to separate audible from visible channels; next to separate audible channels from each other; and most difficult to separate the visible channels from each other in studies where independence of sources of information is necessary to the research design. The participants in the social interaction, of course, do not have these options. They certainly do not look at each other all the time, and are selective as to when they do and do not; but the totality is available all the time, at least in peripheral vision.

The Question of Other Channels

This list of channels is not meant as an exhaustive one. Before presenting it I mentioned some other behaviors that can convey emotional information; and when we look more closely at the concept of channel in the next pages, we shall learn that for some purposes some channels on the list would have to be subdivided. So the question of other channels is not that of whether I have made an adequate list or set too stringent a criterion on what to include. It is, rather, whether there might be other behaviors, ordinarily hidden from our view, which might be vehicles for emotional information. The most obvious case would be any behaviors not receivable through the two main sense modalities of the list: hearing and vision.

Many possibilities have been mentioned by Hall (1963) as part of what calls proxemics, "the study of how man unconsciously structures microspace" (p. 1003). Most of these are not noticeable to American scientists because proxemic stimuli are not part of the mainstream of our social intercourse. We Americans stand too far away from each other, for example, to smell each other's breath in most of our day-to-day contacts. Those relationships in our culture where olfaction could be a part are special intimate ones, according to Hall, and occur only in op- posite-sex couples. How great a distance one maintains varies from culture to culture, as Hall observed, and there is experimental evidence comparing American and Arab subjects in a conversational situation (Watson & Graves, 1966) which bears him out. A number of these proxemic behaviors appear to have emotional significance. Hall gives some excellent examples of Arabs seeming too pushy and overly friendly to Americans, and of Americans seeming too standoffish and disdainful to Arabs, on the basis of the way they handle the space between them.

We may conclude, then, that what one considers a channel for sending and receiving emotional messages must depend upon the group one is studying. We must also conclude that there are behaviors which may well serve as channels within one culture, but which the members of that culture do not recognize because the behaviors are unthinkable in ordinary social interaction. To continue with Hall's acute observations of proxemic behavior, when certain foreigners approach Americans too closely, the Americans back away from them — and because the Americans have interpreted the closeness the way Americans interpret it, as intrusive- ness, not the way the foreigners interpret it, as normal conversational distance. This sort of closeness may be rare between pairs of Americans, but when it happens it certainly seems to carry emotional information for both of them. And of course the subset of social situations among us in which closeness is tolerated, man-woman pairs who are on intimate terms, is a very important subset since, after all, it includes all lovers! Small variations in the various aspects of closeness, as outlined by Hall, undoubt- edly carry emotional information, and there is no reason that they should not be studied.

Another class of behaviors is also worth considering, a class that is hidden from view in another sense: there are many acts which serve functions other than emotional communication most of the time, but, in addition — or in some contexts — convey definite emotional information. Perhaps the best example is eye contact or gaze direction. Kendon's (1967) research shows that a major function of looking alternately toward and away from the other person in conversations is to regulate the interchange, to indicate when one is about to complete an utterance so that the other may have the floor, or to signal that one is about to begin talking, and the like. But total amount of looking, and changes in this amount, vary with the affective quality of the situation, too (for one example, see Exline & Winters, 1965). Quite similarly the head nod has been shown to have an important regulatory function in conversation (Dittmann & Llewellyn, 1968), and is also to be associated with an emotion-related variable, intended persuasiveness (Mehrabian & Williams, 1969). Since these behaviors do serve as conversation regulators, they may be overlooked as emotional responses in the conversation unless there is something very unusual about them — and they may be overlooked by the research investigator altogether. It happens that gaze direction is not currently being neglected by researchers, although it was for many years. But if we take it as a prototype of those behaviors which can serve some common function and, in addition, occasionally be cues to emotional response, we see that the search for channels for emotional messages is by no means completed by making lists like the one earlier in this chapter.

PROBLEMS OF DEFINING THE CONCEPT OF CHANNEL

By this time I have said a good deal about channels, listing six common channels, citing examples of research, and noting a number of relationships among them. All of this discussion has been without benefit of definition, as I indicated at the beginning of this chapter, and so indeed has been the work I have cited. Only one work in the psychological or psycholinguistic literature (Wiener & Mehrabian, 1968) has discussed the concept as a concept or given a working definition of it. Yet it has been used for many years in psychology under a number of different names. Luria (1932) referred to it by the phrase "systems of expression" (p. 172), while Wolff (1943) called it "forms of expression" or, occasionally,

"media of expression." Allport (1937, p. 481) was the first psychologist
to use the word "channel" in this context, but he did not define it in any
other terms. In more recent literature so many writers have used the
concept that it could be said to have achieved currency. The reader
understands it intuitively, so no formal definition is necessary.

A similar intuitive understanding of the concept is assumed by many
writers in telecommunication. In a survey of a dozen texts and other
expositions of various mathematical and engineering aspects of communication theory, six gave no definition of the term "channel"; four,
including Shannon, gave intuitive descriptions like the one I quoted from
Fano (1961) in Chapter 2; and four (also including Fano) gave formal
definitions in terms of input spaces and events, output spaces and events,
and conditional probability distributions over them. These last definitions
are unfortunately too abstract for our purposes, while the intuitive
descriptions are not sufficiently detailed. Some features of each type of
definition, however, may be drawn upon in developing a working definition
appropriate for our purposes here.

First, all agree that channels are media, like wire or air — or
frequency bands within these — through which signals may travel from
one place to another, just as shipping channels are routes along which
goods may be transported from one port to another. Two other features
are variously stressed in the engineering literature. We went into a good
deal of detail about one in describing the list earlier in this chapter,
namely, how effectively one can separate out the information received on
one channel from that received on others. Separability of channels is
explicit in the definition given by the American Standards Association
(1957), but not specifically mentioned in any other works — and this
despite the long history of inventions and research on this problem in
the developing history of radio broadcasting. The other feature variously
stressed is the integral role of the devices that transmit and receive
the signals. Fano (1961) makes the most of this idea, in both his formal
and informal definitions. He includes it in his extra pair of boxes in the
diagram from which Figure 1 in Chapter 2 was taken: the channel encoder
and channel decoder. This feature is acknowledged by some authors other
than Fano, but never spelled out, and it is not even mentioned by many.

In the psychological literature, as I said earlier, only one discussion of the concept of channel has appeared, the one in Wiener and

Mehrabian (1968). They say of it: *"Channel* will define any set of behaviors in a communication which has been systematically denoted by an observer *and* which is considered by that observer to carry information which can be studied (in principle at least) independently of any other co-occurring behaviors" (p. 51). This is a definition which might well be adopted here with only slight modification: I should like to make more explicit the possibility that the observer need not have consciously deliberated about the possible communicative aspects of the behaviors in question.

This definition of channel, like that in telecommunication proposed by the American Standards Association, indicates that channels must be differentiated from each other both from the standpoint of the sender and from that of the receiver. Radio broadcasting and telephone service could not operate if the situation were otherwise. In emotional communication, on the other hand, we have more evidence about receivers than about senders, and this is because of the way most research has been conducted. Of the several studies so far reported in the literature in which different channels for emotional messages were studied, three analyzed their results from the point of view of the sender. Shapiro (1966) had some of his judges watch nonstress interviews on closed circuit TV, some with sound and some without, while others listened to the interviews and still others read typescripts of them. The ratings of the judges (pleasant-unpleasant interviewees' feelings) were averaged within each condition of observation to form the independent variable; messages put out by the senders were free to vary as the dependent variables. Both Beakel and Mehrabian (1969) and Bugental, Love, Kaswan, and April (1971), used grouped judgments of interchannel incongruity in parental communication to children as their dependent variables, and pathology group, sex of parent, and the like, as independent variables. In these studies messages put out by senders were free to vary, and they were studied within different groups or experimental conditions.

In all the other studies of interchannel differences, the reverse was true. Fairbanks and Pronovost (1939), Levitt (1964), Williams and Sundene (1965), Mehrabian and Wiener (1967), Mehrabian and Ferris (1967), Bugental, Kaswan, Love, and Fox (1970), and Bugental, Kaswan, and Love (1970) all used actors to present constant sender stimuli, and studied the variation in the receivers' responses across channels. Our experiment (Dittmann, Parloff, & Boomer, 1965) derived the stimuli from interview material rather than from actors, but selected it carefully to represent constant emotional states in the sending person and analyzed judges' responses across channels and judging groups.

The investigators in these last eight experiments were acting as if they knew there was emotional information available on different channels, but did not know if anyone else were in on the secret. This makes those investigators (including ourselves) sound rather supercilious, but of course it is not the only way of looking at these studies. Another way is to view them as the first and necessary step in the long-range strategy of studying channels. A future step would be to gather more facts about how the sending person uses the various channels at his disposal, how he organizes his communicative activities. I believe, however, that we need to concentrate more now on the first phase, learning how the receiving person operates and refining the methods the research investigator uses to study the whole process. And if we take a somewhat distant position and look at the investigator's methods, we may learn something about the observer in the social situation — just as I said in Chapter 3 we could do in connection with evaluating the amount of emotional information conveyed in a message.

But what does it mean to say that we must start by studying the observer's and the researcher's methods? Let us take the study of body movement as an example, and see what the difficulties are at this stage in our knowledge. A look at the research on body movements shows that two gross sorts of information can be obtained by looking at them, information about their frequency and information about their form. Frequency may be determined by detecting movements with electromyographic methods (as Sainsbury, 1954, did), or by identifying them from motion pictures or with accelerometers, both of which we have done in our laboratory. The fact that there are three measurement techniques does not mean that there are three channels, however, since all three techniques are designed to get at frequency of movements, and they should yield results that are equivalent or at least highly correlated. Form of movement requires quite different techniques for study than frequency; different aspects of form, in turn, require still different techniques. Krout's (1935) sketches of hand postures give one sort of information, and Efron's (1941) tracing of roundness and angularity of hand movements from motion pictures give another. And both of these get at something different than the

SCAN techniques developed by Ekman and Friesen (1968). The differences among these methods are far greater than the differences among the above-cited techniques for counting movement frequencies. From the standpoint of the research investigator, the results of the three methods of analyzing form of movements are clearly distinguishable from each other, and all three are distinguishable from the results of frequency methods. Do form and frequency add up to four channels, then, or should we think of a form channel and a frequency channel? At the present time I believe that there is no rational basis for making a decision. Investigators will have to continue to name channels in accordance with the nature of the research they are conducting, taking into account the techniques they are using for collecting their data. In one study it may be desirable to compare information derived from frequency of movements with that from their form, and these two may well be called channels. In another study it may make more sense to choose one measure of movement and contrast it with the content of the concurrent speech, and refer to each of these as a channel. In both of these cases, the working definition of channel will be bound by the observer's technique of measurement, but the findings may contribute to a knowledge about the whole process and might lay the groundwork for better research on the sender's choice of channels.

These comments have so far been confined to the research investigator and how he might proceed. How do they apply to face-to-face interaction where two persons are communicating to each other? Can the dictum of refining the observer's techniques be applied here as well? Clearly not. In the ongoing social situation it is impossible to separate channels from each other, as I have said before. The receiving person hears both the words and the way they are spoken, and while he probably attends for the most part to the sending person's face, he sees other things about the sending person in peripheral vision and glances elsewhere from time to time, to focus now on hands, now on general posture, then back to the face, and so forth. In view of the obvious differences in what is possible for the research investigator and the social participant, it might be proposed that we have a different definition of channel for the two. At least this would solve the problem of whether to call long-term spoken language and psychophysiological responses channels: for the researcher, yes; for the social participant, no. But such a solution neglects the fact that choice of channel first involves the sending person. A feeling he is trying very hard not to tell about in words, he may be trying just as hard to let us know in other ways, audible or visible. Far from calling for a different definition then, it seems to me that the process of differentiating channels by participants in social situations must be made the subject of intensive study in its own right, using the term "channel" here in the same way as anywhere else. A good deal of the work cited throughout this book can be viewed as first attempts to open up this very area of research.

In the course of continuing this line of research, we will find empirical answers to the question, posed several times in this chapter, about whether seemingly imperceptible activities can be considered channels for emotional messages. Under what circumstances does an observer finally "catch on" to the fact that the sending person is repeating a familiar theme? When does the receiving person note the changes in frequency of foot movements made by his companion in the interaction? Can a person attend to eyeblink rates when an argument is going on? The real question is not whether long-term spoken language or psychophysiological response are channels under our definition, but whether we can collect evidence that they are used as channels — and, if so, when — or evidence about the conditions that facilitate or inhibit such use. If these are the research questions, the definition of channel will serve, not as an admitter or rejecter of certain acts for consideration as research topics but rather as a guideline to research.

CLASSIFICATION OF CHANNELS

In writings on communication theory, channels are classified in a number of ways, having to do with the characteristics of the input and output information to be processed through the channel. Recall that a channel includes not only the physical medium between the transmitter and the receiver, such as air, wire, or whatever, but also the methods used to send and receive the messages. For any given method of transmission and reception, only that sort of information which is appropriate to the methods may be sent and received with greatest efficiency, or in some combinations, sent and received at all. Let us first take up the classification of *discrete and continuous channels,* and these general remarks will become more clear. In a discrete channel, the incoming information must have been quantized so that only a few values of signal are used and coded for transmission. Usually only two values are used in discrete telecommunication channels, *0* and *1*, or *off* and *on*. In a continuous channel, on the other hand, the signal may be any value in the entire range of the apparatus at any given time. It is easy to see, then, that a continuous message can only be sent along a channel whose signal admits of continuous variation. True, any continuous source can be transformed into discrete categories, and coded for transmission on a discrete channel, but the signal as sent and received will be only an approximation of the original information. Conversely, it is possible to send a discrete message on a continuous channel, but this combination does not make most efficient use of the capabilities of the channel.

Now, to apply this way of thinking to channels for emotional messages, we must first have some way of knowing whether emotional information is discrete or continuous in nature, and then learn which channels are capable of handling each type of information. At the present time we do not have many facts on either of these issues, but our reasoning so far gives us some direction as to where to look, and there is some pertinent research in the literature to draw on. The most applicable part of our reasoning is to be found in the structural variable, communicative specificity, which was presented in the last chapter. The closer a message is to the communication end of the continuum, the more likely it is to be discrete in nature, while messages at the expressive end appear to be continuous. This way of looking at it makes a continuum of Ruesch's (1955) dichotomy of the digital versus the analogic in social communication. It also implies that a strict dichotomous classification of channels into either discrete or continuous is not possible as applied to the subject matter of human communication. Indeed, I believe that this is the case. Some messages, like language, can be coded discretely, as Ruesch points out, plus a few facial expressions and symbolic gestures. Others, which we have seen must be described in states-of-being kinds of words are somewhat more continuous in nature. Still other messages must be called truly continuous, like galvanic skin response, degree of muscular tension, and probably frequency of movements or of eyeblinks. These less codable, more continuous messages may occur concomitantly with the discrete ones, sometimes even in the same body area, such as the face. They can thus clarify the coded information if the two are compatible, or confuse it if they are not.

To carry these ideas further, let us refer to some research on the information content of different channels, by P. Ekman (1965) and from our laboratory (Dittmann, Parloff, & Boomer, 1965). In both cases it was body areas which were studied, not channels per se, but the implications for the latter are clear. Ekman used Schlosberg's dimensions of emotion as a basis for obtaining judgments of still photographs taken in an interview situation. He found that judges could agree with each other far better on the pleasant-unpleasant dimension when they saw only the subject's face than when only the body was shown. On judging the same photographs for sleep-tension, on the other hand, the results were almost reversed. Agreement was higher on this dimension when only the body could be seen than when only the face was presented, although there was also significant interjudge agreement under the latter condition. Our experiment corroborated Ekman's findings: using motion picture excerpts from an interview, we found that judges could agree on the pleasant-unpleasant dimension when they saw only the body, but not as highly as when they saw the whole person. Our judges also reported difficulty in applying the terms *pleasant* and *unpleasant* to the body, saying that *tense* and *relaxed* would have been more appropriate. Since we did not use Schlosberg's other dimensions for judging, we have no parallel for comparison with Ekman's very neat converse findings.

Ekman interprets his results this way: the face, while a person is talking, is lively and alert, and thus does not express much of the length of the sleep-tension continuum; the body, on the other hand, while some of its acts can convey pleasant-unpleasant information, does so only infrequently during conversation. This explanation sounds as though there were qualitative differences in the information conveyed by different body areas. But let us look at Schlosberg's two dimensions, and at the body areas which seem to carry them most effectively, from the standpoint of their communicative specificity. The pleasant-unpleasant dimension appears to be more toward the communicative end of the scale, more like the smile and frown in facial expression, while the sleep-tension dimension is toward the expressive end, like the states-of-being facial expressions and degree of muscular tension in the body. Thus the pleasant-unpleasant information seems more amenable to discrete treatment, sleep-tension to continuous treatment, and the channels of face and body in these experiments seem appropriate to these respective treatments. Ekman and Friesen later (1967) refined this interpretation by differentiating between body acts and body positions. The former can convey information about the nature of emotion, like the specific emotional expressions of the face, but they do so less often than the face. Little of this specific information is conveyed by body positions; they serve rather, as cues for intensity of emotion.

At the present time this line of reasoning is conjecture. We know that some emotional information is clearly discrete and that it is carried on channels which appear designed for it. We know, too, that other information is continuous and that the channels seem appropriate to it as well. The conjecture lies in fixing in our minds, at this early date, those channels which we think convey discrete or continuous information. It would probably be possible to collect the data necessary to show whether these matches are accurate or not, and I believe that for some major channels such as facial expression, it would be important to do so. We would have to sharpen our research techniques in useful directions in the course of this work, and it would tell us a great deal about what social participants have to work with in communicating with each other.

The other common way in which channels are described in telecommunication has to do with whether they are *constant* or *possess memory*. The constant channel is characterized by freedom of choice as to which message element may be sent now, regardless of the ones that have preceded it. In the channel with memory, the choice of message element to be sent now is determined to some degree by what has gone before. On first thought there seems to be no possibility for a constant channel in human communication. One seldom weeps immediately after a smile, or is relaxed right after a pent-up rage. And certainly language provides us with many illustrations of complex transitional probabilities, which are not clearly understood after centuries of study.

We must not be too hasty, however, in concluding that the channels we are interested in invariably possess memory. At microscopic levels of analysis some may, indeed, be constant. Nonpurposive body movements, such as both Sainsbury and we have studied by our different methods, will serve as an example. Some of these movements are tied to the rhythm structure of speech while a person is talking (Dittmann & Llewellyn, 1969), and those which are behave like an information source possessing memory. The majority of movements, however, are not related to speech rhythm, and they behave like a constant source (Dittmann, 1972). I shall discuss the results of these studies in more detail in Chapter 7 in connection with measurement problems in research on emotional communication, but suffice it to say here that they make the relationship between channel and constancy of information source in this field appear more complicated than it is in telecommunication. Some channels may be capable of conveying constant information; other channels information that possesses memory. Those are simple cases and can describe telecommunication channels completely. But in our field some information sources may be constant under some circumstances and possess memory under others, and the channel must be capable of handling both types; that is harder to conceptualize and even harder to design studies around. Here again, just as in the classification of the discrete and continuous, we need empirical research to determine which channels are which, and under what circumstances, and the results of this research will teach us a great deal about the whole process of emotional communication.

CHANNEL CAPACITY

It is often said that channel capacity is the most important single characteristic of a channel. It is not a characteristic in the same sense that discreteness and constancy are. Those are classifications: a channel is either discrete or continuous, either constant or possessing memory. Capacity, on the other hand, may be measured for a channel of any type, and is basic in that it tells us how much information the channel may transmit during any given period of time.

Channel capacity is the maximum amount of information per time unit which the channel can possibly transmit. It is not a requirement, but rather a limit: a channel need not always be used up to its maximum, yet it cannot be used at any greater rate without error. To speed up, one must send simpler messages; to send more complicated ones, one must slow down. To make the most of any channel, one must use it as close to its maximum as possible. This means coding incoming information as efficiently as possible, and reducing redundancies, because the channel does not know whether there is needless repetition or not, and redundant message elements take up channel capacity just as much as new ones do. So the limit represented by the capacity of the channel forces the users of the communication system to do continuous cost accounting — and misjudgments are expensive. Channel capacity will be wasted if the channel is not used efficiently, but errors will result if one tries to overuse it. The measure of channel capacity, as we learned in Chapter 2, is the same as the measure of information, plus the added factor of time to yield rate of transmission.

In emotional communication it is intuitively clear that channels differ widely in their capacity. A great many messages can be sent in a small period of time by spoken language, while only a limited number could be sent by body movements. In addition, the average message element in language has a higher inherent information value than that of body movement messages because of the greater variety of possible messages that can be put into words than into movements. Not only is the absolute number of "words" for expressing emotion large in any language, but the variations of their form for expressive purposes, phonemic alterations, morphophonemic changes, and the like (see Stankiewicz, 1964), enrich the vocabulary even more. By comparison, other channels, such as body movement, do not have such large "vocabularies" and can be used for sending only much lower-information messages.

In this brief and intuitive look at the contrasting capacities of language and body movement to carry emotional information, two criteria for channel capacity have been included: the speed with which message elements can be emitted over the channel, and the information value of the message elements the channel can handle. At the beginning of this chapter, speed was mentioned as one of the bases for deciding which modes of expression to include in our list of channels. Posture was described as capable of rapid shifts, and thus able to reflect moment-to-moment changes in emotional state. Grooming, on the other hand, can change only over much longer periods of time, and is thus more suitable for conveying information about more enduring mood swings or about personality traits. Among the channels included in our list, the differences in speed of change are not so great, but they are still important differences. One can mention a change in feeling faster, and have it understood, than one can change posture, tone of voice, or breathing rate, and have any of those changes noticed. An even faster channel is probably to be found in facial expression. Changes here occur in a shorter time than it takes to say the smallest group of words that can convey meaning, as Haggard and Isaacs (1966) have shown. But we must still regard these remarks as an intuitive look, since so little actual work has been done on this aspect of emotional communication.

The other criterion for channel capacity is the information value of the message elements that can be sent on the channel regardless of the speed of transmission. In discussing the classification of channels we noted differences in the discreteness of information they can handle, differences which, it was argued, were also related to how close the messages were to the communicative end of the continuum of communicative specificity. And I have just said that messages sent in language, which is more communicative, have higher inherent information value than those sent in body movement, which is more expressive. The reason for this, we may speculate, is that communicative messages have been coded more efficiently before they are sent. In coding a feeling into language in order to convey it to another person, the sending person has used a most complicated system, one that can give the receiving person a very specific idea of the feeling involved. We might reason, then, that messages toward the expressive end of the continuum give the receiver only a very general idea of the sender's feeling. This sort of reasoning, of course, is closer to hypothesis than to fact at this point.

"Specific" and "general" as used here, are reminiscent of the descriptions applied by Frijda (1953, 1958) to the judges' responses to the facial expression photographs in his experiments. There is good reason for this similarity. Let us recall, from Chapter 3, that when Frijda's judges described a stimulus in general terms, they spoke of the pictured subject's general behavioral attitude, e.g., her state of attention or withdrawal. When they described it more specifically, on the other hand, they spoke of situations which might have led up to what they saw in the stimulus pictures; furthermore, they used emotion names. These words, then, include a whole host of details about what the users of those words expect to be associated with the various emotions. The emotion-naming words themselves are condensations of these expectations, and thus convey a great deal of information. Language is not the only coding system among communication media which has these characteristics, as I have pointed out several times, but it is certainly the most highly developed.

The conclusion we may draw from this argument is that channels which admit of coded material can carry messages of higher information value. Thus we would expect short-term spoken language to fall at one end of any ordering of channels, with facial expression or vocalization probably coming next. The specific rankings from here on down the line will have to await further data, but there are some indications of how they might go, partly from research results and partly from introspection on the part of those who got the results, both of these coming from our laboratory. These, in turn, make sense in the light of results obtained by other workers. Our research results came from the Dittmann, Parloff, and Boomer study (1965) of facial and bodily expression, which showed that judges concentrated more of their attention on the face of the subject pictured in the stimulus material than on the body. Even those judges who turned out later in the experiment to be more influenced by bodily cues started out paying more attention to the face. For most people, then, the face is commanding. It is difficult to look elsewhere even though we know that there is information to be gained from doing so. An even more extreme example may be found in situations where language is involved, and here is where our introspections come in. When we were selecting excerpts from interviews to use as stimuli in this study, we found that the only way we could see either facial or bodily expressions was to turn off the sound as we projected the film. Otherwise we were quickly caught up in the content of the interview — "content," of course, meaning what was being said. With the sound turned on, the visible channels provided information that was like background accompaniment, sometimes complementing, sometimes confusing, but always background — and this despite the fact that we soon knew the "content" of the interviews very well. This experience was not an isolated one in working with films of interviews; we have often found it necessary to eliminate speech when studying other aspects of the communication. The work of decoding speech is so great that it demands virtually full-time attention.

The amount of information in stimulus material had been implicated as a factor in the focus of attention by other research results prior to ours. One bit of evidence comes from Ladefoged and Broadbent's study (1960) of the difficulty listeners have in locating extraneous sounds that are superimposed upon spoken sentences. They relate the amount of attention required of the listener to points of lexical stress in the speech he is listening to, and say that these are also the point of highest information. Other work by Berry (1953) had already shown that information and lexical stress are related. In a large corpus drawn from spontaneous conversations on telephones, Berry did a word-frequency analysis and independently had the material rated for three degrees of stress. Words with the greatest stress tended to be the least frequent words. The reasoning that more attention is demanded at high-information points in the message thus seems firm, even if the evidence for it is adduced in a roundabout way. We may now with some confidence infer an ordering of the amount of information which the three channels — short-term spoken language, facial expression, and body movement — are capable of handling. If we include along with this the differences in speed of change among the channels we have been discussing, an ordering of channel capacity is strongly suggested. There are, as I have said, not yet many facts about this ordering, but the principles by which the facts might be obtained are laid down by communication theory.

Channel capacity has been included in two recent discussions of social communication, one by Wiener and Mehrabian (1968) and the other by Ekman and Friesen (1969a), both published since these pages were first drafted. It should not be surprising that they take very similar factors into account. Wiener and Mehrabian (pp. 55 ff.) write of channel effectiveness, which is made up of efficiency (or the amount of time a channel needs to get a message across under a given condition) and elaboration (or the channel's range of possibilities for communicating various experiences). These authors appear to regard the two components as tending to be dependent upon each other and to be related inversely: to communicate effectively, one may choose a relatively unelaborated channel if it can convey the message very rapidly. Thus Wiener and Mehrabian have posited speed and efficiency as important characteristics of channel effectiveness, corresponding to speed of change and information value of possible message elements that I have used to characterize channel capacity. Ekman and Friesen use the general term "sending capacity" (pp. 93-94), and say it is made up of three factors. The first two are the now-familiar speed and information value of message elements, termed average transmission time and number of discriminable stimulus patterns possible. The third factor is what they call visibility. It seems to me that this is not inherent in the channel itself; rather, it is a threshold problem for the observer, with all of the ramifications we came across when we discussed thresholds under level of awareness in the preceding chapter. As such it presents attention problems for the observer (we shall discuss this more fully in the next chapter) and thus plays a part in determining choice of channels on the part of the sending person.

SUMMARY: CHANNELS OF EMOTIONAL COMMUNICATION

We began this chapter by listing six channels commonly used in communicating emotional messages: short-term spoken language, long-term spoken language, vocalization, facial expression, body movement, and psychophysiological response. These were presented as two groups of channels, with three included in each, based upon the way in which their messages may be perceived: the audible channels and the visible channels. Examination of how these channels work showed that the research investigator may easily separate information coming via these two broad groupings of channels, but that it was more difficult to separate the audible channels from each other, and still more difficult in the case of the visible channels. The social participant, by contrast, always has all channels available to observe. We also considered the possibility that there may be other channels hidden from our daily view because of our culturally determined use of interpersonal space, or because their characteristic behaviors usually serve other interpersonal functions.

We then adopted the definition by Wiener and Mehrabian of the term "channel," in which distinguishing channels from one another was a basic part, and we discussed ways that the observer's channel-discrimination techniques would dictate for some time what one could consider as a channel. The problems of the social participant were seen as vastly more complicated in this respect than those of the research observer, since for the former all the data were at least potentailly available all the time. In spite of these difficulties, which might be called procedural, the principles were seen as the same for the two situations, so that the same definition should be able to cover both.

We then took up two ways of classifying channels: discrete versus continuous and constant versus possessing memory. These classifications really refer to the source information as well as to the design of the channel, and to compatibility or mismatch between the two. At first blush, emotional information seems to be continuous; but there are many messages, such as those cast into language, which have been coded for transmission as discrete signals. These were said to be the ones closest to the communication end of the continuum of communicative specificity (described in Chapter 4). Relating discrete messages to communicative ones led to the argument that this descriptive classification is not properly a dichotomy in our field, as it is in telecommunication, and we tentatively interpreted some experimental results in the literature as being supportive of this view. Less could be said about the other classification: while it was clear that many emotional messages possess memory in that their probabilities are dependent upon previous ones, some at a microscopic level of analysis might well be considered as constant, and there is beginning research evidence to indicate that this may be so.

Finally, we considered the meaning of channel capacity in emotional communication. Two interlocking factors were set forth: the speed at which message elements could succeed each other in the various channels, and the amount of information each message element could convey. There are not many data about the first factor, since so little work has been done on it. There is more to be said about the second, but we needed to get at it by looking at studies that are only peripherally related to the topic of emotional communication. We were nevertheless able to see how the theory provides guidelines to determining at least some ordering of channels on this important variable.

Chapter Six

Emotional Messages in Social Interaction ——————

Communication theory, emotional information, the relationship of message and person, and the channels of transmission — all these topics which we have discussed so far provide us with a language in which to speak of the real meat of emotional communication, namely, the process of transmitting emotional messages in the context of social interaction. That process is the topic of this chapter, and the focus of the discussion will see a definite shift: whereas before we have concentrated on the message itself and how it fits in with the lives of the sending and receiving persons, the emphasis will now be on the interplay between the two persons, with the message being the object of the interplay. In the first section we shall trace the life history of the exchange of an emotional message, so to speak: how it gets started, how it is maintained, and what happens to it later. Then we shall take up some of the things that get in the way of the process, ways in which messages are interfered with or interrupted.

STAGES IN THE LIFE OF AN EMOTIONAL MESSAGE

Initiation

Needless to say, social interactions include all sorts of messages. In some situations, such as angry battling, playing some kinds of games, making love, or sharing aesthetic experiences, for example, the emotional messages predominate. On the other hand, in many other situations of daily life, perhaps the majority of them, emotional messages are not the main point of the transaction. People shop, learn things, work, and conduct all sorts of daily business in social situations. None of these activities absolutely requires emotional messages in order to get done, though a bit of emotional spice adds interest to most of them. In these settings, then, emotional messages may be considered as overlaid upon the other messages that "properly" make up the situation.

Let us take a very simple emotional message of this kind and trace it through. In a work session involving several people, the group is getting good results. One of the people says to the others that he is glad things are going so smoothly, and the group continues with the task. Cases like this are not at all rare, and certainly cause no conceptual difficulty. Other messages pertaining more "directly" to the task are interrupted for a moment, the emotional message is inserted, and then the "real" work continues where it left off. The members of the work group, outside observers, or anyone present can easily tell when the emotional message began, who sent it, how it was sent, and what it consisted of.

Suppose, however, that our protagonist, rather than saying in words that he was pleased, simply looked up at his colleagues and smiled, then looked back at what he was doing. This is perhaps an even more common case, but the example has now been changed so that it includes a number of complications. Did the other workers happen to notice the smile? If so, how were they "cued in" to pay attention to to it? Have there been other indications that this person is glad about the progress they are all making, or does the smile come as a big surprise to everyone? Most of these questions have to do with the very beginning of the exchange, with establishing the fact that there is a message in the first place. There are many cases, of course, where a message is sent and never received: the other people could have continued concentrating on their work and not have seen that one of them looked up and smiled. But let us assume here that they did see it, that the message did get across.

In this example the emotional message is an extraneous one, as I have said, added to those others which "directly" concern the work. But since the work session has been characterized as a successful one, the message is not a surprise to anyone there, so it could not be called a high-information message. The social atmosphere is ripe for some expression of the shared feeling. Yet ripeness is a description of this particular situation, and not an explanation of the beginning of the emotional message. It does not answer the question of how the group's attention was attracted to the smile as a message.

As I see it, paying attention to the smile is really a twofold process. It includes, first, paying attention to the sending person — that is, looking at him or listening, or whatever — and second, recognizing that the smile is an emotional message. Attention is a consequence of the potential receiving persons' interaction with the sender. If the group members are working together closely, there will be messages of all sorts going back and forth, and everyone will be ready for another one, whatever it may be. If they are working in parallel, each on his own aspect of the job, any one person will have to do something definite and attention-attracting to jar the others out of their concentration so that they look at him or listen. Catching the eye of some may be difficult if they are really working, while others may be on the alert for any message to come along — we all know how wide the individual differences are in this respect. Various group-oriented factors will also be playing their roles: group cohesiveness, salience of the various members for others for any of a number of reasons, and the like, factors social psychologists have been studying for years.

Attention to the smile as an emotional message is another matter, about which we can say more from the standpoint of the ideas we have been developing. We concluded in Chapter 3 that general knowledge of the sending person's general cultural heritage, plus specific acquaintance with him as an individual, both combine with knowledge of the stimulus situation to compute the joint probabilities which constitute the measure of information conveyed by any act. The same principles apply to recognizing that an act is an emotional message in the first place. To begin with, we can tell on the basis of what people in our culture do to express themselves. Then, as we get to know a specific person better, we learn of variations on those themes which he uses when he is feeling different ways. Both recognition of the message and evaluation of its information proceed from the general to the specific.

Let us apply these principles to the process of getting acquainted with a person's emotional communication habits. We shall begin with cultural background and look at language usage as a first example. Social class affiliation, regional origin, educational level, and many general cultural factors all combine to set the range of how language is used. These affect the person's vocabulary choice, articulation and pronunciation, grammatical forms considered acceptable, and so on. Stankiewicz (1964) gives a number of examples of the variations used for purposes of emotional communication drawn from many languages. In the same way the manner of sending emotional messages by other means is also socially bound, even though we have few studies of it so far. Efron's (1941) study comparing both form and extent of hand and arm movements of Jewish and Italian immigrants to the U.S. showed dramatic cultural differences. It also showed how those differences disappeared when the people were outside of their ghettos. Hall's book (1959) also contains many examples, as do LaBarre's articles (1947, 1964). Some of Hall's obervations were picked up by Watson and Graves (1966), who studied what Hall had termed the "proxemic behavior" of Arab and American groups and found definite contrasts in acts that are certainly capable of conveying emotional information, as I mentioned in Chapter 5. McNeil's study (1956) compared subcultural rather than general cultural systems. He demonstrated social class differences in expression of emotion among early adolescents. Some of the differences were related to choice of channels: working-class children tended more toward direct bodily expression, while middle-class children used facial expressions more. Since McNeil asked his subjects to act out various emotions, the study was not a completely naturalistic one; but the results reflected the class differences strongly and confirm notions about these manners of expression which we all know about intuitively.

People vary a great deal in how much they participate in the group norms for emotional expression, or at least we can infer this from Estes' results (1938). Subjects in his experiment performed a number of tasks before an audience of judges, who then rated the subjects on several traits. There were wide individual differences as to how easy it was to judge the expressions of the subjects, and the judges also varied in their ability to read the expressions they observed. Those subjects who were hardest to know in Estes' study were introverted and introspective, while those who were least successful at judging others were analytic and scientific in approach. This study was about character traits, but emotional expressiveness was included among the traits studied and was one of the easier ones to judge. The important thing, from the standpoint of my present argument, is that the study was concerned with first impressions, not with expressive patterns among people who knew each other well, so cultural norms were about all the judges had to go on. We may surmise from the results that introspective people are harder to "read" because they do not use the culturally expected means of expression as much as other people do. We may extrapolate that it takes longer to learn the characteristic expressive patterns of introspective people, and that there are some whose feelings their friends can never be entirely sure of.

When we come to acquaintance with idiosyncratic communication habits, we know much less from the results of research studies, but at the same time we know more from our own intuition. If the group we started talking about has been working together for a long time, the members will have got to know each other very well. Their acquaintance may not include socializing outside the job setting, or any specific knowledge of political alignments or personal interests, but they will still know what to expect of this one individual when he looks up at his co-workers. The group will, in short, have developed a certain content-less intimacy by which all sorts of messages can be sent more quickly. "Content-less," of course means the usual thing: the details are difficult, if not impossible, to describe in words. The same sort of intimacy also develops in psychotherapeutic settings. The patient quickly learns about the therapist's communication patterns from speech, from the sound of posture shifts, if the therapy is carried on in the analytic style of therapist-out-of-sight, and so on. He learns these patterns even if he does not "know the therapist," in the sense of having been told in words his stand on any issues which the patient considers important. This is what is meant when writers say that the psychoanalyst cannot maintain a mirror-like objectivity even if he tries most valiantly to adhere to the classical model. Cohen and Cohen (1961) write of this process in detail as they report intensive study of a series of interviews by repeated viewings of motion picture records of each one.

So people know what to expect of each other through knowledge of group membership coupled with knowledge of more individual characteristics. What they get to know will take us further away from the research literature, since we will have less to draw upon other than anecdotal material. Some of what we have to say will be pure speculation, though some of the speculations may be subject to test later on. I believe that the first step in getting acquainted with another person's emotional communication patterns is to learn the habitual channels he uses for sending emotional messages. This is not difficult, since the range of choice is small in any given culture and, if Bernstein's (1962a, 1962b) conclusions about the subculture of the British working class may be generalized, is fairly uniform within the culture. One would then learn the sorts of expressions used by the person on these channels. I shall argue that in the beginning of any acquaintance these expressions will be rather high on the continuum of communicative specificity, and sent on channels that lend themselves best to communicative messages. Thus strangers should be found to concentrate on sending the most discrete, highly coded messages. Words, the best-understood facial expressions, and a few of the most stereotyped gestures should predominate at first. These first acts may, moreover, be performed quite slowly and deliberately for the new acquaintance, in an exaggerated or caricatured way, so as to get the codified meaning across clearly. The code, being agreed upon by the wider community, is thus relied upon to reduce misunderstandings. But communication habits are deeply ingrained and usually removed from awareness, so that misunderstandings, or at best partial understandings, may well be the rule rather than the exception. A person may "blurt out" a response — if this term may be applied to channels other than language — in a way that he does not know about, at any stage of acquaintance. If he does it early, before the other person can be sure what message he is trying to get across, he will lengthen the acquaintance process. The extreme may be seen in ethnologists' reports that in entirely different cultures they are at a loss to understand many aspects of the communications of the strange group. The sources of this strangeness are undoubtedly many. Certainly the visiting ethnologist will fail to understand those messages whose codes he does not know. But he himself, having grown up within his own culture, attaches communicative value to many acts to which his hosts do not attach value. He will thus believe that they are sending some messages which they, in fact, are not sending at all. In this way misunderstandings arise rather than simple failures at understanding.

As time goes on in any relationship, and the strangers become better acquainted, they may supplement the discrete, coded messages with others of a more continuous nature, and the two may branch out and use other channels which are more conducive to expressive messages. Furthermore, even their understanding of each other's coded messages will change, since they will begin to learn to read the codes in use by smaller groups than the total culture, such as regional, subcultural, and family codes. In getting to know someone or, more dramatically, a group of people from a different ethnic background, one learns their "vocabulary" of emotional expression much as one learns the words of a new dialect or language. And in spending a weekend or even an evening with the family of a new friend, one must also learn many new expressions. Some of these will have seemed strange when they first came up with the new friend. Now they seem to make sense in the context of the whole family, and this may sharpen one's perception of the friend's emotional communications in future dealings with him away from his family. Many "family resemblances", by which we ordinarily mean genetic similarities of facial features or body build, are probably really based on family codes of expression. Codified messages are not the only sorts of expression which are influenced in this way, of course, but they are easier to conceptualize and write about. Expressive patterns commonly used within a family or any other highly cohesive group may also be seen in more continuous messages. Choice of channels, no matter what type of information is sent on them, is also subject to group custom and, to some extent too, to individual habit.

These, then, are the factors which I consider as setting the stage for initiating an emotional message: the sending person first does something that attracts the receiver's attention. The likelihood that the receiver's attention will really be attracted depends on his looking at or listening to the sender or being ready to do so, and on his understanding that this act could be an emotional message. He arrives at this understanding on the basis of his general knowledge of the expressive patterns used in the sender's cultural and subcultural group, and of the specific communication habits of the sender. He must first get to know that the act may serve the sender as a channel for emotional messages; second, he must learn the code into which the message might be cast. Once the message is identified as an emotional one, and this is a qualitative judgment, the amount of emotion it conveys can be evaluated, and this is a quantitative judgment. It makes use of the factors outlined in Chapter 3:

the provocativeness of the antecedent act given the social atmosphere of
the stimulus situation, how usual or unusual the sending person's response
is in the light of cultural expectations and of any more specific knowledge
of this particular person's behavioral repertory.

The Fate of the Message

Other stages in the the life of an emotional message are much more
difficult to talk about in such general terms as we have been using
to discuss the beginning of a message. Before we can even start, we must
first distinguish between an individual message about an emotion and
the emotional episode that gives rise to the message. The episode may
be brief, so that there is time for just a single message about it; or it may
last for quite a while and be the occasion for a number of messages. The
duration of any single message will be determined in large part by its
form. The more discrete the message, the more delimited it will be,
and the easier to identify as to its beginning and end. The receiver's attention is drawn to it more definitely, or the sender waits until he has
the receiver's attention before sending it. More continuous messages,
on the other hand, may require more time to identify as such. Tension
or fidgetiness often goes on for quite a while before any inference about
emotion is drawn. And of course long-term messages made up of the
very recurrence of an act or phrase over a span of time will be of
much greater duration.

How long an individual message lasts, then, has to do with the
internal structure of the message itself. How long the emotional episode
lasts is determined by a host of other things, such as how intense it
is, how much the sending person is given to "holding grudges," and
how closely the whole situation fits in with his basic personality makeup,
his loves and hopes and fears. Added to these considerations is the effect
on the social situation of sending an emotional message in the first place,
of how much any message serves in turn as an antecedent stimulus act
for a return message from the person who has up to now been the
receiving one, and so on. Emotional messages may feed each other in
one group or dampen each other in another group, as Raush (1965)
found. In a group of hyperaggressive boys at the beginning of residential
treatment, acts became increasingly unfriendly in comparison with the

extrapolated curve based on initial exchanges, whereas in normal controls definite corrective factors could be seen to counteract this tendency (pp. 496-497). The importance of the social situation in building up or quenching an emotional episode may also be seen in those settings which are designed to minimize the response to any emotional message, such as the psychoanalytic interview. Here some episodes will diminish by simply running down of their own accord, as it were, while others will continue to build up because the analyst's carefully planned behavior is designed to allow emotions to become fully visible to the patient. Some emotions, too, have a "naturally" limited life-span: in selecting passages to represent different feeling states in such interviews for examination of body movements, for example, episodes of overt anger were found to last a maximum of only about a minute and a half (Dittmann, 1962).

Probably the most unnoticed aspect of either an individual emotional message or an emotional episode is when it ends. At the beginning of this section I said that except for a few situations that are given over to emotional interchange, most emotional messages are embedded in situations of other sorts. The onset of such a message would then attract attention because it is something new. But it would have to be an unusual circumstance for the ending to be as commanding. To explain this, let me go back to the example of the work group we started out with. Things are going nicely, you will remember, and one of the people looks up and smiles. When the others see his head movement out of the corner of their eyes, they look up and take in the message. Even though the group is ready for this emotional message and it therefore cannot be described as a high-information one, still it is more unusual than another cognitive message would have been, one related to the work itself, since there have been many of these before the smile. Now how about the end of the message? The man looks back to the work at hand and so do the others. The next message concerns the work, just as many messages had before the smile. Thus this next message is a low-information one, since it is not different from those which preceded the smile. From this explanation we can also see what would make the change back to work-oriented messages convey more information: the building of a new and more recent context consisting of emotional messages. This would ordinarily take some time and involve the interchange of several messages, but it might also result from one very intense, probably inappro-

priate one, the ending of which might be marked in the group by a
sense or relief that this outburst is now over with.

FACTORS INTERFERING WITH EMOTIONAL COMMUNICATION

In the discussion so far about the process of transmitting emotional
messages in the social context, I have been writing as though, once it
was properly started, every message got through quite clearly. If the
receiving person has paid attention to the fact that there is a message, if
he is tuned in on the correct channel and knows the code into which the
message has been cast, then we have assumed that the message was
received with no further difficulty. This is, of course, a very idealized
state of affairs in comparison with what actually happens in social communicative situations. The questions we shall now take up concern
difficulties that arise to make crystal-clear emotional communication a
relative rarity. We shall still be trying to use the mathematical theory of
communication set forth by Shannon in our analysis of the problems, but
we shall find the going harder now. Social interaction uses far more
primitive communicative means than telecommunication to get its messages across, but at the same time it deals with infinitely more complicated
material. It may be expecting too much of a theory developed to deal
with the more straightforward field of telecommunication to cope with
the vagaries of social communication. Perhaps it will be able to handle
only minor aspects of our problems, but we shall see.

Interference in communication systems comes from many sources
and may take on many forms. In the outline of communication theory
in Chapter 2 we found that the main form of interference which the
theory treats of is random noise. "Random" in this context means that the
noise has no predictable pattern of frequency or amplitude. The sources
of this kind of noise may be natural or man-made: natural like light-
ning or other electrical disturbances in the atmosphere, or the thermal
noise resulting from the motion of molecules and smaller particles in
electrical components operating at normal temperatures; man-made noise
comes from motors and switches whose on-off cycles have no predictable
relationship to the signal we wish to send or receive. Since these noises are
random, they may interfere with our signal at any time, they may mask
a message element at any point, thus leading to errors at unknown loca-

tions. It seemed only reasonable to conclude, as engineers did before the time of Shannon's theory, that random noise would reduce the capacity of communication system to transmit the user's signals. Shannon found, however, that this conclusion is unwarranted, that there must be a way of coding the original information so that we can reduce the probability of error to the vanishing point in spite of the noise, provided only the rate of transmission of the signal itself does not exceed the system's capacity. This surprising twist on common sense led to the search for codes capable of approaching Shannon's theoretical result, and to the development of error-correcting codes. As we discovered when we discussed these codes in Chapter 2, we do not get something for nothing from Shannon's finding: the complications of the encoding and decoding may be more expensive than they are worth to get the full measure of benefit from the theoretical prediction. So compromises are sought which can beat the noise problem to some extent, at least, and provide error-free transmission somewhere between the commonsense and theoretical rates. The results have been a boon in many areas of telecommunication.

The question before us now is whether these theoretical findings, which were designed to apply to telecommunication, or to the use of machines for communicative purposes, can also be applied to face-to-face communication of emotional messages. To obtain an answer, we must first ask two prior questions: (1) is the noise we encounter in human communication anything like the random noise I have just been describing; and (2) if not, can the theory be applied to noise of any other description? Let us now take up these questions.

The Nature of Noise in Emotional Communication

The most general way to begin to answer the question of whether there is such a thing as random noise to interfere with emotional communication is to say that there are all kinds, random included. The main point at issue then becomes whether the random sources of noise are important sources, whether they interfere significantly with sending and receiving emotional messages. This is, of course, an empirical point. We will have to wait for a good deal more research before we can say we have any facts about it, even though a few studies can throw some light on the matter. First, let us think about random noise in human communication situations, and see if we can come up with some specific instances to talk about. We will do well to continue with the example of the smile during the work session, since we have filled in a number of details about it and it is familiar. Actually, it is not such a good example because the entire message consists of the one element, the smile; yet this fact itself is instructive.

The reason I have said that the smile in this case is not a good example is that it is such a short message. Its entirety could be said to consist of only one message element, or at most two, if the preparatory lifting of the head were considered an element. By contrast, messages in telecommunication contain hundreds and thousands of elements, consisting of coded numbers, letters, bits. Random noise, where it interferes with those messages, produces errors in some proportion of the entire number of units, and it is this fact which many error-correcting codes have capitalized upon, especially the systems of block encoding and decoding. Here the error-correcting elements added to the message can take up a small part of the total transmission, proportionately smaller and smaller as the source message is longer and longer. Where the total message consists of but one element, as in the emotional message in our example, on the other hand, the effects of random noise are to mask an entire message at random points in a larger interchange which contains many messages in addition to the emotional one. Error-correcting codes for that sort of emotional message would be impossible — but talking about error correction is jumping the gun before we have thought further about what sorts of random interference might affect messages like the smile.

Random events, as I see it, can interfere with the smile at the same two points I introduced in talking about tuning in on an emotional message in the first place: they could interfere with the observer's attention so that he is not in a position to see such a message if it should come along, or they could interfere with the interpretation of the smile as an emotional message. In the case of single-element messages like this one, which occur in the context of a social situation along with other types of message, there are many attention distracters. One of these can come along at any point in time, blocking attention to a brief emotional message being sent at that time. In the work group we have been using as an example, two of the workers might just before have been comparing notes about some implications of the results so far, and could now be thinking about how to follow up on them. For a short message like a smile, a much simpler distraction could effectively block the communication: a worker could be merely brushing a fleck of dust off the page in front if him and miss the smile. Now, how about longer messages? Visible tension in facial or other musculature may last for quite a time, or it may recur during a conversation. Other events competing for attention will happen to block reception of these messages at random points, but the message as a whole will get through if enough of its elements are noticed by the receiving person and are properly interpreted. Some of the competitors will take precedence over others because of what they mean personally to the receiving person. We talked about this in connection with levels of awareness in Chapter 4. Others will take precedence because of their own particular nature. Spoken language is the best example of this. Listening to speech is a very difficult task and demands a great deal of attention. Furthermore, there are times when it is more attention-demanding than others, as we saw in Chapter 5, when we discussed Ladefoged and Broadbent's (1960) interpretation of their data. After language, facial expression seems to come next as an attention absorber. Acts further down the line will be more liable to interference by these more commanding activities. To follow the line of reasoning set forth under channel capacity in Chapter 5, the differences have to do with communcative specificity: the more communicative, the more demanding of attention.

Once attention is focused, external events interfere with the reception of the message by making it difficult for the receiving person to identify the act as an emotional message. First, there can be interruptions because of the physical arrangement of the situation. In our example of the smiling worker, if he were facing toward some of his colleagues and away from others, these latter would not be able to see his smile even if they were attending to him. The lighting in the room might make it difficult to see a smile, too, and so on. But these are trivial interruptions in comparison with the ones involved in discriminating emotional from nonemotional messages in the ongoing social situation. Many acts can serve several different functions in communication. Smiling, as the sending person did in our example, can be a listener response like nodding the head or saying "Um-hmm" (See Dittmann & Llewellyn, 1968). These responses indicate to the speaker that the listener has heard, or has "understood." We have also observed lifting the head to serve the same function, as well as changing the line of regard and a number of other acts. Discriminating these communicative acts from emotional messages is the qualitative judgment we talked about earlier in this chapter in connection with how emotional messages get started. Random events in the communicative context may make this discrimination difficult, and lead to errors in transmitting emotional messages.

Now we have suddenly begun using the word "random" in a different way. When we were talking about attention just now, the random interfering events were thoughts or activities competing for the receiving person's attention, or other sorts of attention-demanding communication going on at the same time. These other events could be of any kind. What made them interfering was their distracting quality. But now, in regard to identifying an act as an emotional message, we are talking about discriminating it from other acts that look or sound very similar. In the case of multipurpose acts like a smile, which may at one point be an emotional message and at another a communicative marker, the discrimination is even more complicated. The smile that says "I am pleased" and the smile that says "I am listening" may be identical, and the observer must discriminate between them by the way they fit into the context, just as the listener must discriminate the word *scale* (which means "to climb") from the word *scale* (which means "instrument for measuring weight"). Emotional messages are composed of communicative elements and must be distinguished from other messages which are made up of the same or very similar elements. In these cases it does not make sense to call the interference random noise and think we are using the term "random" in the same sense that it is used in telecommunication. The interfering material is not random; it has regularities of its own which are understood perfectly well by the receiving person.

Messages whose information is more toward the expressive end of the continuum present the same problem when it comes to identifying them as emotional messages, even though they are basically simpler. Changes in tension level, changes in voice quality or in amount of fidgetiness, for example, are less likely than smiles and head nods to serve other communicative functions such as keeping the conversation going. But tension, too, can arise for a number of reasons other than emotional ones, and the look of tension or the sound of it might be identical no matter what brought it about. Worse yet, the contextual cues by which we tell the difference between smiles that serve different functions are more clear than those which are available in the case of signs of tension, making discriminations of the latter slower and less certain. This is only another way of saying that the information is not so densely packed in these continuous signals as it is in the more discrete and efficiently coded ones, but the problems of distinguishing emotional from nonemotional messages are the same in both. The interfering events may also be relatively low in information value, but they are not necessarily random events either.

Let us now sum up this thinking about the nature of noise in emotional communication. We have separated two points at which interference might make a problem, attending to the message and identifying it as an emotional message rather than some other kind. Attention may be blocked by a number of things: internally, by the thoughts and preoccupations of the receiving person; externally, by the competing demands made upon his attention by other simultaneous messages. The more communicative these other messages are relative to the emotional one, the more demanding they will be of the receiving person's attention, and the more distracting their presence will be. The events competing for attention, be they the receiving person's thoughts or other messages, may not be random each in its own right, but the fact of their existence, the time of their appearance, their demandingness — these may be random in relation to the emotional message at hand, and either block its reception entirely or introduce errors. The next task, that of identifying the message as an emotional one, I have called one of discriminating emotional from nonemotional events. This is a much more complicated process than directing one's attention to a message, and the sorts of events in which the emotional ones are embedded are not at all random, but have meanings of their own. When the elements of an emotional message are recurrences of other sorts of messages, as in long-term spoken language, the discrimination is particularly difficult, and attention to these elements, too, may be interfered with. It is no wonder, then, that so many of these go unnoticed in social interaction and require such complex procedures as content analysis for the research investigator to detect.

In answer to our original question about whether noise in emotional communication is like the noise that communication theory treats of, we must say "maybe," in relation to directing attention to the message, and "no," in relation to discriminating it from other messages. This conclusion, it must be noted, is based not upon research evidence but upon reasoning about the processes and events involved. It could be that in the course of future work we shall come upon some facts which will show randomness in some aspects of interference to emotional messages. For the present, however, it does not appear that we should count on it.

Communication in the Presence of Nonrandom Noise

We have concluded, then, that only part of the interference in transmitting and receiving emotional messages could possibly consist of random noise. We must therefore ask the second question we posed toward the beginning of this section on interference: can the coding theorem of communication theory be applied to interference other than random noise? When we talked about communication theory in Chapter 2, we noted that although the theory had been developed to account for random, that is, white, Gaussian noise, the results of the theory could be generalized to other forms of noise. Shannon (1949) gives approximations for non Gaussian noise, such as impulse noise, by comparing its effects with those of Gaussian noise, which he terms "the worst among all possible noises" (p. 20). He means by this that wherever noise is nonrandom, it must have some regularity that can be taken into account in combating it. There will be predictable times when the probability of error will be greater than for others, or there will be predictable types of error. The engineer can take these factors into account and design some way around the noise. With random noise, on the other hand, there is no predicting what the errors might be or when they might occur, and one must use devices such as error-correcting codes full time to make sure the right message gets across. Thus it is easier to transmit error-free messages through a system perturbed by nonrandom noise than by random noise, by designing coding systems specific to the noise at hand. Applying the theory to emotional communication, we should now be able to say that the task of discriminating emotional messages from other messages is less affected by interference than that of directing attention to the message in the first place. We should furthermore be able to find evidence that where it is done successfully in free social communication, it is accomplished by some specific coding system.

At the present time there is no direct evidence to call upon to show that coding leads to improvement in transmitting emotional messages. True, as I have described the problems of differentiating emotional from nonemotional messages in the last few paragraphs, I have said that communicative, discrete forms like language and facial expression are often easier to discriminate from their contexts than are the more expressive forms like signs of tension. This line of reasoning sounds eminently sensible, but as I have also said that it is not based upon research findings even though the reasoning might point the way to some research in the future. It is also true that the results of some existing studies can be interpreted in this way, as I interpreted P. Ekman's (1965) and ours (Dittmann, Parloff, & Boomer, 1965) in the section on classification of channels in Chapter 5. But there, too, I said that the interpretation was conjecture. What we really need is evidence that human channel capacity is effectively increased by the use of coding.

We can find such evidence only by going quite far afield. Remote as it is, it is still evidence, and while it does not concern emotional communication per se, it has very strong implications for this field. The field we shall go to for our data is human factors engineering or engineering psychology, and it should not be surprising that we do so, since those workers have used communication theory more than any others in psychology. Let us look again at the original use of the theory in psychology — Garner and Hake (1951) — in which the human being himself was considered a communication channel. Stimuli were viewed as sources to this channel, and responses as the user of the information transmitted (see Figure 3, Chapter 2). It is well known that in many situations where men and machines had to operate together, the amount of information fed to the human channel exceeds the channel's capacity to process it, sometimes with disastrous results. In the case of the airplane pilot, for example, a classical subject in much of this research, he is confronted with a staggering number of dials. He must interpret the readings from any of these continuously, especially during landing operations, in order to move the controls correctly so as to get the plane onto the field — and he must also differentiate among the controls and determine their effects on the events that are read out on the dials, thus making the whole process sound like a closed system. With modern, high-speed aircraft he must do even more than this: he must predict what the effect of the controls will be at some later time, since there is an appreciable lag between his actions and the aircraft's movements. In short, the pilot-channel is called upon to handle an enormous amount of information.

Engineering psychologists have made an important contribution to helping pilots and others who deal with complex machinery to increase their capacity to handle information. McCormick (1964) has reviewed a good deal of work in this field, and I shall draw upon his summary. Two examples will suffice to make the point — one from the input side, that is, stimuli to the operator from dials and other displays; the other from the output side, that is, controls by which the operator runs the machinery. Meters and dials of all sorts line the cockpit of the modern airplane like wallpaper. The pilot must have information about his altitude, speed, and the like, as well as about many conditions within the airplane itself. In order to use this information, he must have it in digital form, because everything else he must relate it to is in this form: the maps he uses show the mountain peaks he must avoid in digital form; the instructions to the engines show the many factors he must consider, like rate of fuel consumption and oil pressure, in digital form. If these data are not given him in digital terms by the dials he reads as he operates the plane, he must translate the dial readings into these terms before he can make use of them. In other words, he must code the information himself. Dials do part of this coding ordinarily, but not all of it. There are numbers along the scale swept by the pointer, and regular divisions between the numbers; but those divisions are not numbered, nor are the intermediate positions between them where the pointer might happen to be at some time when the pilot must make a reading. As he watches the pointer move across the dial, he must fill in those numbers by a process he calls interpolation. Thus the pilot is called upon to do that part of the coding involved in the interpolation, and to put his coding and the dial's coding together to yield a number he can use. Both speed and accuracy of display reading have been found in a number of studies to increase when the dial does all the coding and gives the results to the pilot in the form of numbers. Better yet is a combination of these numbers plus the pointer for quick rehearsal of the reading as the pilot's eyes jump from one dial to another during his work. We may conclude that where there are many interfering stimuli, the most complete coding means the greatest amount of information transmitted.

The second example is from the output or motor side of the human channel, from studies of the controls which the pilot must move to get the plane to perform the proper maneuvers. Often a number of control levers must be distinguished from each other, and visual cues may not be used because the pilot is using his visual attention to read all those dials. To make it possible for him to tell one control lever from another, studies have shown that the levers may be coded with differently shaped knobs. In some cases it is possible to tie these shapes symbolically with the functions which the levers control. In this way not only will the knobs be distinguishable from each other, but their functions will be identifiable, and errors in choice among them can be reduced even more. We may conclude again that coding has been demonstrated to increase the amount of information the channel may handle when there are many interferences to contend with.

In terms of communication theory, both of these types of study show that the human channel is capable of handling a great deal more information with more elaborate coding — and this despite the enormous amount of interfering input coming from every direction. We might conclude that Shannon's result that proper encoding can combat noise and make full use of channel capacity is applicable to human communication as well. I believe such a conclusion to be justified, but only at a very high level of abstraction. The crux of the difficulty in applying the theory more concretely lies in the conception of the human being as a channel, and in supposing that measures of his span of attention are in essence measures of his capacity as a channel. Recall that channel capacity in communication theory is made up of another factor in addition to the amount of information to be sent over the channel: that factor is time. The capacity of a channel is the rate of information it can handle. The experiments which led to the conclusions I have summarized above are hampered by their very nature when it comes to studying rates. The subject must respond to the stimulus in order for the experimenter to know if he perceived it correctly. If the experimenter wants to know if the subject's rate of information processing is any higher, he must either feed in stimuli that are each more information-laden, or he must speed up the presentation of the stimuli he is already using. If he does the former, the time it takes to present the stimulus and the time it takes to give the response are part of the total time, and prevent the experimenter from knowing how much time the human channel itself took to process the information. The experimenter can, of course, make some approximation of the time consumed by the channel and the experimental task, but he can never know for sure. If he presents the stimuli at higher speed before he asks for a response, he runs into the limitations of his subject's memory span, which may not be what he is interested in — or he may allow the subject time to group the incoming stimuli or, as G. A. Miller (1956) calls it, recode them, and operate at what seems to be a much higher transmission rate. Thus the finding that coding helps the operator to resist the interfering effects of extraneous input is not a direct application of Shannon's theoretical result about the noisy channel. Even so, however, it is an indirect application and the results are highly suggestive. Furthermore, this work on coding in human factors engineering could probably not have been done without Shannon's theory as a general guide, or it would not have been done for a long time.

Before we leave the topic of codes for combating noise, we should briefly examine the studies of language redundancy and ask about their relevance. Language is, to be sure, a type of code "designed" to transmit mesages between people, and the code imposes so many constraints that language has been estimated to have 50 to 75 per cent redundant information, at least as it occurs in writing. Garner (1962, Chapters 7 and 8) gives a very useful summary of research on language redundancy. Let us remember, though, that a code is a particular form of redundancy, where the constraints have been carefully planned to perform a particular job. Garner points out at some length that a given form of redundancy may be helpful for some purposes and harmful for others. It turns out that the redundancy in natural language does help in recognizing messages in the presence of noise, but there are several problems in interpreting these results. The most familiar words in a language are also redundant words, for example, so we might conclude merely that it is easy to recognize overlearned items. Just how all these complications apply to emotional messages is hard to say, because they probably do not have the structure which language has. At the present state of our knowledge we will do better to look in directions whose relevance is more obvious and whose pitfalls we might hope are less hazardous.

INTERFERENCE BETWEEN CHANNELS

Until now we have been talking about interference by extraneous noise, be it random or of some nonrandom character with a possible meaning of its own. We have been assuming that all sources, noise as well as signal, have been coming through on the same channel. Now we should consider the effects of different channels on each other. In telecommunication this is a much simpler problem, since there is a way around it. Channels in that context are usually frequency bands within which signals may be sent; and interference between channels, or crosstalk, is a matter of design of the equipment. Transmitters must operate so that their signals are confined to the frequency bands assigned to them, and receivers must be able to select only that band within which the desired signal is being transmitted, rejecting even very closely neighboring frequency bands. Things are not so easy in emotional communication, as I said at some length in Chapter 5. An observing person in an ordinary social interchange can shut out the visible channels while still receiving audible ones by simply diverting his eyes; but he cannot do the reverse, and within the visible or auditory classifications he cannot effectively reject one channel and still receive the others. The research investigator can do some of this selective receiving, but only at the expense of using fairly complicated equipment and taking a good deal of time in data analysis before he can recover the message. Still we all know that the social participant does select what he pays attention to. He concentrates on those channels which are most amenable to coded information, and in many cases he acts as if messages on some channels didn't exist. How does he do these things that seem manifestly impossible? After all, stimuli of all sorts are available to him, and not always in such quantity that he should be simply confused by them.

We are not helped by communication theory in dealing with questions like these. We met with this limitation of the theory at the end of Chapter 3, when we first struggled with the issue of qualitative versus quantitative information: it concerns measurement of quantities of information and its transmission, not the means of changing information into transmittable signals. The theory can tell the engineer how to measure the capacity of channels over which information is sent and received, but not how to send or receive on one channel rather than on another. The engineer already has a body of knowledge about maintaining frequency standards, about modulation techniques, about directional antenna systems. He uses communication theory to tell him which direction to go in capitalizing on this knowledge as he designs a system of communication. In the same way we shall have to turn elsewhere to account for selectivity among channels and for understanding the confusion that results when channels interfere with each other. In our case the processes are psychological ones, not electrical, and yet the most attractive psychological theory operates on an electrical model, one which looks rather like the input to a computer.

This is D. E. Broadbent's filter theory, most completely presented in his *Perception and Communication* (1958). The theory was also developed in the human factors context or engineering psychology, in studies not of the pilot in the cockpit of an airplane, but of the man in the control tower trying to keep track of all the signals from incoming planes. Broadbent and his colleagues began their work with auditory perception, and they have applied the thinking they developed to account for their results in order to design experiments involving other sense modalities. The application is not always easy. When Broadbent tries to generalize results on the difference between the two ears to the difference between hearing and vision, the conclusions sometimes seem rather tenuous. The problem is that it is difficult to design experiments which call for information of equal amounts presented, for example, to the ear and the eye, or to the ear and to skin senses. Workers in another field, audiovisual education, have tackled this problem more directly, and I shall refer to some of their results later in this chapter. The underlying principles set forth by Broadbent in his book are directly relevant to our present discussion of cross-talk between channels in emotional communication, and I shall present some of them in detail, since they really have to do with selective attention, a topic we came across earlier in this chapter when we were discussing how emotional messages get started.

Broadbent begins with the Garner-Hake assumption that the person, or the nervous system, as he puts it, acts as a single communication channel with a limited capacity for processing information. In Broadbent's conceptual scheme a selective filter is located ahead of this channel, and picks out what should go through the channel from among the various incoming sensory events. It is influenced both by the nature of the input signals and by the state of the organism. The relevant factors which increase the probability of information passing on to the perceptual channel are: (1) from the input side, (a) the physical intensity of the stimulus, (b) the novelty of the stimulus, that is, its information value, and (c) certain other characteristics specific to different stimuli (Broadbent documents these with considerable research evidence); and (2) from the side of the organism, (a) drive states, in that previously reinforcing stimuli are more likely to be admitted (this is less clearly established), and (b) conditional probabilities in long-term store, a later component in the system. Preceding the selective filter in Broadbent's flow diagram comes a short-term store, which can hold incoming information for a few seconds at most. Following the limited-capacity channel is a long-term store for holding conditional probabilities of past events. Through the operation of a feedback loop, these probabilities may then influence the selective filter, as mentioned: with this idea Broadbent explains very convincingly a number of puzzling facts in learning, such as the difficulty of extinguishing responses learned with partial reinforcement. The model goes on to say that information may return to the short-term store after passing through the limited-capacity channel, but that such looping takes up channel capacity the same as further incoming information. It should be noted that time, an essential to communication theory's definition of channel capacity, is included in Broadbent's conceptual scheme. The means of organizing all these processes and of stimulating effectors are beyond the channel and the long-term store in the flow diagram, and are not completely described in the theory.

Now let us see where all this leads us in our thinking about crosstalk. Since this is a perceptual theory, the limited capacity channel should be thought of as the perceptual system. The model then says that perception can be overloaded by sensory stimuli, and that selection takes place so that a manageable amount of information can be processed further. The capacities of a number of individual sense modalities and stimulus variables is well known by now. Garner gives some selected examples to illustrate the point (1962, pp. 63-75). But what happens when the perceptual system is presented with a number of stimuli at once or within a very short time? We have all heard, from common sense and from classical psychological experiments, that a person cannot attend to two things at once. The experiments reviewed by Broadbent indicate that this is too simple a statement. What a person cannot do is process too great an amount of information in too little time, or, in other words, exceed the capacity of the perceptual channel. Usually two separate stimuli or sets of stimuli do just this, but not always. When neither one of them conveys much information in itself, then both can be processed. When both stimuli are high in information value, they both suffer some loss in perception, or, in some cases, complete blockage of both. If they are unequal, and this important point is quite well supported by research evidence, the high-information stimulus gets through at the expense of the low-information one. A problem with the "at once" part of the familiar statement about attending to two things is that it may include the short time span necessary for the filter to select one stimulus and then shift to the other.

This very shifting takes up some of the channel capacity of the entire system. A disadvantage of the system, both for control tower operations and for the psychological experimenter, is that when the person is required to give a response to both stimuli, either by the job he is performing in the tower or for the experimenter in the laboratory, some time is needed by the short-term store to act as a sort of buffer register, as the person rehearses one response while giving the other. That the rehearsing takes up channel capacity has been firmly supported by later experimentation (see Posner & Rossman, 1965, for a summary of this work).

None of these conclusions is completely new to those familiar with the classical literature on attention, as Broadbent points out. But he goes on to say that his formulation is a more exact version of what was already known — and that a number of its parts were not known at all, such as the influence of the relative information values of competing stimuli on the likelihood of their being "perceived". The relevance of Broadbent's theory to cross-talk in our work on emotional communication is quite obvious: attention to messages coming in from the different sense modalities (or from two organs of the same modality, e.g., the two ears) applies directly to our thinking about attention to messages from different communication channels. The receiving person's ability to attend to all these messages is limited, and those channels which are most capable of attracting attention and those capable of handling messages of the highest information value take precedence in his attention, as selected by the process Broadbent has called the filter. In order to perform a selective function, the filter must be influenced by memory of how long it has been since that channel was used or since that sort of message came through. As a fairly long-term memory, it might also influence, and be influenced by, other factors, such as the wishes and fears of the receiving person. The idea of a short-term memory for temporary storage of incoming information awaiting processing is a very useful one for our thinking. It clarifies the problems involved in attending to messages whose elements are repetitions of messages, such as those of long-term spoken language.

There are a number of differences between Broadbent's theory and the one being presented here, differences that it will be useful for us to examine. One is that he takes the Garner-Hake position of channel as being contained within one person, its input being perceptions and its output being motor responses. This contrasts with our way of seeing the channel as a connecting link between two persons, with the motor responses of the first person being the channel's input and the perceptions of the other, its output. A consequence of our conception is that it enables us to see limitations in channel capacity at two points, input to the channel and output. Limitation at the input is easily seen in the case of speech: people can talk faster than usual when asked to, but not much. Listeners' ability to understand speech, on the other hand, is not so limited by its speed. We may artificially increase the speed of speech two to fivefold by clipping small time segments and eliminating hesitation pauses with little loss in intelligibility. Hence speech is more limited at the input of our channel, at the channel encoder, than at its output, at the channel decoder. On the other hand, the capacity of psychophysiological responses to transmit information is probably more limited at the output of the channel. Changes in these events can be quite rapid in the sending person, but these changes are difficult for the receiver to pay attention to or even to observe at all. Finally, in many cases there are limitations at both ends of the channel. Recall again the first criterion I used for including a means of expression in our list of channels: changes should occur rapidly enough to reflect moment-to-moment changes in feeling. Many changes, such as neatness of grooming, could not be produced any faster by the sending person than they could be observed by the receiver, or vice versa, so that channel

would be severely limited at both ends as a means for conveying
emotional messages.

Broadbent's theory concentrates on the receiving person's capacity
for processing incoming information from the various channels at his
disposal. After all, that is what he was studying when he developed the
theory. As I have just pointed out, however, there is a parallel capacity
in the sending person to transmit messages on different channels. Based
on a number of experiments in which different messages, sometimes
incompatible ones, were sent on different channels, we now know that
multiple transmission is possible. Broadbent is mute on this point, but
his theory is not necessarily inapplicable to it. The theory will need to
be extended to cover these instances, and just where various components
like filter, short-term store, and feedback loops will fit in we cannot say
until the relevant research has been done. Then we will have a more
balanced picture of the entire communication process.

When I began describing Broadbent's work, I noted that his experimental representative of different channels was the pair of organs of
the same sense modality, such as the two ears. Just how well that pair
compares to a pair of modalities was difficult to say from his evidence.
In quite another field there has been a good deal of work comparing
the visual and auditory senses, the field of audiovisual education. The
practical problem there is to determine on some basis other than artistic
preference what modes should be used to present material to students so
that they will get the most out of it. It is not surprising that most
of the research on the problem has been done with Broadbent's theory
as a model. Travers (1964) reviews a number of experiments by himself
and his students, which show that when the perceptual system is overloaded
multiplying inputs does not help. In fact, there is some loss from the
dual inputs if audio and video information are at all different, because
switching from one sense modality to another takes some time for the
function Broadbent calls the selective filter to perform, and this must
be subtracted from the total capacity of the system (see Reid, 1965).
Jester and Travers (1966) report that some subjects tried actively to
blot out one input or the other when the load was too great. These
investigators concluded that there is no improvement from presenting
the same material by means of two sense modalities, attractive as the
idea sounds to the uninitiated. Hsia (1968), on the other hand, found

that under certain conditions audio plus video presentation was more successful than either alone. These conditions were that the overlap between the two should be very carefully regulated so that the redundant information can be used to reduce errors. In this sense redundancy is a form of coding — in more general terms, of course, coding is a particular kind of redundancy, as was noted earlier in the case of language — and is used to combat whatever noise is present. If the total information the perceptual system is required to handle, the new information plus the planned redundant information, is beyond capacity, then adding the redundant information does no good.

From these studies we may conclude that Broadbent's conception of the perceptual system as a limited capacity channel applies to the situation where different sense modalities are the inputs, as well as to his original work on the two organs of the same modality. As a matter of fact, the various features of his model have been found to account for the results in so many experiments that we should consider it a well-established way of looking at the perceptual system.

SUMMARY: THE PROCESS OF TRANSMITTING EMOTIONAL MESSAGES

We began this chapter by tracing the life history of an emotional message, using a very simple one as an example, and discussing the many factors which enter in at each point. First, for the message to get across from sender to receiver, the latter must be paying attention to the former, and recognize that an emotional message is being sent. For this to happen the people must be well enough acquainted with each other's communicative habits to know when an emotional message is being sent. This acquaintance is made up of the same factors as the background data for evaluating the information in an emotional message: knowledge of cultural heritage plus knowledge of the more individual ways of expression. The content of this acquaintance, I have said, is a two-stage affair: first the channels which the other person habitually uses for emotional messages, and next the way he uses these channels — in other words, the codes he uses for his emotional messages. Early in an acquaintance, according to the argument presented, people will use more communicative codes so as to avoid misunderstandings;

later they branch out into more expressive means. For an emotional message to start, then, the receiver must be attending to the sender and know him well enough that he can be attuned to the message when it comes. Later stages in the life of the message are more difficult to talk about. The message itself may call for further ones, either from its originator or from others. And the end of a message usually goes unnoticed, since everyone's attention is drawn to the next message, which may be another emotional one or one of some other sort.

Our next topic was the sources of interference to transmission of emotional messages. From a communication theory standpoint, the most obvious of these to discuss is noise, because we would be eager to see if Shannon's most surprising result would hold for emotional communication. Can proper coding of emotional information at least partially circumvent the interfering effects of noise? Since the noise which communication theory deals with is random noise, we first looked carefully at our subject matter to see if any meaningful part of the interferences could be called random. We looked at two points at which there might be interference, paying attention to the message and identifying it as an emotional one rather than some other kind. The conclusion was that some things that interfere with attention might be called random, but interferences to discriminating emotional messages from others could not.

Using this conclusion, we looked next at the possibilities for combating nonrandom noise. Communication theory states that this type is easier to deal with than random noise; since it is nonrandom, it would have to contain some kind of regularity which could be taken account of in coding the material to be transmitted. In the absence of any research evidence on this matter in the field of emotional communication, we went to a quite distant territory to find some — to human factors engineering. There we learned that coding does help to increase channel capacity in the presence of nonrandom interference, but only if we consider the human being as a channel and the amount of material he can perceive accurately as his capacity. There are problems with this conception, chiefly because the essential ingredient of time is not included in it, so that channel capacity cannot be spoken of in terms of rate of transmission of information. Hence the results of communication theory apply here only at a very high level of abstraction.

As to the effects of cross-talk, or interference from one channel to another, we found that there was more to say. Communication theory does not help with this problem, since in telecommunication the solution may be found on a technical level. Our purposes are better served by Broadbent's theory of attention, in which a selective filter mediates between the various channels feeding in information and the perceptual processes which digest it. Broadbent, too, adheres to the human-as-chanel model, but for him rate of information processing is of paramount importance, and thus his conception of channel capacity is more like the original one. The important part of this theory for our topic is the basis on which the filter selects from the various channels competing for input to the perceptual system: the characteristics of the various signals, such as their relative intensity and their relative information value; and the state of the organism, such as drives and the history of reinforcement of those drives, and the history of what the filter has selected most recently. Broadbent's theory has its weaknesses when applied to emotional communication, e.g., its neglect of the motor side of the processes it spells out so well on the perceptual side. Consequently it does not help us in studying the selection of channels by the sending person, but the theory may be very useful in designing experiments on cross-talk among channels so far as the receiving person is concerned.

RESEARCH ON EMOTIONAL PROBLEMS ———

In Part I we looked at information measurement in emotional communication and at the process of transmitting messages in vivo between participants in the social situation. By the last chapter the key characters in the discussion were the participants and how they make use of the various cues and contexts in reading each others' emotional states. In Part II we leave the social situation and turn our attention to the research investigator's methods of studying emotional communication. What we see in the laboratory will be a good deal simpler, yet the principles are the same. Methods in social research are only sketches of the real thing, like stick figures, because we can take so few factors into account and because our methods are ponderously slow. We can consequently take these operations apart more thoroughly here and examine them in detail.

The general topic of Part II is precisely these operations. After an investigator has decided on what aspect of emotional communication he is going to study, he must choose methods for realizing his goal. His choice is based in large part upon how he conceptualizes the nature of the information he is studying. In Chapter 7 we shall look at some of the ways an investigator may think of his variables and how these make a difference both to the design of a study and to the interpretation of its results. The framework will come from the structural variables and classifications of channels explicated in Part I. Chapter 8 will take up more specific problems of strategy, those which arise in day-to-day laboratory work. While many of these are general in that they are with us no matter what we are investigating, some are more frequent in research on emotional communication because of the very nature of the subject matter.

Chapter Seven

Systematic Research Issues

The theoretical issues we shall take up in this chapter all stem from the structural variables introduced in Chapter 4, and from the classifications of channels first explained in Chapter 2 and given more detail in Chapter 5. The ones we will begin with are perhaps the more fundamental: they concern the ways an investigator may conceptualize the information source underlying the data he is collecting. They are basic because they determine the methods he will use to collect the data in the first place, as well as the methods he will analyze them with later on. The first of these issues is communicative specificity, closely related, as we have noted a number of times, to the channel classification of discrete versus continuous. The second is the other channel classification: constant versus possessing memory. Later on we will come to the second and third structural variables, level of awareness and intentional control, and the emphasis will be on how the investigator might get at these variables in his research.

COMMUNICATIVE SPECIFICITY

In Chapter 5 the description of communicative specificity as a variable began with Charles Morris's (1946) definition of language; it was stated that messages cast in terms most in line with that definition were the most communicative: they would be based upon a set of agreed-upon, systematically related signs, suitable for any occasion. In terms of communication theory, ideas expressed in highly communicative form have been coded for easy transmittal and understanding. Messages made up of less communicative elements, on the other hand, lack one or another of the

167

features of Morris's definition, perhaps first the system of connecting relations, or syntax, and then the universality of the elements. Messages at the expressive end of the continuum are not even made up of individual elements in the same sense; they are, rather, continuing changes of some bodily processes such as muscular tonus or intensity of activity. So at one extreme lie the truly communicative, discrete acts; at the other, the truly expressive or continuous activities or states.

We have already talked about the implications of this difference to the people who are trying to communicate with each other: more communicative messages convey more information and thus demand more attention of the beholder. Now how about the research investigator who is trying to observe and study the communicative situation? The main point I wish to make here involves a special case of a general problem of research, namely, that the investigator's concept of what he is observing dictates his methods of observation, and that the type of observations he makes, in turn, dictates the way he may analyze his data. As the principle is applied here, we must know in advance about the communicative specificity of the particular sort of messages we are interested in so that we may collect appropriate data and use an appropriate method of measurement and data analysis. Otherwise the measurement will be less precise than it needs to be and the resulting research will yield less information than it might be capable of.

In some cases it is easy to match the measurement techniques to the phenomenon under observation. In our laboratory, for example, we drew upon short-term spoken language in developing one part of an indexing system for interviews. Our "indicator" for the presence of emotion was simply the presence of names or references to emotions. This sort of information is the most discrete and categorical one could think of, comparable to the dots, dashes, and spaces of telegraphy. To be sure, some judgment was occasionally involved in identifying these emotion names since they are not inherently different from other words. In addition, from time to time there would be a phrase which one judge would identify as an emotion name while another judge would not. These, however, were rare exceptions. The number of emotion names mentioned in well over a hundred interviews was 336, a large but certainly manageable number of categories. The number could be reduced by noting the overlap among many of them and by combining synonymous words into fewer categories.

One could even be guided by some of the available results on the categories of emotion or on dimensionality, as reviewed in Chapter 3. The combining of categories is possible because of the very nature of words: the names *are* discrete categories and there is a finite number of them — be that number 300 or 30 or whatever as they are finally boiled down for data analysis. It would not make sense to treat them as though they were continua. As we have seen, there are few other events outside the short-term spoken language channel which can also be fitted into a framework of discrete categories, but there are many others which obviously cannot be treated in this way — degree of muscular tension, for example, and many other psychophysiological responses.

Many of us have gotten ourselves into trouble on this issue, however, by assuming that more of the behaviors that make up human communication are distributed discretely than may actually be the case. In part this is because of the results of recent research in language. These have been so revealing that we have been intrigued into supposing that the methods used in that research could be applied elsewhere in human communication. Consisting as it does of sounds and groupings of sounds which are separated in the minds of both speaker and hearer into discrete events, language is clearly a code which both have somehow agreed to use. The details of that code are far from clear, despite an enormous amount of very sophisticated work on it; but that fact only adds to our interest in, not to say awe of, the entire process. As we look at information transmitted by means other than language, it is only logical that we should try to conceptualize those other means in the same terms. The prime mover of this approach has been Birdwhistell, who has conceptualized the study of body movement and facial expression by the system he has called kinesics.*

In the past decade we have seen a flowering of research on communication by facial expression, body movement, and other behaviors, research which was stirred up largely by Birdwhistell's many presentations.

---

* An analysis related to the one presented below was developed as part of an assessment of the theoretical structure of kinesics in a review (Dittmann, 1971) of a recent book by Birdwhistell (1970). The present analysis is specifically devoted to those behaviors easily thought of as making up emotional messages, and is not limited, as is the earlier one, to body movement material.

He has been able to get the point across very forcefully that researchers in the past have missed the boat by concentrating on what people say and paying little attention to all the other things they do to communicate with each other. His methodological approach has been to assume that these behaviors, insofar as they are used for communication, are arranged like language, that they are discrete, categorical events which are put together in a way parallel to syntax and grammar. This is an oversimplified view of how people communicate. In the meantime there is by now a rich literature on these various other-than-language behaviors in communication, and we now examine them to see what we know of them from the standpoint of communicative specificity. The material will be presented in terms of the list of channels from Chapter 5. That list is inadequate in detail, however, especially for the body movement channel, and other classifications will be superimposed to cover the ground more usefully.

Short-term Spoken Language. As I have said many times in this book, and reiterated in the last few paragraphs, short-term spoken language is built for discrete, categorical information. But this propensity does not mean that continuous information cannot also be transmitted on this channel. The indexing scheme developed in our laboratory, using emotion names mentioned above, is an illustration of the discrete use of the channel. Another is Freud's (1901) discovery of certain types of tongue-slips as revealing unconscious processes, and George's (1959) method of finding unusual words and phrases in content analysis. In all these examples, words are completely communicative. Emotional information of a more expressive type, on the other hand, may also be conveyed by the nuances of which words and their combinations are capable. Wiener and Mehrabian's (1968) immediacy and Howe's (1970) grammatical qualifications are examples of research instruments using this sort of information. We need only one instance of nonimmediacy to recognize a speaker's feelings about his addressee or the topic he is talking about, and we need only one instance of a complicated set of qualifiers, yet in each case the measure is continuous. Usually, of course, a listener does not make up his mind so quickly about what he hears, but waits for further instances to add up. In that case we are talking not about short-term but about long-term spoken language — the difference between the two is often vague. The important point here is that even in short-term language, fine shadings of meaning are expressed by what appear on the surface to be quite discrete words. In sum, information of varying degrees of communicative specificity may be transmitted on this one channel, though weighted in frequency toward the communicative.

Long-term Spoken Language. Let us recall the differences between these first two channels: short-term spoken language consists of individual events, each of which can be understood by itself. The messages are complete as they are sent or as they arrive. Long-term spoken language, on the other hand, is made up of the patterning among groups of events. Here lies an important difference between the sorts of information one can expect to find on the two channels: short-term events, be they discrete or continuous, may be added up over a period of time to yield other information, which may itself turn out to be different in communicative specificity than the events that made it up. In the usual case the short-term events are discrete and the long-term message is continuous — as in content analysis, where words of a certain category are counted over some period of time and the total is considered an index of how "important" this category is to the author of the text, or of whether it is more important now than it was when he wrote that other text five years ago. We must keep in mind that the content analyst may derive some discrete information in the process as well: the very content categories he uses in his analysis may be visible only in the long term, for the individual events may fit together only after a number of them are collected. Most often, probably nothing new is added by this process. The content analyst who prides himself on being completely empirical will say that the text determines the categories; he means that no great inferential feat was needed to see what topics the author was writing about in the text. There are still important occasions where something new is added, where the short-term messages combine to lead the analyst to infer something quite different, and the appearance of this newly inferred fact is itself a single, discrete event, toward the communication end of the continuum of communicative specificity. Thus we may say that the long-term spoken language channel represents the whole range of the continuum, although probably in the majority of cases the information used on this channel is more expressive than communicative.

Vocalization. Several kinds of variables have been studied on this channel, and they must be treated separately in the present analysis. Those concerned with "tone of voice" have been both discrete and continuous. Dusenbury and Knower (1939) cast their "tone of voice" experiment in terms of eleven categories similar to those used later by Tomkins and McCarter (1964) and others. The high accuracy of judgments of acted portrayals while saying part of the alphabet, only slightly lower than that of their earlier results (Dusenbury & Knower, 1938) with facial expressions under the same conditions, indicates that both actors and observers are capable of finding discrete information on this channel. Such a conclusion is strengthened by another study done at about the same time. Fairbanks and Pronovost (1939) used five emotions for their actors to portray a standard-content passage, but they also included ambiguous readings in the stimulus material "to prevent the observers from deducing that only five different emotions were being portrayed" (p. 89). They gave the observers a list of twelve emotional states to choose from as they listened to the recordings. Accuracy of identifying the categories was still high. Kramer (1964) used the Fairbanks-Pronovost material for a similar study, and in addition used a sharp cut-off low pass filter to make the words unintelligible, and also had the passage translated for readings in Japanese.

To get at continuous information in "tone of voice", Starkweather (1956a) also used filtered speech and had judges make ratings of amount of emotion expressed and pleasantness. Waskow (1963) obtained ratings on four different scales from filtered speech. Both of these investigators were studying natural speech in real social situations, Starkweather of a Congressional hearing and Waskow of counseling interviews.

Studies of emotional information in speech other than tone of voice have included nonfluency and linguistically derived features as variables. Nonfluencies were first classified by Dibner (1956) and Mahl (1956), and these classifications were found to be highly related by Krause (1961). Krause and Pilisuk (1961) combined the Dibner and Mahl lists and found only a few to discriminate in a study of imagined anxiety. Boomer (1963) reclassified the Mahl list to take account of "linguistic and syntactical differences among the disturbances" (p. 264). Whatever the list, the disturbances have been used to form indices of "anxiety" or some related variable that can be compared across conditions or subjects. So while each instance of a nonfluency is a discrete event, the investigators have been less interested in the individual events than in the indices they have developed from them. The indices, of course, are continuous variables, and are always treated as continuous in data analysis.

The most influential figure in applying linguistic analysis to social and emotional communication research has been George Trager. Originally he expected all elements of speech to vary discretely, as phonemes do (see Trager & Smith, 1951), but as he examined more material it looked as if some features might better be conceptualized as varying continuously. These are the paralinguistic events (see Trager, 1958), superimposed upon those features of speech which are necessary for comprehension of "content". Pitch and loudness extremes, changes in tempo, voice openness, and the like, are included among the paralinguistic variables. So far only one pair of experiments has used paralanguage as a measure of anything like emotional tone or attitude. These are by Duncan and Rosenthal (1968) and Duncan and Rosenberg (1969), who rated various paralinguistic features and then averaged the ratings to obtain an index. Each individual rating was itself a continuous variable, and the final index, as an average of these, was also continuous.

We may conclude that the vocalization channel is capable of conveying information all along the continuum of communicative specificity. The particularly communicative messages found by Dusenbury and Knower, Fairbanks and Pronovost, and Kramer were obtained in a highly structured situation in which actors portrayed various emotions, and may thus not be completely representative of the way things happen in social interaction. More research has been done on the more expressive, continuous information, but whether this is any more representative must remain an open question at the present stage of the data in the field.

Facial Expression. We need not review this channel in great detail here, but refer back to the discussion in Chapter 3 about the kind of information available on this channel. The research on categories of emotion in facial expression shows clearly that people are able to send and receive very definitely communicative messages via facial behavior. The research on dimensions shows that quite expressive messages are also sent and received by these means. In addition, Leventhal and Sharp's (1965) research is another example of the use of an index made up of ratings of specific facial behaviors. Their measurement method is worth describing more completely since they have some relevant things to say about the discrete-continuous issue. Leventhal and Sharp used a notational system derived from Birdwhistell's (1952) as a starting point for their measuring instrument. The independent variables in the study centered around the increasing distress of labor in women delivering babies; the dependent variables were the facial expressions of the mothers, recorded during observations. The facial features which Birdwhistell covered — forehead and brow, eyes and eyelids, mouth and nose — were included in the study and specific symbols were developed from the more general ones he suggested. Leventhal and Sharp finally used the symbols within each facial area not as categories, but as items to be added up for a total index of distress, a continuous variable. The facial areas were analyzed separately to learn which ones provided significant amounts of information about the distress conditions. They found that the scores based upon the upper facial features (forehead and brow) differentiated among the increasing degrees of distress with advancing labor, while those from the lower features (mouth and nose) did not.

In their discussion (see especially pp. 315-316) they see their finding about the contrast between upper and lower facial features as being in accord with other research results in which upper features gave reliable information about intensity of feeling, and lower features about its quality — especially those qualities associated with the smile. Intensity of feeling, a continuous variable, is the keynote of the labor room — intensity of one quality of emotion, distress. It is this intensity that advances as labor progresses, not variety of emotional qualities. There would, of course, be different qualities of emotions in the labor room as well as intensities, for women interpret the childbirth experience in many different ways. Thus qualities would be more likely to vary between subjects, the error term of the analysis, not between stages of labor within subjects.

Body Movement. In comparison to the channels discussed so far, body movement is very complicated. There are many body areas to be moved, to begin with, and in many circumstances they can be moved quite independently. Where the whole body moves in concert, postural changes result, and the person may move toward or away from his conversational partner. In addition, one specific set of behaviors relating the two partners in conversation — eye contact — does not fit easily into any of the categories in the list of channels. Since it is related to certain body movements during speech, however, I have included it here.

Several body movements have been treated as discrete, categorical events in research. These are *head nods, gaze direction,* and certain body positions. Head nods (Dittmann & Llewellyn, 1968) are easily identifiable as responses of listeners to indicate keeping up with the conversation as in saying "Uh-huh" or "Yeah", and may be located quite precisely in relation to other events such as speech rhythms. In addition to the listening function, they also serve, in conjunction with other behaviors (the vocal listener response was specifically identified in our study), as conversation regulators in much the same way that Kendon (1967) found changes in gaze direction to do. Gaze direction, however, is a more complex set of behaviors, functioning more directly to indicate, as the person looks away from his partner, that he wishes to begin talking, for example. Of all the postural features studied so far, only *arm position* of standing persons, namely, the arms *akimbo* position (see Mehrabian, 1968a), can be called a discrete variable. Several other arm and trunk positions have been made into discrete variables by instructing actors to pose in discretely different positions (see James, 1932), but the underlying variables are continuous and have been measured directly as continuous variables in other studies (Mehrabian, 1968a, 1968b).

One of the most interesting possibilities for consideration as discrete body movements is to be found in the movements accompanying speech. Two distinct types of movements have been identified by Freedman and Hoffman (1967) and by Ekman and Friesen (1969b). Those most obviously related to ongoing speech are the object-focused movements (Freedman & Hoffman) or illustrators (Ekman & Friesen). Since many of them accompany the rhythmical features of speech, their onset and cessation are abrupt, with the result that they appear to be discrete movements. But now we are using the term "discrete" differently than we were just before. Until now "discrete" referred to the nature of the classification scheme: its categories are separate and non-overlapping if the variable is to be called discrete, and if the events being examined lend themselves to such classification, we say that the events are discrete. The head nod is a good example. A head movement either falls within the category of the nod or it does not. The movement could be separated in time from those preceding it, as object-focused movements are (most nods are, too), or it could be difficult to tell exactly when it starts. But in either case the movement may be classified according to the discrete category of nod. Whether object-focused movements are discrete in this sense is an open question. To begin with, there are many kinds of object-focused movements. Ekman and Friesen (1969b) and Freedman (1972) point out some of the issues which have to be taken into account in studying them. From what they say, it appears that some of these movements should probably be considered discrete and some continuous, but the data are not all in yet.

Among the discrete acts we have been discussing so far on the body movement channel, we find another feature of interest to their communicative specificity. It is like the difference between the short-term and long-term channels of spoken language: discrete events added up over a period of time can yield a continuously varying total. While Kendon has treated gaze direction as a discrete variable, for example, and has used as his data the events surrounding each instance of change in direction of gaze, Exline and his colleagues (Exline & Winters, 1965; Exline, Gray, & Schuette, 1965) have counted frequency of eye contact or measured the amount of time of eye contact between subjects over the period of time of an experimental condition lasting several minutes. These totals may then be used to compare different experimental conditions or types of subjects, or whatever.

Many inherently continuous variables have been studied in the body movement *channel. Body orientation*, or how squarely one person faces another; *body accessibility*, or whether the body is kept covered by the arms with legs close together, or relatively open; *body lean* toward or away from the partner; *distance* between conversational partners — all are continuous (Mehrabian, 1968a, 1968b). There may be discrete aspects to some of these, however, which the investigator should be on the lookout for: Garfinkel (1964) found that when one person comes up very close to another, the second becomes suddenly very upset, as if an offer of an intimacy were being strongly communicated whether the second person wanted it or not.

We may summarize the body movement channel by saying that there are a few behaviors which are discrete and many others which are continuous. In addition, many of the discrete events may be treated as continuous ones if they are grouped together and the totals are used as variables.

Psychophysiological Responses. We have very little to go on from the published literature to make much sense of this channel from a discrete-continuous point of view. Virtually everything I have seen is of continuous sources of information: heart rate, skin resistance, and so on down the channels of the polygraph — all are continuous variables. This also obtains for their few visible manifestations, such as obvious sweating, blushing, and the like. It may be that the question for this channel is: can there in principle be such a thing as a discrete variable? Perhaps some data will one day turn up to answer this question.

In this survey of the sorts of variables into which to cast the basic data of emotional messages, we have seen that the investigator must look carefully at the type of information yielded by the various behaviors. Whether that information is discrete or continuous, communicative or expressive, determines the form of his data. In the next step, data analysis, the type of information makes a difference, too. Psychologists very commonly make discrete variables out of data that are really continuous. They do this in order to use statistical methods which they have been brought up to believe are highly sophisticated, the most outstanding example being the analysis of variance. The danger of this procedure is that information is always lost in breaking up a continuum into step intervals, and we learned why in Chapter 2. Recall the first principle governing the amount of information possible in any message element: it is a direct function of the number of categories into which the message elements may be classified. How much information one is willing to sacrifice for the sake of categorization depends on the fidelity criterion he has set up for his results.

In research on emotional communication, of course, this may all seem like a rather precious overexactness. Our uncertainties of what to measure may be so great, and the possibility for artifacts so omnipresent, that the question of fidelity criterion may often more properly be turned around the other way: rather than worrying about how much information he might lose by categorizing, the investigator may well wonder how much loss there would have to be before he could even notice it through all the confusion around him. It is often obvious that we have lost information when we categorize in the extreme by dichotomizing an entire range — "high" muscle tension as compared with "low," for example. But for many studies it may not make much difference whether we end up with three or seven step intervals in the final measurements.

The fact is, however, that we have statistical methods for handling all sorts of data. In most experiments several variables are included in some form of factorial design. By analyzing all the variables at once, we are able to learn about the many interrelationships among them. If all the variables are continuous, we can recover the maximum information about their interrelationships by analyzing the intercorrelations among them. If the dependent variable is continuous and some of the independent variables are inherently discrete, it will then be necessary to reduce the remaining ones to discrete variables so that analysis of variance techniques may be applied. One thus loses the information of the metric only in those variables which have been categorized. Where the dependent variable is discrete, it is easiest to make all variables discrete and perform some multivariate analysis applicable to categories such as information transmission analysis. Garner and McGill (1956) have shown the relationship between these latter methods quite clearly. In short, we have quite a bit of leeway in fitting our analytic methods to the data on hand.

CONSTANCY OF INFORMATION SOURCES

We referred briefly to constancy versus possessing memory in Chapters 2 and 5 as a classification of channels. This means the relationship between probabilities of message elements and their sequence in the message as a whole: in the constant information source the probabilities are the same no matter when they occur, while in the source possessing memory the probability of any one message element occurring depends at least partly on the element that came before it. In both earlier chapters I said that common sense pointed strongly to considering all emotional messages as possessing memory — any message element in emotional communication would be strongly influenced by those which preceded it.

In this case, too, however, we must take an empirical position about the acceptance of such a commonsense conclusion. It may be true with respect to some variables under study, and not for others. An illustrative example is provided by my own recent study of body movement frequencies. Let me emphasize that the variable is *frequency* of movements over some finite period of time, and not the form or "meaning" of individual movements or types of movement. The movements we have examined are the nervous, jittery, fidgety movements which each person produces at a more or less constant rate, and which have been shown to vary in rate with feeling state or with mood or emotional involvement (Sainsbury,

1955; Dittmann, 1962). Our research on body movements came to a standstill because of a real question as to their independence — as a measurement device — from speech output (Boomer, 1963). Subsequent experimental results (Boomer and Dittmann, 1964) exonerated the original findings, but by then the relationship between speech and body movement took a different turn because of other theoretical developments. These concerned work with a unit of speech that is marked by the rhythmical or prosodic features of speech, a unit named the phonemic clause, first described by Trager and Smith (1951). It was to this unit that Boomer (1965) ordered the occurrence of hesitation forms in speech. He learned that hesitations were to be found predominantly at the outset of phonemic clauses. A similar analysis of movements (Dittmann & Llewellyn, 1969) showed that a similar ordering obtained for these phenomena as well, but with a slight difference. Rather than occurring chiefly at the beginnings of clauses, movements occurred at the beginnings of speech, whether the speaker was getting started on a clause, or on the fluent speech following a nonfluency within a clause. This relationship was examined for a large mass of material on three samples using two quite different data-recording methods — motion picture and accelerometer records of movements — and held up for all subjects. The actual amount of movement variance accounted for by the relationship, however, while statistically significant, was still relatively small: about 7 per cent. Thus it seemed that movements were quite independent of the effects of speech rhythm, although not entirely so.

A further analysis (Dittmann, 1972) showed where the lack of independence resided. This was an analysis of sequential probabilities of movements, to determine in what way the probability of movements as elements in a larger message are dependent on those preceding them. If there are sequentially dependent probabilities, then frequency of body movement should be considered an information source possessing memory. If not, then movements of the sort that can be picked up by our accelerometers would appear to be a constant source. Movements were coded in terms of their locations within the rhythmical structure of the phonemic clauses during which they appeared, and successive, overlapping pairs of them were tabulated for computation of contingent probabilities. Since the rhythmical components of the clause are sometimes broken up by nonfluencies, fluent and nonfluent clauses needed to be analyzed separately.

The rhythmical locations coded for fluent clauses were the juncture pause (if any); the main body of the clause; and the final part, including the stressed word or the final word of the clause (earlier research had shown that the stressed word *is* the final one in four-fifths of clauses). For nonfluent clauses they were the juncture pause (if any); the material before the nonfluency; the nonfluency itself; the material following the nonfluency; and the final part of the clause. The location of each movement was tabulated in relationship to the location of the movement following it. This second movement then became the first in the next pair to be tabulated, and so on. Movement pairs that were confined to the same clause were separated from those in which a juncture intervened between first and second movements, and also from those few cases where more than one juncture came between the two successive movements.

The basic finding of the analysis was that sequential probabilities for movement pairs which begin in fluent clauses are vastly different from those which begin in nonfluent clauses. Briefly, movements in fluent clauses behave like a constant information source, while those in nonfluent clauses appear to come from a source possessing memory. The details are interesting. Where the first movement of a pair comes in a fluent clause, the second movement is as likely as not to follow within the same clause. But if the first movement is in a nonfluent clause, the chances of the second movement's also appearing in that same clause are about two to one. Movements thus bunch up in nonfluent clauses. Further study leads to the conclusion that this bunching may be ascribed to the nonfluency itself. Where the first movement of a pair coincides with the material just before the nonfluency or along with the nonfluency, fully 62 per cent of second movements will occur before or during that same nonfluency. There seems to be a very rapid firing of movements whenever a nonfluency is on its way. Otherwise, movements appear at a leisurely rate which depends on the individual's style and on what emotional or other state he is in at the time.

Thus movements surrounding nonfluencies appear to be the source that possesses memory, while all other movements, both those in fluent clauses and those in the final fluent part of otherwise nonfluent clauses, may be regarded as a constant source. The amount of movement information lost to the movement-rhythm relationship is directly measurable by the methods developed by communication theorists (for a clear and concise statement of these methods — and of their pitfalls — see Binder & Wolin,

1964). The bunching of movements within nonfluent clauses means that some of the movement information is redundant, since it contributes less information than it could if the movements were spread out evenly. The amount of redundancy is 21.9 per cent. The comparable figure for fluent clauses is 5.3 per cent. The concentration of movements around the nonfluencies, themselves, yields even higher figures of redundancy, up to 50.2 per cent, for movement pairs where the first movement occurs just before the nonfluency. These results show dramatically that consideration of measurement methods in communication theory terms can tell us not only whether we are on the right track but also how much difference it makes.

The usefulness of knowing how much information was lost in those message elements which possess memory has yet to be tested in the case of this illustration. The direction to which the results point, however is obvious: if the investigator wants the information conveyed by the constant source of movements, he will then try to get rid of the apparently different source which overlaps to such a great extent with speech rhythm. With modern technology this is not as difficult as it sounds, since most of the nonfluencies that seem to induce movements consist of pauses, and these can be detected easily and used to control the apparatus for counting the movements. The details of such an application of the findings, however, are not so important here as the fact of the findings. This classification of information sources, constant versus possessing memory, was applied here as a way of looking at a measurement technique used for studying emotional communication so as to learn if the most effective use is being made of the technique. If we are to get as much as we can out of our measurements, we should look at other variables in the same way and apply what we learn to improving our measures.

OTHER STRUCTURAL VARIABLES

Communicative specificity and constancy are variables that were developed directly out of considerations of communication, both communication theory itself and linguistics. The remaining structural variables — level of awareness and intentional control — are old ones in psychology, and the systematic problems they present to the investigator are well known. This is not to say that the problems have all been solved: there are many loose ends in conceptualizing these variables in research generally, and a number of specific problems in applying them to research in emotional communication. It is these latter that I shall try to explicate here.

Level of Awareness

The most obvious systematic issue connected with the variable of level of awareness is that it consists of two dimensions, aware-repressed and aware-subliminal. It is important to keep these two separated in any research; for even though their results are superficially similar, they imply quite different things about the individual who is the subject in the research and about what he may be expected to do next. Whether he is repressing knowledge of an emotional message or cannot see or hear it, the overt result is that the message is not there for him. If it is subliminal, then an increase in its intensity (or its duration, or whatever) will enable him to perceive it and react to it. If, on the other hand, he is witholding it from awareness through repressive maneuvers, he may still not perceive it even if its intensity increases markedly. In the case of high stimulus levels it is easy to tell the difference between the subject who is repressing and the one who is not, and there really is no systematic problem in keeping the two dimensions straight. In the not-so-extreme case the difference is not so obvious, and opportunities for muddy thinking abound.

Chief among these is the old familiar logical fallacy of affirming the consequent in a syllogism: if a subject is repressing, then he will not recognize the message despite several increases in its intensity; this subject has not recognized the message after a number of increases in intensity; therefore he is repressing. When we look at this reasoning coldly and logically, we all know that it is wrong. Subjects may not recognize a message for other reasons than those which have to do with the variable of level of awareness in either of its dimensions. A key reason centers around whether the subject is paying attention to the stimulus person or to that aspect of his behavior where an emotional message might be perceived. Attention by now is a familiar theme here. It came up quite early in the exposition of the aware-subliminal continuum in Chapter 4, and led to a brief discussion of the decision theory model for conceptualizing thresholds as compared with the model of classical psychophysical methods. It came up again in Chapter 6, first in connection with how an emotional message gets started in the social situation, and later in listing factors that interfere with emotional communication.

In the laboratory, as in the social situation, there are also extraneous stimuli, all competing for the subject's attention. Some of these the experimenter takes into account in analyzing his data, and some he misses. The obvious ones he tries to control: by telling the subject where to look in the apparatus, by providing only one other person for him to interact with, by limiting the task to only certain kinds of message, and the like. But the subject often misunderstands, and may bring to any given trial in the experiment a set left over from the last trial or the last social situation he was involved in. More importantly, he may try to guess the experimenter's "real intentions" and not hear the instructions, much less attend to the stimulus the experimenter hopes he will concentrate on. Thus attention is as important for receiving emotional messages in the laboratory as it is in the social situation, and many lapses of attention will be interpreted as problems of awareness.

The discussion thus far makes it seem hopeless for the research investigator to know, when a subject does not respond to given stimulus, whether he is paying attention or not, or if so, whether the stimulus is being repressed or is below the subject's threshold. All the investigator has to go on is the subject's behavior: he does not respond. From there on the researcher, like the participant in the social situation trying to read emotions, must infer the reason for the lack of response. If he is not to be satisfied by pure guessing, the researcher has to seek outside information to help him make the correct inference. The nature of repression furnishes him with some means for increasing his chances for success when repression is involved. Repression is not instituted randomly against recognition of all sorts of material, but selectively against ideas, feelings, or representations of things the person is disturbed about. Thus only emotional messages which themselves stir up an emotional response will be cast out of awareness through repression. The research investigator can make use of this fact by looking for emotional concomitants of the subject's absence of response. If he finds some evidence of upset in the subject, by whatever means the investigator has to collect this evidence, he can then be more sure that repression is at work. If he finds no such evidence, of course, he cannot say simply that the lack of response is due to some factor other than repression, since there may be some emotional reaction the experimenter cannot read. But he has looked for outside evidence, and conclusions are therefore on safer ground. Other outside evidence may come from marked inconsistencies between the message and other behavior the subject is engaged in. A person may produce obviously emotional behavior, but at the same time do other things to indicate that he has not the slightest idea that he is producing such a message. Inconsistent communications on different channels are especially susceptible to this interpretation. Still other outside evidence may come from the subject's later behavior, but this begins to tread on dangerous ground — first, because retrospection on matters as evanescent as feelings is subject to many well-known ills, and, second, because some research designs base their dependent variables on the following responses and would thereby be confounded. A final, more general outside evidence comes from the experimenter's experience with how subjects have behaved in his experiment before, and, in the case of any individual subject, how he himself has behaved in previous trials in the experiment.

In short, the experimenter is not completely helpless in differentiating the two dimensions of level of awareness, even though he cannot be entirely sure of his conclusions in all cases. Having made the distinction, or at least having made a stab at it, the researcher is next faced with the problems of using the two dimensions of repression and perceptual sensitivity in describing the emotional messages he is interested in studying. As I have observed, the topics are old ones in psychology: limens were at the very root of the development of a scientific psychology, and repression was a sort of touchstone of the struggle to admit psychoanalytic principles to the psychology laboratory. Many studies of repression have been done in the field of perception, and would seem to offer ready-made models for studies of repression in emotional expression. I believe, however, that there are some basic differences between the old repression studies and what we are discussing here: many of the early studies of repression had as their aim either to demonstrate or to deny repressive forces, to show that repression exists or that it doesn't. All effort was concentrated on this one phenomenon. In research on emotional expression, on the other hand, repression is one factor among many which join to determine the effectiveness of a communication, and it interacts at every point with the other factors. In the context of the present discussion, repressive forces affect limens by altering the criteria by which subjects make their judgments. Even before that it affects the extent to which subjects pay attention to the stimuli presented by the experimenter. And the stimuli themselves are often so fleeting and the repressive mechanism so fast that the time available for the experimenter to make his observations may be almost infinitesimally short.

Let us turn now to some illustrations of the principles I have been developing. The most extensive analyses of awareness in messages have been done by content analysis of verbal material, and I shall only refer to a few of these here, for the techniques are well known and I discussed them at greater length in Chapter 4. There are in addition analyses of other material which I shall review more fully, since the investigators' solutions of the methodological problems involved are instructive.

Illustrating a point by referring to content analysis has the disadvantage that it restricts us almost entirely to long-term spoken language as a channel of emotional communication. More than that, most studies using content analysis are not about face-to-face communication of immediate feelings, but about longer-term expressions of what might better be called character traits and motivational structures. Still, in some studies we can see how inconsistency of expression, one of the main criteria of repression, is detected, both in the sending person and in the receiver. I shall use as my example here the project reported by Coffey et al. (1950) and by Freedman et al. (1951), since in that work the procedures of the investigators are spelled out in clearest detail. In their system of analysis three levels of personality are separated, and are called the Public, the Conscious, and the Private levels. The Public Level is seen through the subject's actual behavior toward others in a group situation — in this case, group psychotherapy sessions. The data are judgments by observers who listen to recordings of the sessions and code interactions according to a scheme of two dimensions, one of which is an affective one. This is the familiar circular system first set forth by Freedman et al., and which appears in several subsequent publications by Leary. The Conscious Level is also conceptualized in the same circular form, but the data come not from what the subject does to the others in the group, but from what he says about himself or about people who are important to him. Most of these descriptions are presumably fully available to his awareness — although of course their long-term trends might not be. The Private Level resembles the Conscious, only the data come from how the subject describes the hero and those the hero interacts with in TAT stories and dreams.

On the surface it might seem that events at the Public and Conscious levels would be available to the subject's awareness, and those at the Private Level would be repressed. This is not the way the system of analysis works, however. It works rather through analysis of discrepencies between the Conscious Level and the other two. If the profile of Public and Conscious levels are similar — if, for example, the subject says he is a friendly person and indeed the predominant affect of his interactions toward others in the group is friendly — then we say that this sort of message is within his awareness. If, however, he describes himself as friendly and yet actually behaves hostilely toward others, we say that the hostile expression is not within his awareness. We say further that he has repressed these expressions if we judge that they come so often and so intensely that they should be above his sensory threshold. This is not simply a matter of the social undesirability of hostility, incidentally: some people value hostile expression as a sign of "strength of character" and may be quite consistent on the matter at the Public and Conscious levels. The same sort of analysis is made of the comparison of dream and projective material with respect to level of awareness, but is not so directly relevant to our theme.

Another example of content analysis as a source of inference about repression is provided by Osgood (1959). In explaining the procedures of contingency analysis (defined briefly in Chapter 4), Osgood illustrates its use in clinical work by the analysis of a set of psychotherapy interviews. Content categories that are mentioned together more often than chance are clearly associated in the patient's thinking. Those which occur together far less often than chance are said to be dissociated. An obvious interpretation of these latter instances is that there is some unconscious avoidance of the implications of any possible association between these topics, because of fear or whatever. Osgood is careful to point out, however, that one cannot make an automatic interpretation of negative contingencies: "The contingency method provides evidence for nonchance structure; interpretation of this structure is still the job of the skilled analyst." (p. 75).

Analyses of material other than verbal from the standpoint of awareness are much rarer than the content analyses we have just been reviewing. I shall confine my remarks to two studies, since they will suffice to illustrate the methodological problems involved. The first is one of the series by Krout (1935) on what he calls autistic gestures. The main body of his work is concerned with hand gestures, but the study outlined here includes some other types as well. It was Krout's impression that people are not aware of the movements they produce, and that they do not notice those of other people either. Even so, he felt that these movements had symbolic significance based usually on the individual's own personal history. In addition he showed in a later study (1954a, 1954b) that some gestures are commonly enough associated with specific emotional themes that they might well serve communicative purposes. But an explanation of that study would take us far afield from our present topic. The question here is what evidence he had that gestures are produced out of awareness and are not noticed by other people.

The most direct evidence is anecdotal. Krout found in his experiments that subjects had to be kept naive about what the observers in experiments were recording; for if they thought their gestures were being observed, they paid closer attention to what they were doing and inhibited their movements. He also found that in ordinary circumstances subjects could not recall what their movements had been a short time before, and that observers had to be specially trained to see movements. The systematic evidence, though indirect, pointed to the conclusion that gestures have symbolic meaning connected with anxiety-laden conflicts which lead people to keep their occurrence out of awareness. In one study subjects were asked to associate to the names of 160 gestures, and then later to imagine someone performing each gesture and associate to that image. In the first task only the most superficial associations usually came to the subjects' minds, often a simple restatement of the description. At the same time a number of idiosyncratic responses occurred to several of the items on the list. To the images of someone performing the movements, subjects very often blocked completely and did not complete the task. Krout concluded that:

> ... intimate complexes can be touched off in the process of free-associating to gesture-stimuli, and gestures are thus probably charged with emotion ... with the result that gestures cannot be interpreted by conscious procedures, and that they are apparently difficult to approach by any technique because of the conflicts which they are likely to set off (1935, p. 33).

Krout then went on to an ingenious experiment to demonstrate the emotional aspects of gestures. Each subject was observed in a classroom by two observers who noted each gesture produced by the subject while the lecture was going on. Along with the notation of the gesture itself, the observers also recorded the words said by the instructor just beforehand. Then in the laboratory the subjects were given a list of words to associate to, some of which came from the classroom situation (the crucial words) and some of which were drawn from the Kent-Rosanoff list (the controls). The subjects were instructed to associate to the words, and a number of measures were taken of their responses. Reaction times were uniformly greater in the responses to the crucial words, on the average by a factor of over 1½ to 1, and signs of "complexes" associated with the crucial words were also more frequent. A number of controls were instituted to insure these results, but their analysis was only at the level of the psychological statistics of that time, and the data were not completely enough presented for reanalysis. Nevertheless, from the data presented, the results seemed to hold up; the subjects' movements were apparently responses to emotional stimuli. Krout concluded that his conception of gestures had been supported. He put it this way:

> The theory of autistic gestures is that, in the presence of conflict and blockage, there may be an escape of impulses into effector-systems which, were the impulses uninhibited, would provide normal outlets for them (1935, p. 120).

This conception is very much like Luria's (1932) idea of spillover of cognitive tension into the motor sphere, and Krout refers to that work. He later used the idea to build an experimental situation to produce larger numbers of gestures, and found, as I mentioned above, some identifiable emotion-gesture combinations. There, too, the subjects appeared to be largely unaware that they were making these movements, though they seemed to be wary enough about them that the experimenters had to say that they were recording verbal responses in order to prevent the subjects from inhibiting their movements.

The practical problems of doing this sort of research are enormous, and it is no wonder that Krout's approach has lain fallow these many years. Only very recently, with the advent of more advanced methods of handling motion picture film and the possibility of controlling videotape machines by computers, has anything been done even in the same general area as Krout's research. I refer here to the work on Micromomentary Facial Expressions, or MMEs (Haggard & Isaacs, 1966), and to the System for Classification and Analysis of Nonverbal Behavior, or SCAN (Ekman, Friesen, & Taussig, 1969). Both of these have direct reference to the level of awareness issue. Haggard and Isaacs' work with motion picture films of interviews was discussed in Chapter 4. Both dimensions of awareness are involved here: the expressions occur so fast that they are invisible at ordinary speeds of projection. On the other hand, the authors raise the question of whether the expressions are really subliminal, or not noticed because we have learned not to notice them by some ego mechanism akin to perceptual defense. This is from the side of the viewer and by extension of the research investigator. Haggard and Isaacs have indeed provided the researcher with a method for getting at these messages, but the researcher may need some way of telling whether their production is conscious or not on the part of the sender, too. Here things are even less clear. The subject himself is probably not aware of the expressions, and Haggard and Isaacs postulate a type of ego mechanism to explain this, called temporal censorship.

> . . . the MME may serve as a safety valve to permit at least the very brief expression of unacceptable impulses and affects. From this point of view the MMEs have a double benefit to the individual: he may indulge in some impulse expression with minimal risk of retaliation or rejection by the observer, and without arousing the anxiety that would ensue if he himself were aware of, or of having expressed, the unacceptable impulse or affect (p. 165).

A hint of how these processes might be studied may be seen in the finding that the expressions tended to be incompatible with those which preceded and followed them in the context of the interview.

Ekman and Friesen (1968) have taken on the most ambitious project of determining the meaning of movements. They take as their basic records the behaviors of patients in actual interviews. Briefly the program, as they put it:

... applied to each body area separately, isolates each movement in terms of beginning and end points and then, through paired comparison procedures, groups movements similar is visual appearance into act types. The SCAN output for each body area lists the location, duration and classification of each act (p. 198).

The locations can then be referred to other variables, such as time in the course of the patient's treatment, content under discussion, or whatever. Only very small amounts of material have been analyzed in this way so far, since the recording medium for the first efforts was the motion picture and the investigators were working by hand. They now have a computer-controlled videotape chain by which they will be able to cover far more territory (see Ekman, Friesen & Taussig, 1969, for more detailed description).

Ekman and Friesen relate movements of different body areas and of different forms within body areas to concurrent verbal material in their 1968 study. Sometimes similar emotions are expressed both verbally and nonverbally, and sometimes not. When they are not, the question is whether the message expressed in movements is unconscious. Mere comparison of the verbal and nonverbal cannot answer this question. Certain incompatibilities that would imply nonawareness can be looked for, as in a content analysis, or the patient could be asked later on. Ekman and Friesen did ask one of their patients, and all the types of movement had a familiar ring to her save one — and that was the one which was most difficult for the investigators to interpret, too, since it did not have a consistent topic of content attached to it. We will need a good deal more exploration in this area before we can make definitive statements about methods for getting at the two continua of level of awareness, and the apparatus and program Ekman and Friesen have developed offer hope that this work is under way.

Intentional Control

The systematic problems connected with research on intentional control are no less difficult than those we have just been discussing under level of awareness, but we shall need less space for their exposition because there has been very little empirical work to back up what we can say. Most of the available references are two studies using content analysis, where one of the chief goals is to discover the motivations of the communicator, especially in analyzing propaganda materials. In Berelson's (1952) early but still valuable review of the content analysis literature, intent figures in two of the three assumptions which he posits as underlying the method: first, "that inferences about the relationship between intent and content ... can validly be made" (p. 18), and second, "that the 'meanings' which [the content analyst] ascribes to the content ... correspond to the 'meanings' intended by the communicator and/or understood by the audience" (p. 19). And among the five major uses of content analysis which Berelson has found in his survey, one is "to identify the intentions and other characteristics of the communicators" (pp. 72 ff.). Intentions are thus only one among a number of other characteristics which the content analyst tries to make inferences about. Personality traits, psychological states, changes in tension level — the content analyst is also interested in information about these.

In working with propaganda the analyst assumes that the material has been planned carefully in the light of policy decisions made by the rulers of the country concerned. By studying the propaganda systematically, the analyst hopes to learn of these plans and infer the underlying policy. A good example is cited by George (1959) from World War II, when a division of the Federal Communications Commission examined the Nazi propaganda output from broadcasts and newspapers. At the time when Mussolini tried to reestablish a fascist goverment to fight alongside the Germans, the Nazi propaganda was at first very enthusiastic, but within a few days a note of caution was injected into the stories in a few newspapers. These were taken by the FCC analysts to mean that the top German command did not wish its people to expect too much from the new fascist government. A change of policy regarding the possibilities for Italian support of the German war effort was thus predicted, a change later verified by entries in the Goebbels diary when it was recovered at the end of the war (Lochner, 1948). In this case, then, the intention of the propagandists was read through the appearance of new information in their communications, information which was inconsistent with their earlier statements, but which was quite in line with the change in plans of what they now wished the people to believe. These plans or intentions, in turn, reflected new policy in the way the war was to be conducted, and knowledge of these changes could be used in military planning on the Allied side.

The analysis made by the FCC content analysts of the German propaganda material is a good representative of the method George (1959) advocates for content analysis. He calls it a nonfrequency approach, which he contrasts with the original methods of categorizing content and counting the frequencies of each category. What he relies upon for his data is precisely what the social participant relies on as he is receiving messages from his conversational partner, namely, the appearance of something new or unusual in the content, something which may occur only infrequently, perhaps only once, and which tips him off that a message of high information value is at hand. The research investigator observing the whole proceeding will also use this approach in part as a way of learning about the communicator's intent. Fearing (1953) listed this as the second method by which the researcher learns about intention. His first method is stated somewhat vaguely as "statements by or information about communicators" (p. 81). As I understand "statements by communicators," Fearing supposes that one can ask the communicator what he intended to say and accept his answer at face value. According to the reasoning we have been following, this is certainly a feasible procedure, but yields results only when the communicator is aware of what his intentions are and is willing to tell the investigator about them. Otherwise the investigator must rely upon "information about the communicator," in Fearing's words. This, it seems to me, returns him to methods of content analysis, or to whatever information he can derive from other channels the communicator is using at the same time. If the messages from various channels are inconsistent, the investigator will not know where to turn.

Since the work that led Fearing to the thoughts which finally appeared in this article had been on mass media, not on face-to-face social interaction, his remarks about methodology are more cogent to the former than to the latter. But the formulation of intent which he gave earlier in the paper provides a valuable methodological cue for getting at what I call intentional control. Recall that, for Fearing, the idea of intent refers to the directedness of communication, to the communicator's planning for his message to elicit some effect on the person or persons receiving it. Thus the communicator, to the extent that he is exercising this planning and control, focuses his attention upon the receiver to see if the intended effect has come about. Nowadays the research investigator has good techniques for seeing how closely the sending person is following his receiver's reactions, as provided by mutual glances (see Exline, Gray, & Schuette, 1965; Exile & Winters, 1965; Kendon, 1967; Cranach, 1971). The relationship between mutual glance and intentional control is not a simple one: a subject who believes that the interviewer thinks badly of him looks at this interviewer less (Exline & Winters), as does the subject who is asked embarrassing questions (Exline, Gray, & Schuette). Nevertheless, in a study of the finer details of gazes, Kendon (pp. 53 ff.) posited as a major function of gaze direction a monitoring one, in which the subject gathers information about the behavior of his conversational partner, checking to see at key points if he is still attending, and presumably to see how he is taking whatever message the subject is trying to get across. Kendon is careful to point out that all we can tell with the methods used to study gaze direction to date is whether the person is looking, not specifically what he is looking at or looking for as he glances at the other person. Other methods would have to be added, as well as other experimental conditions, to get at these issues. But my point is that Fearing's conceptualization of intent as the communicator's planning focused upon the receiving person, plus the more recent technical innovations in research on visual behavior, points the way to study of intentional control.

Before we close the discussion of Fearing's contribution to measurement of this structural variable on such an optimistic note, we need to remember another aspect of intentional control as it was presented in Chapter 4, and this complicates matters considerably. This is that the sending person himself is one of the receivers on whose reactions a great deal of attention is focused. "What sort of a person am I," he asks himself, "if I feel such-and-such in this situation?" True, he assumes that other people share his values and he watches for their reactions accordingly, and to this extent we can study his intentions through that behavior. But he can often exercise controls over his own responses even before they are expressed, and the research investigator will miss this planning unless it manifests itself in some other way that can be clearly attributed to controls from within. This last point, of course, is the methodological stinger: suppose that the visible manifestation of all this inner activity is a lapse of attention to the ongoing conversation, so that the subject's next statement is a bit out of context. The researcher observing this event will have to make some inference about it which will lead him to the correct interpretation. Lapses of attention can occur for many different reasons — a special intellectual interest in that point back there in the conversation, for instance, about which there is no particular need to control emotional responses. The researcher cannot be sure, and will probably conclude that he will best confine his efforts to the study of the subject's attention to others if he wants any good information about intentions.

Some additional leads to measurements of intentional control are given by Ekman and Friesen's (1969a) study of the mechanisms involved in deception. These writers reason that control is most carefully exercised over those channels which have the highest capacity and which are ordinarily attended to most closely by others. Thus the face is most subject to inhibition and dissimulation and provides the fewest cues to deception, while the legs and feet are least responded to and least subject to conscious control, and are thus a good source of leakage cues. The hands give an intermediate source of information about deception. A preliminary examination of these ideas contrasted head and body cues, using films of interviews with patients who were trying to give the impression of being in much better shape than they actually were. Adjectives consistently checked by viewers of the patients' heads painted much more healthy pictures than these derived from the patients' bodies only. The idea of deception sounds like conscious, deliberate control, but in one of the patients this did not seem to be the case: her interviewer was impressed that she was still suffering considerable anxiety despite her initial improvement since admission to the hospital, and she herself substantiated his impression during a later discussion. At the time of the interview, then, she seemed to be trying to deceive herself as much as her interviewer about her condition. Ekman and Friesen are continuing to work on the deception situation, using more refined methods, and their developments may be expected to make a substantial contribution to our understanding and methods for studying control over emotional expression.

Summary: Systematic Issues in Research
on Emotional Communication

One of the important results of theorizing in the way we have
been doing throughout this book is that it leads us to look not only at
our results, but also at our research methods, from the standpoint of
that theory. In this chapter we have examined a number of methodological
problems in the area of emotional communication, based upon issues
which grow out of the way the investigator thinks about what he is
studying. In each case we have traced the results of confusions about the
issues in terms of the resulting measurement problems.

Four systematic issues were identified. The first was related to
communicative specificity. Starting from the premise that it is important
for the investigator to know about the nature of the information source
of his data before he starts his measurements, we examined the growing
literature on behaviors that might convey emotional messages from the
standpoint of their communicative specificity. The way of classifying the
research was the list of channels first explicated in Chapter 5. We found
that in the first channel, short-term spoken language, most of the information is communicative, as we might expect from the definition of this
structural variable. In the last channel, psychophysiological responses,
everything studied so far is at the expressive end of the continuum. For
all the other channels the events measured so far lie at various points
between the communicative and the expressive — more communicative
events in facial expression, more expressive events in long-term spoken
language and body movement. We then examined briefly one of the consequences of knowing what sort of events one is studying: the methods
one uses in analyzing the data.

Another systematic problem area was the classification of sources
as constant or possessing memory. It confronts the investigator with a
problem much like that of communicative specificity, although less is
known about it in human communication. We probably accept as a given
that in most acts which we see in studying emotional communication,
the probability of each act depends largely upon what type of act
preceded it. Where they do depend on each other in this way, some
redundancy is involved, and we can get less than maximum information
from our measures. But this sort of redundancy may turn out to be tied

to some quite circumscribed relationship with another variable. It is therefore worth an investigator's while to examine his variables in advance from the standpoint of their constancy. Then he can know if he will encounter inevitable loss of information — or if he has just been thinking about his research question in an inefficient way.

Two other systematic problems largely concerned measurement: how do you measure just one variable and avoid confusing it with others? The first of these was level of awareness, which has the additional problem of really being two dimensions or variables. Content analysis methods have been used to measure the repression side of it, and some ways of differentiating the repression and subliminal aspects of level of awareness were suggested: repression results from some upset or anxiety, and there should be other signs of this; repressions also usually involve the individual in inconsistencies, which may be picked up by other signs. Below threshold stimuli, on the other hand, can be raised to threshold level by simply manipulating intensity or duration — if the investigator is sure the subject is paying attention. As a matter of fact, attention problems play havoc with methods of getting at both the repression and the subliminal dimensions of level of awareness.

Intentional control was the other variable for which measurement methods were discussed. It, too, is subject to confusion by the subject's alterations of attention. Much of the traditional measurement of intention has also been done by content analysis. Characterizing it as a sharply focused directing of communication toward the receiver was seen as a cue to the way intentional control could be detected by the researcher.

Chapter Eight

Strategic Problems

In the preceding chapter several issues were discussed which regularly lead to problems in the methodology of research on emotional communication. These are issues that stem from the way in which the investigator thinks of his research area to begin with, even before he sets out to study some part of it. In this chapter we take the investigator at this next step in his work: he has decided what to study, and perhaps even in general how to go about it. He is now confronted with a number of practical problems of the strategy of his work, of how to plan the details of his study.

Most of these problems are of the same sort as those facing investigators in any field. Samples must be chosen carefully so that the results will be generalizable to known populations; measures must be well established beforehand so that the investigator and his audience will know what the resulting numbers refer to; procedures must follow directly from the principles under study — and a host of other admonitions which have been written about so extensively in the literature on research design.

There are always some special problems that arise within any one field of research in addition to the general ones, problems inherent to the nature of that field. In most areas there is an unwritten body of know-how which all beginning researchers must become acquainted with, and which readers outside of those areas may not realize, or may have forgotten about if they ever knew. This chapter will discuss three of these within the confines of research on emotional communication. The first one is related to the theory we have been developing in earlier chapters of this book, that of the context the investigator uses to evaluate emotional information. The other two grow out of problems which the investigator himself has in his daily work: how the human observer can pay attention to complicated interactions without selecting what he sees, and how he can maintain any emotional distance from his subject matter, which is itself emotional in nature.

THE CONTEXT FOR EVALUATING EMOTIONAL INFORMATION

The information value of behaviors classified as emotional messages cannot be measured in a vacuum. The idea of using the relationship between an act and its context as the basis for measurement first came up in Chapter 3, where I said that one must know something about the background of the person under observation in order to evaluate a given act, and that one must also know about the background of the stimulus situation in order to evaluate the antecedent act. In Chapter 6 we examined these same factors from a different standpoint, that of what makes any act attract the attention of the social participants as a possible emotional message. At that point we went into greater detail about context. For purposes of analysis we broke it down into several parts, layered, as it were, one upon the next — from the most general to the most specific. At the general end was the knowledge one person would have about another simply on the basis that both belong to the same culture and know what to expect in a wide range of situations from anyone who shares the same cultural heritage. Below this came the layers of subcultural patterns, family traditions, and finally, idiosyncratic ways of reacting. The better a person knows another person within these several contexts, the greater will be his knowledge of the probability of the other person's behavior in this or that specific situation.

That the distinctions among these layers are reasonable there is no doubt, but the distinctions are certainly easier to maintain in the armchair than in the laboratory. The investigator's problem with them is that he cannot tell if they really make a difference, because, as we shall see, the research evidence has not really added up to a demonstration of the entire series. In this section we shall examine the results of several studies of these various contexts to see how well they have been separated in fact. We shall look at the results of each study from two standpoints: first, how well it shows the context effect within the layer it was designed to examine, and second, what evidence it provides about the relationships among different layers. We must bear in mind that at this stage of research in this area most studies are about one layer only, and we should not expect to find very much about inter-layer relationships. Still, there is some of this sort of evidence, mostly as by-products of the main purpose of some of the studies, and as such it is worth reviewing.

Cultural differences in communication have been well established by now, but only indirectly as they relate to emotional messages. I shall cite two studies as examples. The first is the classical one by Efron (1941), who compared gesture patterns of immigrant Jewish and Italian people in New York. His methods were painstaking and thorough. The differences between these two main groups were very clear-cut by several measures: extent of movement, form of movement, and parts of the arm and hand involved. Equally striking was the finding that the children of immigrants from these same areas could not be distinguished on the same variables. Some differences that might be interpreted as subcultural were also found: when the immigrants were in their closely populated neighborhoods of the city and talking with each other, their gestures were most like those of their fellows. When they were outside, talking with those who had already been in this country for a long time, their gestures were more like those of the "standard American," if such a speech-derived term may be applied to gesture patterns. But Efron was not interested in subcultural differences when he was making this observation. He was concerned instead with the changes that could be seen to occur with the passage of time as the immigrant learned new ways of behaving. The other cultural study is that of Watson and Graves (1966), which was a quantitative follow-up of some culture patterns observed less formally by Hall (1963), for which he had coined the term *proxemics,* or how people use and manipulate the physical distance between each other in social situations. Hall's observations had been very explicit about the difference between Arab and American people in this regard: the former stand closer to each other in conversations than the latter, face each other more directly, look each other more squarely in the eye, talk in a louder voice, and touch each other more. Watson and Graves studied these variables in 32 students, 4 from each of four Arab countries and 4 from each of four geographical regions of the United States. The six possible pairs of students within each region were ob-

served in a brief conversation, and their behavior was tabulated in terms
of the notational system proposed by Hall. There were small and occasionally significant differences in the five variables between subgroups
of Arabs and the Americans, and large and impressive as well as significant differences between the Arab and American groups. In fact there
was no overlap on any variable between subgroup means from the two
cultures.

Again, as in Efron's study, the goal of this work was to explore
cultural differences, not subcultural ones. The N's per subgroup were too
small for any comparisons and, at any rate, since the authors do not say
that they chose the subgroups to represent subcultures, any inferences
would likely be farfetched. Watson and Graves do, however, bring up the
possibility of differences of yet another of the layers we are discussing:

> ... *within* a culture area, are differences in proxemic style —
> a tendency to confront others more directly, to avoid looking
> them in the eye more than most, etc. — associated with other
> personality traits. What kinds of things are communicated by
> such subtle deviations (p. 984)?

This question is about individual differences in relation to cultural
background, not about individual style as a context for evaluating a
single act; yet raising the question recognizes individual as well as
cultural patterns.

Among studies examining subcultural differences, those by McNeil
(1956) and Bernstein (1962a, 1962b) will serve as good illustrations.
McNeil's study was referred to briefly in the last chapter. It showed that
middle-class children were more restricted in their expression of emotions
when using their bodies as a means of communication, while lower-class
children are more restricted when expressing them conceptually. Bernstein's
study was of language usage, so it does not speak of emotional communication so directly. He found that working-class children's language
in many details was a more restricted code, while that of middle-class
children was more elaborated. By this he meant that middle-class children
could express much of their feelings and attitudes through language,
while working-class children could express only factual information
through this medium, and needed other means, like direct action.

to convey messages about their feelings.* Thus McNeil and Bernstein both found gross differences in channels chosen for emotional communication between children of these two social classes. In both studies the groups distinguished were social class groups within the same culture, American for McNeil and British for Bernstein. The differences in which the investigators were interested were discrete ones that made the groups look like subcultures rather than the differences in degree ordinarily found in research on social class. The larger cultural differences, the subject of the two studies I have just referred to, were not at issue here, but both McNeil's and Bernstein's results show less mutual interclass comprehensibility than we had suspected before. Individual differences among the subjects within the social class groups were hardly mentioned; they made up the error terms in the statistical analyses.

Only Krout (1954a, 1954b) has studied individual patterns of expression in substantial numbers of subjects, but he did not exploit his methods to the fullest degree for our purposes. It was his hypothesis that the movements he called autistic gestures were born of conflict in the individual's past. He did obtain some evidence, on the basis of conflicts induced in an experimental situation, that there were some commonalities across individuals in the resulting movements. He could have used the same methods to search further for the study of movement patterns within individuals, as he began to do with the two cases he wrote about more extensively in an earlier report (1935). My own work in this field (Dittmann, 1962) began by showing that there are stable patterns of movement frequencies from one body area to another, patterns that convey considerable information about emotional states or moods. That first study used only one subject, so no comparisons could be made of idiosyncratic response patterns. Subsequent work, as yet unreported, suggests that there are stable base-line patterns for each individual, and that these patterns change in idiosyncratic ways when changes analogous to emotional states are introduced into the experimental situation.

This work on individual expressive patterns is quite the opposite

* Bernstein's conclusions were challenged in one respect by Robinson (1965), who found that working-class children have both codes available to them in some circumstances, but the basic differences Bernstein found were still viable when applied to everyday situations.

of those of Efron and of Watson and Graves, with which we began this discussion, and those of McNeil and Bernstein as well: whereas those investigators were studying cultural differences with little mention of individual differences, Krout and I focused on individual differences with little reference to culture — although Krout somewhat piously recommended studies of autistic gestures in other cultures (1954b, p. 149). As to the issue of evidence about more than one layer of context, part of his work included comparison of expressive differences between the men and women who made up his sample of American college students, and sex differences in this instance should probably be considered subcultural.

Thus we have seen from this brief review that there are a number of contexts — from the most general to the most specific — against which an observer may view a given act in order to evaluate its unusualness as a message of emotion, the amount of information the message conveys. I began the review with two aims: (1) to see how well the differences were shown, and (2) to learn whether the several layers of context were distinguished from one another. The first aim has been met quite well: the differences were adequately demonstrated in each of the studies; and when we take them all together, we may conclude with a good deal of confidence that many kinds of differences in emotional expressiveness are very well established. With respect to the second aim, things are not quite so clear, since the studies do not add up to such a neat whole. Each has focused on one or another of the levels as its topic for investigation; and while there has been an occasional mention of other levels, the investigators were not centrally interested in the relationships among them. The reason that we have no overall study including many levels is clear. Raush (1965) hinted of it in the article I discussed at some length in Chapter 3: the number of data it would be necessary to collect in order to compare the relative contribution of all levels at once would be enormous. But not all studies in which acts are evaluated in relationship to their context would require simultaneous knowledge of all levels. The idea of levels has been opened up, and the studies themselves represent methods that could be drawn upon in future work. We can only hope that in the course of later studies some multilevel results will turn up.

The form of these results will probably be that of norms for contexts of different levels. The methods used by past studies lend themselves to the development of norms, which after all are nothing but frequency distributions of various sorts of acts for people within some specified reference group. Indeed the substantive results of many of the studies I have referred to here can be viewed as first steps in building norms for the reference groups of the various levels of context.

ATTENTION PROBLEMS IN HUMAN OBSERVERS

By now the subject of attention is a familiar one in this book. We heard about it several times in connection with the participants in social interaction. Chiefly it is a problem for the receiving person as he tries to make his way through all the many competing inputs which are always present in interaction with others. Attention is a problem for the sending person, too, since only by attending to his receiver can he know how well he is communicating, or whether he is communicating at all — and this is especially important, as we saw in the last chapter, when he intends to get a certain message across. We turn now to the research investigator as he applies his various methods to studying the whole process. The strategies he employs are no different from those used by social psychologists or by anyone else studying complicated relationships, but some of them are rather specialized in work on emotional communication, particularly work in which the separation of different channels is essential to the study.

Briefly, the investigator is immune to attention problems only if his methods allow him to be. The easiest way to gain this immunity is by using some of the mechanical and electronic instruments currently available for making original records of the communication situation. These devices suffer no lapses of attention as they work for the investigator, and while he is using them he need not worry about anyone's alertness. When the time comes for him to turn the resulting records into data,* he can still avoid attention problems if the devices have produced records that are amenable to mechanical analysis, as are digital outputs on paper tape or traces from a pen recorder, which may be reduced to digital data in an optical scanner.

---

* Ekman and Friesen (1968) have pointed out the difference between records and data.

Most records in studies of human communication, however, are not of this nature at all. They are, rather, notes and tallies by observers who were present in the actual situation under study or who watched it through a one-way screen. If the recording was done mechanically by tape recorder or film, the records must still be reduced to the sort of notes and tallies that make up data in this type of research. In this case the observer has many of the same attention problems that the social participant has. There should be no misunderstanding about the difference between the social participant and the research observer in this respect, however: the participant has a much harder time of it. The people taking part in free social interaction are not studying emotional communication. For a true exchange to take place among them, they must keep up with all the many messages that are being sent, or at least try to, including any emotional ones that may be present. The observer, on the other hand, being at one remove from the social situation, can focus his attention only on those aspects of the interaction that are germane to his task (see Goodrich & Dittmann, 1960). Those aspects are not themselves all-inclusive, since every research study must abstract only a few variables out of all the possible ones, even in these days of multivariate designs. In addition, a particular observer may be assigned only one of those variables to concentrate on; he may even be prevented from seeing other events which would interfere with his part of the job. Thus there is a reduction in the amount of input he is subjected to, a reduction that derives from the very nature of his task as contrasted with the task of the social participant.

Even with this added distance and lower quantity of input, however, he is still prey to some of the same interferences of attention as the social participant. These are the interferences inherent in the perceptual process itself. We discussed a principal one in Chapter 5 in connection with channel capacity, and again in Chapter 6 when we took up interference between channels. To recapitulate briefly, there is a built-in tendency for the human observer to find higher-information signals more commanding, and to pay attention to them at the expense of lower-information ones. This tendency is present in all people: in the social participants trying to maintain the pace of the conversation and at the same time to figure out what the others in the situation are feeling; and in the researcher as well, watching the scene from his slightly removed and less involved position. There is a good deal of evidence about this source of interference from studies of perception, summarized, as I have said before, by Broadbent (1958). Our study on facial and bodily expression (Dittmann, Parloff, & Boomer, 1965) provides additional evidence with a more direct bearing on observational methods in research. The observers in that study clearly concentrated on the face, not the body, when they were forming their judgments about how another person was feeling. Some of the observers concentrated less on the face, but they were special observers, having had professional training and experience in the field of dancing, where the body *is* the medium of expression. They may also have had some specific perceptual-personality orientation, which predisposed them to be interested in bodily expression and led them to become dancers in the first place. All observers were able to take in the emotional messages provided by body areas other than the face, as evidenced by performance when the face was masked so that they could not see it, and they were surprised to find how much they could see there. But when both face and body were made visible again, they all looked at the face — even the dancers. The difference was that the dancers, having been cued in to the information from the body, now paid significantly more attention to it than the other subjects were able to.

It is not only high-information messages that are more likely to get through the perceptual system, Broadbent goes on to say, but also high-intensity messages, to the detriment of other, lower-intensity ones. As a result the observer has two factors to contend with as he tries to concentrate on those aspects of the social situation which his research calls upon him to observe. He is helped, as I have already said, by his very position as an observer, removed a bit from the situation he is watching. For even greater objectivity he must exclude those parts of the total communication which interfere, and there are various methods and mechanical aids designed to improve his chances. Some of these have been used for many years and are thoroughly familiar to social psychologists and observers of small children, like the pre-categorized coding sheet in time-sampling studies. Every minute, or whatever time interval has been decided upon, the observer looks at the categories and checks those which apply to his subjects during that interval. Since he has all the categories in front of him, the observer is less likely to forget any one of them as a possibility in the speed of the interchange. His attention is forced to comply with the task.

A more complete method of excluding irrelevant signals for the observer is to mask them mechanically. This technique is possible in all research where records are made by filming or videotaping, and in a few others as well. We discussed the many possibilities for masking when we were listing the audible and visible channels in Chapter 5, and several of the articles cited there included information on how masking was done. Here are a few more examples: the facial and bodily expression study in our laboratory used masking in one condition, preventing the judges from seeing the subject's face while allowing full view of the body. Once that was done there was a good deal of agreement about emotional information available from bodily cues. The judges' surprise at finding this was because they had never in the ordinary course of events been able to look for this sort of information in other than the facial area — except for the professional dancers, who behaved quite differently. Ekman (1965) used the same procedure, but even more completely. For one of his experimental conditions he masked the face and left the body in view as we did. For another, he masked the body and left only facial cues available to his judges. A number of other bases for masking one information source or another have also been used by various researchers. The recent studies of interchannel differences, reviewed in Chapter 5, provide examples.

Content analysis methods provide the same sort of aids to attention as the pre-categorized coding sheet, only they enable the investigator to handle considerably more complicated conceptualizations. The observer in the time-sampling study who is present in the social situation as a nonparticipant is limited by his span of apprehension. His coding sheet cannot contain more categories than he can take in at once. The content analyst, on the other hand, can look over a much longer list at his leisure, referring back to his original protocol as often as he needs to in order to refresh his memory. Indeed, the procedure of coding material from written records quite often becomes almost as mechanical as work with the "meaningless" output of psychophysiological recording apparatus. The investigator's problems of coping with the interfering effects of strong stimuli or high-information stimuli from other sources are considerably reduced by these methods.

PROBLEMS OF EMOTIONAL INVOLVEMENT IN OBSERVERS

The attention problems we have been discussing are perceptual-cognitive ones, stemming from the fact that the human observer can process only so much material at a time. The nature of the raw material in research on emotional communication imposes upon the observer a whole other set of problems in addition. These come from his very strong tendency to become emotionally involved in the social situation he is called upon to observe. He becomes involved because he is a human being watching his fellow human beings, and he feels their feelings empathically, just as any person feels what others are going through. The difficulty with the observer's empathizing is that what he observes is subject to distortions based upon his own emotional history, just as in the case of the social participant. Again, he is helped to overcome this difficulty by his position as an observer, slightly removed from the situation, just as he is helped with his information processing task, but probably not as much, because of the very subject matter of emotions. Emotions are at once what he empathizes with, what he is likely to distort, and what the task asks him to be objective about in his observations.

There is a special problem with using films as records of social interaction: the person analyzing the material has two stimuli to contend with — the social situation depicted in the film, and the film itself. Film as a unique psychological stimulus has received more attention in Europe than in the United States. I do not know any direct reason for this, but I feel that it may be related to the greater emphasis on the phenomenological approach there. As time has gone on, a number of experiments have been conducted in this area, and while it is not always easy to tie the results together, by now a body of knowledge has developed which we in the United States should know more about. The field as it has grown is called filmology. It was developed in Paris by Gilbert Cohen-Séat, and recently most of the research has been done in Milan, at the Agostino Gemelli Institute. The work began with a dual concern for the film as an experience in the theater and as an educational aid. In the former, many variables — such as the power of the story, the quality of the acting, and so on — enter into the effects on the individual viewer. In the latter, many factors that are far removed from our topic are understandably involved. In addition to these more general concerns, there have been a number of studies in more specialized areas like perception, its distortions and its neurophysiological substrate, using short experimental films as the stimulus material. These have included many variables of greater interest to us here, and we need not think of filmological research results being confined to "the movies" and instructional films. Some preliminary thinking, but so far as I know no empirical work, has also been devoted to television as a medium. I assume that effects comparable to those I shall be discussing below are also present there.

The nature of the viewer's response to the film situation is, briefly, that he loses himself in it. He becomes less critical, more empathic, more emotionally involved with these events and people on the screen than he is in everyday life. He identifies emotionally with the actors and their roles, projects himself into them in the full sense of the word. He chooses the character on the screen he is to identify with on the basis of how well that character fits in with his own needs and history. Among the scholars who have tried to puzzle out the nature of the phenomenon is Albert Michotte, of Louvain. His first paper on the subject (1948) ranged through a number of possible explanations for the powerful experience of reality in films: movement, lighting, covering and uncovering of distant objects by nearer ones, the brilliance of the picture on the screen as contrasted with its dark surround, and the like. By 1953 (published 1960) he had centered on movement as being the most important of these. He reasoned that the movement of objects on the screen provokes empathic movements in the viewer,

> ... reactions on a reduced scale, perhaps incipient movements, but generalized and affecting his entire motor apparatus. In such a way there commonly comes to be a true fusion between visual events (the actor's movements) and proprioceptive tactile-kinesthetic events (the viewer's movements) to the point where there is only one movement for him (p. 66; my translation).

Michotte goes on to explain emotional empathy by a parallel process: both the movements and the emotional expressions of the actor on the screen become part of the viewer (p. 72).

These ideas, though they come out of a phenomenological tradition, have found a good deal of confirmation in empirical work. The response people have to movements on the screen, for example, has been demonstrated in EEG studies. In one of these (Cohen-Séat, Lelord, & Jampolsky, 1960) 28 out of 60 subjects showed clear changes in alpha rhythm at the onset or cessation of movements on the screen; in 9 of these there was a specific alpha response to human movements in the film. Another study (Romano & Botson, 1963) demonstrated that objects and events central to the action of a short film, the things the actors picked up and handled, and the movements they performed, were remembered far better than other aspects of the film. Thus movement is responded to quite specifically, thus supporting Michotte's theory of the realism in response to film.

As to emotional involvement, everyone knows about it as an everyday occurrence in the theater. Some of the specific details have in addition been documented by Ancona and his colleagues in studies using methods akin to those in the achievement-motive literature, and based on Murray needs. Different types of film (exciting and action-oriented as compared with introspective ones depicting interpersonal problems) stimulate different needs, as shown by Ancona (1963) and by Croce (1964). Furthermore, those subjects who said they participated very fully in the films showed those effects even more strongly. Finally, watching an exciting film can serve as a catharsis for strong emotion, especially for those who do not allow themselves consciously to feel the impact of the emotion very fully (Ancona & Bertini, 1966). *

* This is not the place to go into the details of the research on catharsis of aggression through viewing films (or television). It has quite a long history in the U. S., and has usually been spurred on by our interest in whether television is "good for" our children or productive of violence in those who watch all the blood and thunder available to them through this medium. A number of short-term studies have been reported where the immediate effects of single presentations are compared; there is also one long-term study of programming available television over a more representative period. See Feshbach (1961) for a study and references relating to the catharsis point of view, and Berkowitz (1970) for a review of studies opposing that position. The long-term study is reported in Feshbach and Singer (1971). It is symptomatic of the insularity in psychology today that the work of the European filmologists is never cited by the American workers who are plowing the same fields — and that the Europeans in the articles referred to above do not cite the American work either, although most other filmological research reports do.

The studies on emotional involvement and other effects of film on viewers are all about the usual application of motion pictures, namely, the dramatic film in the theater. They thus may seem far removed from our concerns here. But films used as records in research are also films, and they produce many of the same effects on their viewers in the laboratory as filmed drama does on its viewers in the movie house. Cohen and Cohen (1961), for example, wrote eloquently of their response to the filmed interviews they were examining in detail at the National Institute of Mental Health:

> We anticipated that we would be even more detached in studying a film [than in clinical consultation], because now we had no responsibility to any but ourselves; no need to be useful or penetrating. Whatever the reasons, it took us months to achieve a modest degree of objectivity. At first we found ourselves responding constantly to the therapist — he should have been silent when he spoke; he should have spoken when he was silent; and when he said anything useful, he said it too late or too soon... It has been hard to focus attention on our task... We are capable of feeling outraged... We have learned from our contacts with a number of other groups engaged in similar efforts that this reaction is a common one (p. 49).

It has been my strong impression, after a good deal of experience, that similar reactions occur when investigators use tape-recorded material as their research protocols, and I would imagine that videotape recordings would also have the same effect. I do not, however, have any research evidence about these two types of recording of the kind I have referred to in the case of films.

We may conclude, then, that motion picture records of social situations, rather than opening for the observer a window to reality through which he can view his subject matter objectively, confront him instead with an additional input which is a stimulus situation in its own right. Fortunately there are ways to break into this involvement, just as there are aids to the observer in overcoming the more general attention problems discussed in the last section of this chapter. As a matter of fact, some of the same methods also serve admirably here: some data-handling techniques used in content analysis, for example, introduce a mechanical quality to work with any material that helps cut through an investigator's emotional involvement with it. When the investigator working with films uses methods similar to those of the observer who is present in the situation with his inevitable coding sheet, he is also insulated to some extent by the mechanics of that device. His attention to the task of keeping track of the time on his stopwatch and filling in the categories at required intervals tends to preclude too much emotional involvement with what he is viewing on the screen.

The observer of research records on film may also increase his distance from the experimental material by other means. An obvious one is to break up the replay of these recordings so as to interrupt the continuity of the situation, and thus prevent himself from getting into it so deeply. The observer can also take small passages of the material and repeat them over and over again, reducing in this way any involvement he may have begun to develop in the material. A test of the effectiveness of this last technique (Dittmann & Colombo, 1965) demonstrated measurable habituation with repetition. The film used for this test was not itself research material, but it did concentrate on a dramatic emotional interchange between two central characters. Several psychophysiological measures were used which are generally thought to be related to subjects' involvement with experimental situations: GSR, frequency of spontaneous GSRs, respiration rate, and heart rate. Three groups of subjects saw the three-minute film excerpt five times with varying intervals between repetitions, and a control group saw other parts of the same film, balanced for dramatic content and totaling the same length of time as the five repetitions of the experimental excerpt. Heart rate showed a clear habituation to repetition of the film excerpt, and nonspecific GSRs supported this trend, though not significantly. The control group showed no evidence of habituation, despite the fact that they saw just as much film and were exposed to the experimental setup for the same period of time. The intervals between repetitions made no difference in the results. This variable was included because of the findings of an earlier study (Dittmann, 1964) on the effects of repetition on the amount of information judges were able to glean from films. There it was shown that repetitions increased information yield, as we should expect from the results of a number of studies of instructional films, and that in addition those subjects who had a day's interval between showings of the film retained still more information from it. This result, it should be noted, is consonant with the well-established principle of the superiority of spaced learning over massed learning, but it had not been demonstrated before using this sort of material. In this first study, too, there was an effort to rate subjects' involvement with the film, and although the measure was not completely satisfactory, there was some trend toward less involvement with an interval between repetitions than without. This trend did not, however, hold up in the later, more extended study of involvement. The solid finding, then, is that repetition of short excerpts can help the observer to break through his involvement with the material.

In most investigations in psychology the experimenter uses not one, but several different methods in collecting his data. In many cases it is possible to arrange things so that the methods can serve as checks on each other to assure that bias is not introduced. In these days of a growing literature on experimenter effects in research, more and more psychologists are instituting checks of this sort in their work. It goes without saying that they are even more necessary in research where the very nature of the subject matter is close to or identical with the nature of bias, as in emotional communication, social influence techniques, and the like.

SUMMARY: PROBLEMS OF STRATEGY IN RESEARCH ON EMOTIONAL COMMUNICATION

This chapter dealt with problems faced by the researcher when he gets down to the practical steps of carrying out studies in emotional communication. While not confined to research in this area, they are so characteristic of it that a beginning body of know-how has developed which is useful for investigators to share with each other.

Three problems of strategy were discussed. The first concerned how the investigator learns about the context within which he looks at the individual act to determine its unusualness or information value. Three levels of context were discussed: the cultural, the subcultural, and the idiosyncratic. The studies cited illustrate how each researcher adhered strictly to one level, with only occasional mention that the others might exist. For many purposes this isolation will do no harm to the conclusions that might be drawn, but in some cases we will need to take greater account of the relationships among the levels. The studies thus far done may serve as models for developing norms at different levels against which to measure the given act.

The other two practical problems are of the investigator himself, as observer. One is how to keep his attention focused upon the signal source. When he can turn this observational task over to a machine, his attention problems are over, but he cannot always do this. When an observer is personally present in the situation, he has the advantage over the social participant that he is not directly involved, but he still confronts the same two difficulties of the social participant in that both are attracted by high-information and high-intensity signals and have difficulty attending to concurrent low-information and low-level ones. Some aids to the researcher in dealing with this problem were mentioned (along with some research results to show their effectiveness) : excluding the unwanted signals, directly translating observed events to research language, masking, and content analysis.

Finally we discussed the practical problem of the research observer's emotional involvement with the people who serve as his subjects. The techniques just mentioned under attention problems help to some degree, but where the research protocol is the motion picture (and perhaps also the tape recording or videotape), an additional problem is introduced: the psychological stimulus presented by the recording medium itself. I outlined very briefly some of the thinking and research on this process which has been done in Europe, and two of my own experiments in attempting to find ways around the involvement. The conclusions were that breaking the material up into small bits helps, as does repeating these over and over so that the observer habituates to the initial emotional impact of the material.

References ———————————————————

Abelson, R. P., & V. Sermat. Multidimensional scaling of facial expressions. *Journal of Experimental Psychology*, 1962, *63*, 546-554.

Allport, G. W. *Personality: A psychological interpretation.* New York: Henry Holt, 1937.

Allport, G. W., & H. S. Odbert. Trait names: a psycholexical study. *Psychological Monographs*, 1936, *47*, Whole No. 211.

Allport, G. W., & P. E. Vernon. *Studies in expressive movement.* New York: Macmillan, 1933.

American Standards Association. Definition of electrical terms. Group 65: Communication. American Institute of Electrical Engineers, 1957.

Ancona, L. Il film come elemento nella dinamica della aggressività. *IKON*, 1963, *13*, No. 46, 27-32.

Ancona, L., & M. Bertini. Aggressivity discharge effect through films causing strong emotional stress. *IKON*, 1966, *16*, No. 57, 7-27.

Andersen, M. P. A mid-century survey of books on communication. *Journal of Communication*, 1964, *14*, 203-214.

Attneave, F. *Applications of information theory to psychology.* New York: Holt, Rinehart, and Winston, 1959.

Beakel, Nancy G., & A. Mehrabian. Inconsistent communications and psychopathology. *Journal of Abnormal Psychology*, 1969, *74*, 126-130.

Beebe-Center, J. G. *The psychology of pleasantness and unpleasantness.* New York: D. Van Nostrand, 1932.

Berelson, B. *Content analysis in communication research.* Glencoe, Ill.: Free Press, 1952.

Berkowitz, L. Experimental investigations of hostility catharsis. *Journal of Consulting and Clinical Psychology*, 1970, *35*, 1-7.

Bernstein, B. Linguistic codes, hesitation phenomena and intelligence. *Language and Speech*, 1962, *5*, 31-46. (a)

Bernstein, B. Social class, linguistic codes, and grammatical elements. *Language and Speech*, 1962, *5*, 221-240. (b)

Berry, J. Some statistical aspects of conversational speech. Chap. 28, pp. 392-401 in W. Jackson (Ed.) *Communication theory.* New York: Academic Press, 1953.

Binder, A., & B. R. Wolin. Informational models and their uses. *Psychometrika*, 1964, *29*, 29-54.

Birdwhistell, R. L. *Introduction to kinesics: An annotation system for analysis of body motion and gesture.* Louisville, Ky.: University of Louisville, 1952.

Birdwhistell, R. L. An approach to communication. *Family Process,* 1962, *1,* 194-201.

Birdwhistell, R. L. *Kinesics and context.* Philadelphia: University of Pennsylvania Press, 1970.

Block, J. Studies in the phenomenology of emotions. *Journal of Abnormal and Social Psychology,* 1957, *54,* 358-363.

Boomer, D. S. Speech disturbance and body movement in interviews. *Journal of Nervous and Mental Disease,* 1963, *136,* 263-266.

Boomer, D. S. Hesitation and grammatical encoding. *Language and Speech,* 1965, *8,* 148-158.

Boomer, D. S., & A. T. Dittmann. Speech rate, filled pause, and body movement in interviews. *Journal of Nervous and Mental Disease,* 1964, *139,* 324-327.

Brillouin, L. *Science and information theory.* 2nd ed. New York: Academic Press, 1962.

Broadbent, D. E. *Perception and communication.* Oxford: Pergamon Press, 1958.

Bugental, Daphne E., J. W. Kaswan, & Leonore R. Love. Perception of contradictory meanings conveyed by verbal and nonverbal channels. *Journal of Personality and Social Psychology,* 1970, *16,* 647-655.

Bugental, Daphne E., J. W. Kaswan, Leonore R. Love, & M. N. Fox. Child versus adult perception of evaluative messages in verbal, vocal, and visual channels. *Developmental Psychology,* 1970, *2,* 367-375.

Bugental, Daphne E., Leonore R. Love, J. W. Kaswan, & Carol April. Verbal-nonverbal conflict in parental messages to normal and disturbed children. *Journal of Abnormal Psychology,* 1971, *77,* 6-10.

Bühler, K. *Sprachtheorie.* Jena: G. Fischer, 1934.

Burt, C. The factorial study of emotions. Chap. 46, pp. 531-551, in M. L. Reymert (Ed.), *Feelings and emotions.* New York: McGraw-Hill, 1950.

Carmichael, L., S. O. Roberts, & N. Y. Wessell. A study of the judgment of manual expression as presented in still and motion pictures. *Journal of Social Psychology,* 1937, *8,* 115-142.

Cherry, E. C. The communication of information (an historical review). *American Scientist,* 1952, *40,* 640-663.

Cherry, C. *On human communication. A review, a survey, and a criticism.* New York: John Wiley & Sons, 1957.

Chomsky, N. *Syntactic structures.* The Hague: Mouton, 1957.

Coffey, H., M. Freedman, T. Leary, & A. Ossorio. Community service and social research — group psychotherapy in a church program. *Journal of Social Issues,* 1950, *6,* No. 1.

Cohen, R. A., & Mabel B. Cohen. Research in psychotherapy: preliminary report. *Psychiatry,* 1961, *24,* 46-61.

Cohen-Séat, G., G. LeLord, & R. Jampolsky. Études comparées de divers types de réponse à la présentation filmique du mouvement. Réactions psycho-physiologiques et problèmes de personalité, *Revue Internationale de Filmologie*, 1960, *10*, No. 32, 37-50.

Cranach, M. v. The role of orienting behavior in human interactions. pp. 217-237 in A. H. Esser (Ed.), *Behavior and environment: The use of space by animals and men*. New York: Plenum Press, 1971.

Croce, Maria A. Condizionamenti sociali attraverso tecniche cinematografiche: determinazione dell'effetto "power" di proiezione filmiche. *IKON*, 1964, *14*, No. 48, 53-58.

Dance, F. E. X. The "concept" of communication. *Journal of Communication*, 1970, *20*, 201-210.

Darwin, C. *The expression of the emotions in man and animals*. London: Murray, 1872.

Davitz, J. R. *The communication of emotional meaning*. New York: McGraw-Hill, 1964.

deLaguna, Grace A. *Speech, its function and development*. New Haven, Conn.: Yale University Press, 1927.

Dibner, A. S. Cue-counting: a measure of anxiety of interviews. *Journal of Consulting Psychology*, 1956, *20*, 475-478.

Dittmann, A. T. The relationship between body movements and moods in interviews. *Journal of Consulting Psychology*, 1962, *26*, 480.

Dittmann, A. T. Nuove tecniche per aumentare la resa di informazioni del mezzo cinematografico. *IKON*, 1964, *14*, No. 49, 79-81.

Dittmann, A. T. Review of *Kinesics and Context* by Ray L. Birdwhistell. *Psychiatry*, 1971, *34*, 334-342.

Dittmann, A. T. The body movement-speech rhythm relationship as a cue to speech encoding. Chap 7, pp. 135-152 in A. W. Siegman and B. Pope (Eds.), *Studies in dyadic communication*. New York: Pergamon, 1972.

Dittmann, A. T., and G. Colombo. The effects of repetition of motion picture excerpts on viewers' emotional response. *IKON*, 1965, *15*, No. 54, 7-14.

Dittmann, A. T., & L. G. Llewellyn. Relationship between vocalizations and head nods as listener responses. *Journal of Personality and Social Psychology*, 1968, *9*, 79-84.

Dittmann, A. T., & L. G. Llewellyn. Body movement and speech rhythm in social conversation. *Journal of Personality and Social Psychology*, 1969, *11*, 98-106.

Dittmann, A. T., & H. L. Raush. The psychoanalytic theory of conflict: Structure and methodology. *Psychological Review*, 1954, *61*, 386-400.

Dittmann, A. T., & L. C. Wynne. Linguistic techniques and the analysis of emotionality in interviews. *Journal of Abnormal and Social Psychology*, 1961, *63*, 201-204.

Dittmann, A. T., M. B. Parloff, & D. S. Boomer. Facial and bodily expression: A study of receptivity of emotional cues. *Psychiatry*, 1965, *28*, 239-244.

Driessel, A. B. Communications theory and research strategy: A metatheoretical analysis. *Journal of Communication*, 1967, *17*, 92-108.

Duncan, S., Jr. Nonverbal communication. *Psychological Bulletin*, 1969, *72*, 118-137.

Duncan, S., Jr., & M. J. Rosenberg. The paralanguage of experimenter bias. *Sociometry*, 1969, *32*, 207-219.

Duncan, S., Jr., & R. Rosenthal. Vocal emphasis in experimenters' instruction reading as unintended determinant of subjects' responses. *Language and Speech*, 1968, *11*, 20-26.

Dusenbury, D., & F. H. Knower. Experimental studies of the symbolism of action and voice — I: A study of the specificity of meaning in facial expression. *Quarterly Journal of Speech*, 1938, *24*, 424-436.

Dusenbury, D., & F. H. Knower. Experimental studies of the symbolism of action and voice — II. A study of the specificity of meaning in abstract tonal symbols. *Quarterly Journal of Speech*, 1939, *25*, 67-75.

Efron, D. *Gesture and environment.* New York: King's Crown Press, 1941.

Eiman, P. D., E. R. Siqueland, P. Jusczyk, & J. Vigorito. Speech perception in infants. *Science*, 1971, *171*, 303-306.

Ekman, G. Dimensions of emotion. *Acta Psychologica*, 1955, *11*, 279-288.

Ekman, P. Body position, facial expression, and verbal behavior during interviews. *Journal of Abnormal and Social Psychology*, 1964, *68*, 295-301.

Ekman, P. The differential communication of affect by head and body cues. *Journal of Personality and Social Psychology*, 1965, *2*, 726-735.

Ekman, P., & W. V. Friesen. Head and body cues in the judgment of emotion: A reformulation. *Perceptual and Motor Skills*, 1967, *24*, 711-724.

Ekman, P., & W. V. Friesen. Nonverbal behavior in psychotherapy research. pp. 179-216 in J. M. Schlein (Ed.), *Research in psychotherapy*, Volume III. Washington, D. C.: American Psychological Association, 1968.

Ekman, P. & W .V. Friesen. Nonverbal leakage and cues to deception. *Psychiatry*. 1969, *32*, 88-106. (a)

Ekman, P., & W. V. Friesen. The repertoire of nonverbal behavior: categories, origins, usage, and coding. *Semiotica*, 1969, *1*, 49-98. (b)

Ekman, P., & W. V. Friesen. Constants across culture in the face and emotion. *Journal of Personality and Social Psychology*, 1971, *17*, 124-129.

Ekman, P., W. V. Friesen, & T. G. Taussig. VID-R and SCAN: tools and methods for the automated analysis of visual records. Chap. 16, pp. 297-312, in G. Gerbner, O. R. Holsti, K. Krippendorff, W. J. Paisley, & P. J. Stone (Eds.), *The analysis of communication content.* New York: Wiley, 1969.

Ekman, P., W. V. Friesen, & S. S. Tomkins. Facial affect scoring technique: a first validity study. *Semiotica*, 1971, *3*, 37-58.

Ekman, P., E. R. Sorenson, & W. V. Friesen. Pan-cultural elements in facial displays of emotion. *Science*, 1969, *164*, 86-88.

Eldred, S. H., & D. B. Price. A linguistic evaluation of feeling states in psychotherapy. *Psychiatry*, 1958, *21*, 115-121.

Engen, T., N. Levy, & H. Schlosberg. A new series of facial expressions. *American Psychologist*, 1957, *12*, 264-266.

Engen, T., N. Levy, & H. Schlosberg. The dimensional analysis of a new series of facial expressions. *Journal of Experimental Psychology*, 1958, *55*, 454-458.

Estes, S. G. Judging personality from expressive behavior. *Journal of Abnormal and Social Psychology*, 1938, *33*, 217-236.

Exline, R. V., & L. C. Winters. Affective relations and mutual glances in dyads. Chap. 11, pp. 319-350, in S. S. Tomkins & C. E. Izard (Eds.), *Affect, cognition, and personality*. New York: Springer, 1965.

Exline, R., D. Gray, & Dorothy Schuette. Visual behavior in a dyad as affected by interview content and sex of respondent. *Journal of Personality and Social Psychology*, 1965, *1*, 201-209.

Fairbanks, G., & W. Pronovost. An experimental study of the pitch characteristics of the voice during the expression of emotion. *Speech Monographs*, 1939, *6*, 87-104.

Fano, R. M. *Transmission of information*: A statistical theory of communications. Cambridge, Mass.: MIT Press, 1961.

Fearing, F. Toward a psychological theory of human communication. *Journal of Personality*, 1953, *22*, 71-88.

Fenichel, O. *Problems of psychoanalytic technique*. Albany, N. Y.: Psychoanalytic Quarterly, Inc., 1941.

Fenichel, O. Psychoanalytic method. 1935. In *Collected Papers, First Series*. New York: Norton, 1953, 318-330.

Feshbach, S. The stimulating versus cathartic effects of a vicarious aggressive activity. *Journal of Abnormal and Social Psychology*, 1961, *63*, 381-385.

Feshbach, S., & R. D. Singer. *Television and aggression*. San Francisco: Jossey-Bass, 1971.

Frankena, W. K. Some aspects of language. Chap. 5, pp. 121-145, in O. Henle (Ed.), *Language, thought, and culture*. Ann Arbor: University of Michigan Press, 1958. (a)

Frankena, W. K. 'Cognitive' and 'non-cognitive.' Chap. 6, pp. 146-172, in P. Henle (Ed.), *Language, thought, and culture*. Ann Arbor: University of Michigan Press, 1958. (b)

Freedman, M. B., T. F. Leary, A. G. Ossorio, & H. S. Coffey. The interpersonal dimension of personality. *Journal of Personality*, 1951, *20*, 143-161.

Freedman, N. The analysis of movement behavior during the clinical interview. Chap. 8, pp. 153-175, in A. W. Siegman & B. Pope (Eds.), *Studies in dyadic communication*. New York: Pergamon Press, 1972.

Freedman, N., & S. P. Hoffman. Kinetic behavior in altered clinical states: Approach to objective analysis of motor behavior during clinical interviews. *Perceptual and Motor Skills*, 1967, *24*, 527-539.

Freud, S. The psychopathology of everyday life. Vol. VI (1901), *Standard Edition of the Complete Psychological Works*. London: Hogarth Press, 1960.

Freud, S. Further recommendations in the technique of psycho-analysis. 1913. J. Riviere (Trans.), Vol. II, No. 31, pp. 342-365, in *Collected Papers*. London: Hogarth Press, 1946.

Frijda, N. H. The understanding of facial expression of emotion. *Acta Psychologica*, 1953, *9*, 294-362.

Frijda, N. H. Facial expression and situational cues. *Journal of Abnormal and Social Psychology*, 1958, *57*, 149-154.

Frijda, N. H. Facial expression and situational cues: A control. *Acta Psychologica*, 1961, *18*, 239-244.

Frijda, N. H. Recognition of emotion. Pp. 167-223 in L. Berkowitz (Ed.), *Advances in experimental social psychology*, vol. 4, New York: Academic Press, 1969.

Frijda, N. H., & E. Philipszoon. Dimensions of recognition of expression. *Journal of Abnormal and Social Psychology*, 1963, *66*, 45-51.

Gardner, R. A., & Beatrice T. Gardner. Teaching sign language to a chimpanzee. *Science*, 1969, *165*, 664-672.

Garfinkel, H. Studies of the routine grounds of everyday activities. *Social Problems*, 1964, *11*, 225-250.

Garner, W. R. *Uncertainty and structure as psychological concepts*. New York: Wiley, 1962.

Garner, W. R., & H. W. Hake. The amount of information in absolute judgments. *Psychological Review*, 1951, *58*, 446-459.

Garner, W. R. & W. J. McGill. The relation between information and variance analyses. *Psychometrika*, 1956, *21*, 219-228.

Garvin, P. L. The place of heuristics in the fulcrum approach to machine translation. *Lingua*, 1968, *21*, 162-182.

George, A. L. Quantitative and qualitative approaches to content analysis. Chap. 1, pp. 7-32, in I. deS. Pool (Ed.), *Trends in content analysis*. Urbana, Ill.: University of Illinois Press, 1959.

Gerbner, G. On defining communication. Still another view. *Journal of Communication*, 1966, *16*, 99-103.

Gilbert, E. N. Information theory after 18 years. *Science*, 1966, *152*, 320-326.

Gladstones, W. H. A multidimensional study of facial expression of emotion. *Australian Journal of Psychology*, 1962, *14*, 95-100.

Goodrich D. W. & A. T. Dittmann. Observing interactional behavior in residential treatment. *AMA Archives of General Psychiatry*, 1960, 2, 421-428.

Haggard, E. A., & K. S. Isaacs. Micromomentary facial expressions as indicators of ego mechanisms in psychotherapy. Chap. 14, pp. 154-165, in L. A. Gottschalk & A. H. Auerbach (Eds.), *Methods of research in psychotherapy*. New York: Appleton-Century-Crofts, 1966.

Hall, E. T. *The silent language*. New York: Doubleday, 1959.

Hall, E. T. A system for the notation of proxemic behavior. *American Anthropologist*, 1963, *65*, 1003-1026.

Hebb, D. O. Emotion in man and animal: An analysis of the intuitive processes of recognition. *Psychological Review*, 1946, *53*, 88-106.

Hebb, D. O., & W. R. Thompson. The social significance of animal studies. Chap. 15, pp. 532-561, in G. Lindzey (Ed.), *Handbook of social psychology*. Cambridge, Mass.: Addison-Wesley, 1954.

Howe, E. S. Effects of grammatical qualifications on judgments of the depth and of the anxiety arousal potential of interpretive statements. *Journal of Consulting and Clinical Psychology*, 1970, *34*, 159-163.

Hsia, H. Output, error, equivocation, and recalled information in auditory, visual, and audiovisual processing with constraint and noise. *Journal of Communication*, 1968, *18*, 325-353.

Jakobson, R. Closing statement: linguistics and poetics. pp. 350-377 in T. A. Sebeok (Ed.), *Style in language*. Cambridge, Mass.: Technology Press of Massachusetts Institute of Technology, and New York: Wiley, 1960.

James, W. T. A study of the expression of bodily posture. *Journal of General Psychology*, 1932, *7*, 405-436.

Jester, R. E., & R. M. Travers. Comprehension of connected meaningful discourse as a function of rate and mode of presentation. *Journal of Educational Research*, 1966, *59*, 297-302.

Jowett, B. (Transl.) *The dialogues of Plato*. London: Macmillan, 1892.

Kanfer, F. H. Verbal rate, eyeblink, and content in structured psychiatric interviews. *Journal of Abnormal and Social Psychology*, 1960, *61*, 341-347.

Kasl S. V., & G. F. Mahl. The relationship of disturbances and hesitations in spontaneous speech to anxiety. *Journal of Personality and Social Psychology*, 1965, *1*, 425-433.

Kauranne, U. Qualitative factors of facial expression. *Scandanavian Journal of Psychology*, 1964, *5*, 136-142.

Kelman, H. C., & Alice H. Eagly. Attitude toward the communicator, perception of communication content, and attitude change. *Journal of Personality and Social Psychology*, 1965, *1*, 63-78.

Kendon, A. Some functions of gaze direction in social interaction. *Acta Psychologica*, 1967, *26*, 22-63.

Kramer, E. Elimination of verbal cues in judgments of emotion from voice. *Journal of Abnormal and Social Psychology*, 1964, *68*, 390-396.

Krause, M. S. Anxiety in verbal behavior: A correlational study. *Journal of Consulting Psychology*, 1961, *25*, 272.

Krause, M. S., & M. Pilisuk. Anxiety in verbal behavior: A validation study. *Journal of Consulting Psychology*, 1961, *25*, 414-419.

Krippendorff, K. Values, modes and domains of inquiry into communication. *Journal of Communication*, 1969, *19*, 105-133.

Krout, M. H. Autistic gestures: an experimental study in symbolic movement. *Psychological Monographs*, 1935, *46*, No. 208.

Krout, M. H. An experimental attempt to produce unconscious manual symbolic movements. *Journal of General Psychology*, 1954, *51*, 93-120. (a)

Krout, M. H. An experimental attempt to determine the significance of unconscious manual symbolic movements. *Journal of General Psychology*, 1954, *51*, 121-152. (b)

LaBarre, W. The cultural basis of emotions and gestures. *Journal of Personality*, 1947, *16*, 49-68.

LaBarre, W. Paralanguage, kinesics, and cultural anthropology. pp. 191-220 in T. A. Sebeok, A. S. Hayes, & Mary C. Bateson (Eds.), *Approaches to semiotics*. The Hague: Mouton, 1964.

Lacey, J. I. Psychophysiological approaches to the evaluation of psychotherapeutic process and outcome. pp. 160-208 in E. A. Rubinstein & M. B. Parloff (Eds.), *Research in psychotherapy*. Washington, D. C.: American Psychological Association, 1959.

Lacey, J. I., J. Kagan, Beatrice C. Lacey, & H. A. Moss. The viceral level: Situational determinants and behavioral correlates of autonomic response patterns. Chap. 9, pp. 161-196, in P. H. Knapp (Ed.), *Expression of the emotions in man*. New York: International Universities Press, 1963.

Ladefoged, P., & D. E. Broadbent. Perception of sequence in auditory events. *Quarterly Journal of Experimental Psychology*, 1960, *12*, 162-170.

Lasswell, H. D., N. Leites, et al. *The language of politics*. New York: George Stewart, 1949.

Leventhal, H., & Elizabeth Sharp. Facial expressions as indicators of distress. Chap. 10, pp. 296-318, in S. S. Tomkins & C. E. Izard (Eds.) *Affect, cognition, and personality*. New York: Springer, 1965.

Levitt, E. A. The reationship between abilities to express emotional meanings vocally and facially. Chap. 7, pp. 87-100, in J. R. Davitz (Ed.), *The communication of emotional meaning*. New York: McGraw-Hill, 1964.

Liberman, A. M., F. S. Cooper, D. P. Shankweiler, & M. Studdert-Kennedy. Perception of the speech code. *Psychological Review*, 1967, *74*, 431-461.

Lochner, L. (Ed.). *The Goebbels diaries, 1942-1943*. Garden City, N. Y.: Doubleday, 1948.

Luria, A. *The nature of human conflicts*. (W. H. Gannt, Transl.) New York: Liveright, 1932.

Mahl, G. F. Disturbances and silences in the patient's speech in psychotherapy. *Journal of Abnormal and Social Psychology*, 1956, *53*, 1-15.

Mahl, G. F., & G. Schulze. Psychological research in the extralinguistic area. pp. 51-124 in T. A. Sebeok, A. S. Hayes, & Mary C. Bateson (Eds.), *Approaches to semiotics*. The Hague: Mouton, 1964.

Malinowski, B. The problem of meaning in primitive languages. Supplement I, pp. 296-336, in C. K. Ogden & I. A. Richards, *The meaning of meaning*. London: Routledge & Keegan Paul, 1923 (10th edition, 1949).

McCormick, E. J. *Human factors engineering*. New York: McGraw-Hill, 1964.

McGill, W. J. Multivariate information transmission. *Psychometrika*, 1954,

19, 97-116.

McGranahan, D. V. The psychology of language. *Psychological Bulletin*, 1936, 33, 178-218.

McNeil, E. B. Social class and the expression of emotion. *Papers of the Michigan Academy of Science, Arts, and Letters*, 1956, *41*, 341-348.

McQuown, N. A. Linguistic transcription and specification of psychiatric interview materials. *Psychiatry*, 1957, *20*, 79-86.

Mehrabian, A. Inference of attitudes from the posture, orientation, and distance of a communicator. *Journal of Consulting and Clinical Psychology*, 1968, *32*, 296-308. (a)

Mehrabian, A. Relationship of attitude to seated posture, orientation, and distance. *Journal of Personality and Social Psychology*, 1968, *10*, 26-30. (b)

Mehrabian, A. Significance of posture and position in the communication of attitudes and status relationships. *Psychological Bulletin*, 1969, *71*, 359-372.

Mehrabian, A., & Susan R. Ferris. Inference of attitudes from nonverbal communication in two channels. *Journal of Consulting Psychology*, 1967, *31*, 248-252.

Mehrabian, A., & M. Wiener. Decoding of inconsistent communications. *Journal of Personality and Social Psychology*, 1967, *6*, 109-114.

Mehrabian, A., & M. Williams. Nonverbal concomitants of perceived and intended persuasiveness. *Journal of Personality and Social Psychology*, 1969, *13*, 37-58.

Meyer, D. R., H. P. Bahrick, & P. M. Fitts. Incentive, anxiety, and the human blink rate. *Journal of Experimental Psychology*, 1953, *45*, 183-187.

Michotte van den Berck, A. Le caractère de "réalité" des projections cinématographiques. *Revue Internationale de Filmologie*, 1948, *1*, No. 3, 249-261.

Michotte van den Berck, A. La participation émotionelle du spectateur a l'action représentée à l'écran. *Revue Internationale de Filmologie*, 1960, *10*, No. 35, 64-74.

Miller, G. A. *Language and communication*. New York: McGraw-Hill, 1951.

Miller, G. A. The magical number seven, plus or minus two. *Psychological Review*, 1956, *63*, 81-97.

Miller, G. A. & F. C. Frick. Statistical behavioristics and sequences of responses. *Psychological Review*, 1949, *56*, 311-324.

Miller, G. A., & D. McNeill. Psycholinguistics. Chap. 26, Vol. III, pp. 666-794, in G. Lindzey & E. Aronson (Eds.), *The handbook of social psychology*. Reading, Mass.: Addison-Wesley, 1969.

Miller, G. R. On defining communication: Another stab. *Journal of Communication*, 1966, *16*, 88-98.

Minter, R. L. A denotative and connotative study in communication. *Journal of Communication*, 1968, *18*, 26-36.

Morris, C. *Signs, language and behavior.* New York: Prentice-Hall, 1946.

Newman, S. S. Personal symbolism in language patterns. *Psychiatry*, 1939, 2, 177-184.

Nummenmaa, T., & U. Kauranne. Dimensions of facial expression. Reports from Department of Psychology, Institute of Pedagogy, Jyväskyläz 3, Finland, No. 20, 1958.

Ogden, C. K., & I. A. Richards. *The meaning of meaning.* London: Routledge & Keegan Paul, 1923 (10th edition, 1949).

Olson, W. C. *The measurement of nervous habits in normal children.* Minneapolis, Minn.: University of Minnesota Press, 1929.

Osgood, C. E. The nature and measurement of meaning. *Psychological Bulletin*, 1952, 49, 197-237.

Osgood, C. E. Fidelity and reliability. pp. 374-384 in H. Quastler (Ed.) *Information theory in psychology. Problems and methods.* Glencoe, Ill.: The Free Press, 1955.

Osgood, C. E. The representational model and relevant research methods. Chap. 2, pp. 33-88, in I. deS. Pool (Ed.), *Trends in content analysis.* Urbana, Ill.: University of Illinois Press, 1959.

Osgood, C. E. Dimensionality of the semantic space for communication via facial expressions. *Scandinavian Journal of Psychology*, 1966, 7, 1-30.

Osgood, C. E., & G. J. Suci. Factor analysis of meaning. *Journal of Experimental Psychology*, 1955, 50, 325-338.

Pierce, J. R. *Symbols, signals and noise: The nature and process of communication.* New York: Harper, 1961.

Pittenger, R. E., & H. L. Smith. A basis for some contributions of linguistics to psychiatry. *Psychiatry*, 1957, 20, 61-78.

Pittenger, R. E., C. F. Hockett, & J. J. Danehy. *The first five minutes: A sample of microscopic interview analysis.* Ithaca, N. Y.: Paul Martineau, 1960.

Ponder, E., & W. P. Kennedy. On the act of blinking. *Quarterly Journal of Experimental Physiology*, 1927, 18, 89-110.

Popper, K. R. *Conjectures and refutations.* London: Routledge & Keegan Paul, 1963.

Posner, M. I., & Ellen Rossman. Effect of size and location of informational transforms upon short-term retention. *Journal of Experimental Psychology*, 1965, 70, 496-505.

Premack, D. A functional analysis of language. *Journal of the Experimental Analysis of Behavior.* 1970, 14, 107-125.

Premack, D. Language in chimpanzee? *Science*, 1971, 172, 808-822.

Quastler, H. (Ed.) *Information theory in psychology. Problems and methods.* Glencoe, Ill.: The Free Press, 1955.

Raush, H. L. Interaction sequences. *Journal of Personality and Social Psychology*, 1965, 2, 487-499.

Reid, I. E. Sense modality switching in relation to learning. Unpublished doctoral dissertation, University of Utah, 1965.

Renneker, R. Kinesic research and therapeutic process: Further discussion. pp. 147-160 in P. H. Knapp (Ed.), *Expression of the emotions in man.* New York: International Universities Press, 1963.

Robinson, W. P. The elaborated code in working class language. *Language and Speech*, 1965, *8*, 243-252.

Romano, D., & C. Botson. Strutturalità e rimemorizzazione del materiale filmico. *IKON* 1963, *13*, No. 45, 39-58.

Royal, D. C. A multidimensional analysis of perception of emotion from schematic facial expressions. Unpublished doctoral dissertation, University of Michigan, 1959.

Royal, D. C., & W. L. Hays. Empirical dimensions of emotional behavior. *Acta Psychologica*, 1959, *15*, 419 (Abstract).

Ruesch J. Psychiatry and the challenge of communication. *Psychiatry*, 1954, *17*, 1-18.

Ruesch, J. Nonverbal language and therapy. *Psychiatry*, 1955, 18, 323-330.

Ruesch, J. & W. Kees. *Nonverbal communication: notes on the visual perception of human relations.* Berkeley & Los Angeles: University of California Press 1961.

Rump, E. E. Facial expression and situational cues: Demonstration of a logical error in Frijda's report. *Acta Psychologica*, 1960, *17*, 31-38.

Sainsbury, P. Gestural movement during psychiatric interview. *Psychosomatic Medicine* 1955, *17*, 458-469.

Sapir, E. Language as a form of human behavior. *English Journal*, 1927, *16*, 421-433.

Scheflen, A. E. Communication and regulation in psychotherapy. *Psychiatry*, 1963, *26*, 126-136.

Scheflen A. E. The significance of posture in communication systems. *Psychiatry*, 1964, *27*, 316-331.

Scheflen, A. E. Quasi-courtship behavior in psychotherapy. *Psychiatry*, 1965, *28*, 245-257.

Schlosberg, H. A scale for the judgment of facial expressions. *Journal of Experimental Psychology*, 1941, *29*, 497-510.

Schlosberg, H. The description of facial expressions in terms of two dimensions. *Journal of Experimental Psychology*, 1952, *44*, 229-237.

Schlosberg, H. Three dimensions of emotion. *Psychological Review*, 1954, *61*, 81-88.

Shannon C. E. A mathematical theory of communication. *Bell System Technical Journal*, 1948, *27*, 379-423, 623-656.

Shannon C. E. Communication in the presence of noise. *Proceedings of the I.R.E.*, 1949, *37*, 10-21.

Shannon, C. E. & W. Weaver. *The mathematical theory of communication.* Urbana: University of Illinois Press, 1949.

Shapiro, J. G. Agreement between channels of communication in interviews.

Journal of Consulting Psychology, 1966, *30*, 535-538.

Siegman, A. W., & B. Pope. Effects of question specificity and anxiety-producing messages on verbal fluency in the initial interview. *Journal of Personality and Social Psychology*, 1965, *2*, 522-530.

Soskin, W. F. Some aspects of communication and interpretation in psychotherapy. Paper in a symposium, Communication in the counseling situation. *American Psychologist*, 1953, *8*, 272.

Soskin, W. F., & P. Kaufmann. Judgment of emotion in word-free voice samples. *Journal of Communication*, 1961, *11*, 73-80.

Stankiewicz, E. Problems of emotive language. pp. 239-264 in T.A. Sebeok, A. S. Hayes, & Mary C. Bateson (Eds.), *Approaches to semiotics*. The Hague: Mouton, 1964.

Starkweather, J. A. The communication-value of content-free speech. *American Journal of Psychology*, 1956, *69*, 121-123. (a)

Starkweather J. A. Content-free speech as a source of information about the speaker. *Journal of Abnormal and Social Psychology*, 1956, *52*, 394-402. (b)

Stevens, S. S. Introduction: A definition of communication. *Journal of the Acoustical Society of America*, 1950, *22*, 689-690.

Stokoe, W. C., Dorothy C. Casterline, & C. G. Croneberg. *A dictionary of American sign language on linguistic principles*. Washington, D. C.: Galaudet College Press, 1965.

Swets, J. A. Is there a sensory threshold? *Science*, 1961, *134*, 168-177.

Thayer, L. O. On theory-building in communication: Some conceptual problems. *Journal of Communication*, 1963, *13*, 217-235.

Thompson, Claire W. & Katherine Bradway. The teaching of psychotherapy through content-free interviews. *Journal of Consulting Psychology*, 1950, *14*, 321-323.

Thompson, Diana F., & L. Melzer. Communication of emotional intent by facial expression. *Journal of Abnormal and Social Psychology*, 1964, *68*, 129-135.

Tislow, R. An aversive-thought/belching syndrome: A somatic expression of unpleasant thought content. *Life Sciences*, 1964, *3*, 1501-1503.

Titchener, E. B. *An outline of psychology*. 3rd. ed. New York: Macmillan, 1900.

Tomkins, S. S. *Affect, imagery, consciousness. Vol. 1: The positive affects*. New York: Springer, 1962.

Tomkins, S. S., & R. McCarter. What and where are the primary affects? Some evidence for a theory. *Perceptual and Motor Skills*, 1964, *18*, 119-158.

Trager, G. L. Paralanguage: A first approximation. *Studies in Linguistics*, 1958, *13*, 1-12.

Trager, G. L. & Smith, H. L., Jr. *An outline of English structure. (Studies in Linguistics: Occasional Papers, 3)*. Norman, Okla.: Battenberg Press, 1951 (Republished: New York: American Council of Learned Societies, 1965.)

Travers, R. M. W. The transmission of information to human receivers. *AV Communication Review*, 1964, *12*, 373-385.

Triandis, H. C., & W. W. Lambert. A restatement and test of Schlosberg's theory of emotion with two kinds of subjects from Greece. *Journal of Abnormal and Social Psychology*, 1958, *56*, 321-328.

Waskow, Irene E. Counselor attitudes and client behavior. *Journal of Consulting Psychology*, 1963, *27*, 405-412.

Watson, O. M., & T. D. Graves. Quantitative research in proxemic behavior. *American Anthropologist* 1966, *68*, 971-985.

Wiener, M., & A. Mehrabian. *Language within languages: Immediacy, a channel in verbal communication.* New York: Appleton-Century-Crofts, 1968.

Williams, F., & Barbara Sundene. Dimensions of recognition: Visual vs. vocal expression of emotion. *Audiovisual Communication Review*, 1965, *13*, 44-52.

Wolff, W. Involuntary self-expression in gait and other movements: An experimental study. *Character and Personality*, 1935, *3*, 327-344.

Wolff, W. *The expression of personality.* New York: Harper, 1943.

Wood, Lucie A., & J. C. Saunders. Blinking frequency: A neurophysiological measurement of psychological stress. *Diseases of the Nervous System*, 1962, *23*, 158-163.

Woodworth, R. S. *Experimental psychology.* New York: Holt, 1938.

Woodworth, R. S., & H. Schlosberg. *Experimental psychology.* New York: Holt, 1954.

Wundt, W. *Outlines of Psychology.* Translation of the 7th ed. (C. H. Judd, Trans.). Leipzig: Wilhelm Engelmann, 1907.

Name Index

228

Subject Index ———————————————————